# A Guide to the

# Math SAT®

by

Richard F. Corn

# A Guide to the Math SAT®

## by

## Richard F. Corn

ISBN: 978-0-9985849-0-4

Library of Congress Control Number:  2017900566

Errata or supplemental information for this book may be found at
http://www.mathprepbooks.com/errata.com

Published by Richard Corn, LLC

# TABLE OF CONTENTS

# 1. Introduction

This book contains all the information needed to achieve your full potential in SAT® math. This book can be used as a standalone text or it can be used in combination with the official practice tests published by the College Board on their web site and in their book, The Official SAT Study Guide (ISBN 978-1-4573-0430-9). Official practice tests are also posted on the Khan Academy web site.

The first part of the book contains a review of math topics that you are likely to encounter on the test. The math review is organized into lessons, and each lesson ends with practice problems and solutions to the problems.

The second part of the book contains advice on how to take the math SAT®. Because the SAT® is probably very different from tests you have seen in school, you may find this advice to be very helpful.

If your target date is less than six weeks away, go directly to Part Two of this book and start taking practice tests. If your target date is more than six weeks away then start with Part One of this book, which contains a review of the math that you need to know. When the six week mark arrives, switch to Part Two.

## Calculators
The SAT® has two math sections. The first section is shorter and calculators are not allowed. The second section is longer and calculators are allowed. This book contains practice problems where you can use calculators and problems where you cannot. On some problems it is recommended that you solve them first by hand and then use a calculator to verify your answer.

There are virtually no restrictions on the calculator you can use on the test. The SAT® even permits the usage of calculators with CAS (the Computer Algebra System, which can be used to solve equations with variables). You can check whether your particular calculator is allowed by going to the College Board web site https://collegereadiness.collegeboard.org/sat/taking-the-test/calculator-policy.

Some students are highly proficient with calculators whereas others hardly use them. Throughout this book you will find calculator tips. The tips and screen shots are based on the TI-83 and TI-84 family of calculators. If you are using the TI-89 or the TI-Nspire calculators, your steps, keystrokes and screens may be different.

## Reader feedback, errors and supplements
I enjoy hearing from readers, so please feel free to send email to mathprepbooks@gmail.com. Despite a thorough editing of the material in this book it is inevitable that mistakes were missed and I apologize for them in advance. If you find an error please send an email. Errors that are found in the book will be posted promptly at http://www.mathprepbooks.com/errata.html . That same web page will contain a link to any supplemental materials that were written after publication of this book. The current SAT® is a relatively new test that is evolving, so some supplements may be needed.

# PART ONE:  Math review

We begin a review of the math that is on the syllabus for the SAT®, starting with middle school math and ending with statistics.

Most students will not have the time to review every topic in the syllabus. You should choose topics where you feel less confident, and/or topics that appear most frequently on the SAT®. The Appendix lists the math topics covered in this book, in order of popularity on the SAT®. However if your goal is a high score, say 750+, then you should have a sound understanding of every topic.

To a reasonable extent, units in the book are independent and can be studied in any order. But you will find some lesson examples and homework problems in one unit that make use of information in another unit. This is intentional because the SAT® places emphasis on an integrated knowledge of math and because overlap is desirable in some areas of math, especially algebra.

# 2.  Pre-Algebra

Math review begins by covering the math that you were supposed to have mastered in middle school.

## 2.1    Multiplication and long division

You may well wonder why math review begins with multiplication and long division. It is because the SAT® contains a no calculator section and some problems in that section may require you to multiply or divide by hand without a calculator.

**Multiplication**
No decimals: Sometimes you will simply have to multiply two integers (numbers without a decimal place). To do this just line one number above the other and multiply one row at a time, as shown below.

To multiply 123 by 45:

$$
\begin{array}{r}
123 \\
\times\ 45 \\
\hline
615 \\
4920 \\
\hline
5535
\end{array}
$$

align the numbers so they are right-justified

multiply 123 by 5 to get 615

place a zero in the last position, multiply 123 by 4 to get 492

add

One decimal: Sometimes you will have to multiply an integer (a number without a decimal) with another number that has a decimal.

To multiply 123 by 4.5 start by counting the number of decimal places there are in the decimal number. In this example there is one decimal place. Then set up the problem exactly as if no decimal points existed (ignore the decimal points) and multiply as if both numbers were integers.

| | |
|---|---|
| 123 | |
| x 45 | ignore the decimal places and align the numbers so they are right-justified |
| 615 | multiply 123 by 5 to get 615 |
| 4920 | place a zero in the last position, multiply 123 by 4 to get 492 |
| 5535 | add |
| 553.5 | adjust the decimal (see instructions in the text) |

Because the decimal number had one decimal place, the answer must also have one decimal place. Instead of 5535 the correct answer is 553.5. Check this on a calculator to see that it is correct.

Both decimals: Sometimes both numbers will have decimal places.

To multiply 1.23 by 4.5 start by counting the total number of decimal places in both numbers. In this example there is a total of three decimal places. Then set up the problem exactly as if both numbers had no decimal points (ignore the decimal points) and multiply as if both numbers were integers.

| | |
|---|---|
| 123 | |
| x 45 | ignore the decimal places and align the numbers so they are right-justified |
| 615 | multiply 123 by 5 to get 615 |
| 4920 | place a zero in the last position, multiply 123 by 4 to get 492 |
| 5535 | add |
| 5.535 | adjust the decimal (see instructions in the text) |

Because the decimal numbers had a total of three decimal places, the answer must also have three decimal places. Instead of 5535 the correct answer is 5.535. Check this on a calculator to see that it is correct.

**Long division**

Now that you have mastered the art of multiplication you can take on long division which, unfortunately is more complicated. We start out by trying to divide an integer by an integer; in other words neither number has a decimal place.

Case 1: Dividing integers (with no remainder)

We start with a simple situation where there is no remainder. Suppose we want to divide 24 into 1272. The problem might ask "what is the quotient when 1272 is divided by 24" or you might be trying to simplify $\dfrac{1272}{24}$. The steps are shown below.

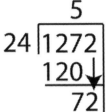

24 cannot divide into 1, so do nothing

24 cannot divide into 12, so do nothing

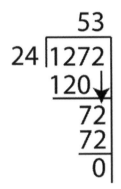

24 divides into 127 five times, so place a 5 above the 7 in 127. Then muliply 5 by 24 to get 120 and place 120. Then subtract 120 from 127 to get 7. Then bring down the 2 to make 72.

24 divides into 72 three times, so place a 3 above the last 2 in 1272. Then multiply 3 by 24 to get 72 and place 72. Then subtract 72 from 72 to get 0. There is no remainder in this problem because 24 x 52=1272.

<u>Case 2: Dividing integers (with a remainder)</u>

Next take a look at dividing integers when there is a remainder. Suppose we want to divide 16 into 1272. The problem might ask "what is the quotient when 1272 is divided by 16" or you might be trying to simplify $\dfrac{1272}{16}$. The steps are shown below.

$16\overline{\smash{\big)}\,1272}$

16 cannot divide into 1, so do nothing

$16\overline{\smash{\big)}\,1272}$

16 cannot divide into 12, so do nothing

$$
\begin{array}{r}
7\phantom{000} \\
16\overline{\smash{\big)}\,1272\phantom{0}} \\
112\phantom{0}\downarrow \\
\hline
152\phantom{0}
\end{array}
$$

16 divides into 127 seven times, so place a 7 above the 7 in 127. Then muliply 7 by 16 to get 112 and place 112. Then subtract 112 from 127 to get 15. Then bring down the 2 to make 152.

$$
\begin{array}{r}
79 \\
16\overline{\smash{\big)}\,1272} \\
112\phantom{0}\downarrow \\
\hline
152 \\
144 \\
\hline
8
\end{array}
$$

16 divides into 152 nine times, so place a 9 above the last 2 in 1272. Then multiply 9 by 16 to get 144 and place 144. Then subtract 144 from 152 to get 8. The remainder in this problem is 8 but we need to express the answer in decimal.

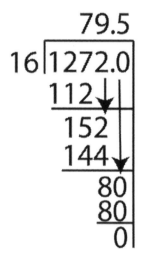

Re-write 1272 as 1272.0 and place a decimal after 79 on top. Then bring down the zero from 1272.0 to make 80. 16 goes into 80 five times so place a 5 in the first decimal place on top. Multiply 16 by 5 to get 80. Now the problem is completed.

If you had not reached zero at this point you would need to re-write 1272.0 as 1272.00. Then you would bring down another zero and repeat the process.

## Case 3:  Dividing with decimals

Suppose you have to divide two numbers and one or both of them has a decimal.  That situation is easily addressed by multiplying the numerator and denominator by 10 until all decimals are removed.  At that point you can divide as shown above in the earlier cases.  For example, if we want to divide 1.6 into 12.72 we just follow the steps below:

$$\frac{12.72}{1.6} \qquad \text{the original problem}$$

$$\left(\frac{12.72}{1.6}\right)\left(\frac{10}{10}\right) = \frac{127.2}{16} \qquad \text{multiply by } \frac{10}{10}, \text{ and repeat as needed}$$

$$\left(\frac{127.2}{16}\right)\left(\frac{10}{10}\right) = \frac{1272}{160} \qquad \text{now all decimals have been removed}$$

Now the problem has been transformed into dividing one integer by another and the process is the same as case 1 or case 2, depending on whether there is a remainder.  In this example,

$$160\overline{)1272} \qquad$$ 160 cannot divide into 1, so do nothing

$$160\overline{)1272} \qquad$$ 160 cannot divide into 12, so do nothing

$$160\overline{)1272} \qquad$$ 160 cannot divide into 127, so do nothing

$$\begin{array}{r} 7 \\ 160\overline{)1272} \\ 1120 \\ \hline 152 \end{array}$$

160 divides into 1272 seven times, so place a 7 above the last 2 in 1272. Then muliply 7 by 160 to get 1120 and place 1120. Then subtract 1120 from 1272 to get 152. The remainder in this problem is 152 but we need to express the answer in decimal.

$$\begin{array}{r} 7.9 \\ 160\overline{)1272.0} \\ 1120 \\ \hline 1520 \\ 1440 \\ \hline 80 \end{array}$$

Re-write 1272 as 1272.0 and place a decimal after the 7 on top. Then bring down the zero from 1272.0 to make 1520. 160 goes into 1520 nine times so place a 9 in the first decimal place on top. Multiply 160 by 9 to get 1440. Place the 1440 and subtract to get 80. There is still a remainder so the process repeats.

$$\begin{array}{r} 7.95 \\ 160\overline{)1272.00} \\ 1120 \\ \hline 1520 \\ 1440 \\ \hline 800 \\ 800 \\ \hline 0 \end{array}$$

Re-write 1272.0 as 1272.00  Then bring down the last zero from 1272.00 to make 800.  160 goes into 800 five times so place a 5 in the second decimal place on top. Multiply 160 by 5 to get 800. Subtract to see that there is no remainder and you are done!

## 2.1 Practice problems on multiplication and long division

1. Without a calculator: What is the product when 12 is multiplied by 53?

A)    4.4

B)    159

C)    636

D)    646

2. Without a calculator: What is the quotient when 3588 is divided by 156?

A)    0.04

B)    2.3

C)    23

D)    559,728

3. Without a calculator: If $x = 3.6$ and $y = 25.6$ what is the value of $xy$?

A)    2.3

B)    9.21

C)    23.04

D)    92.10

4. Without a calculator: If $xy = 5244$ and $x = 15.2$ what is the value of $y$?

A)    34.5

B)    43.7

C)    345

D)    437

5. Without a calculator: If Jordan can run 12.5 miles in 50 minutes, on average how many minutes does it take Jordan to run a mile?

A)    2.5

B)    4

C)    25

D)    40

6. Without a calculator: If Meaghan buys 5 avocados for her party and each avocado costs $1.25 how much money will she spend on avocados?

A)    $6.25

B)    $6.75

C)    $6.75

D)    $8.75

7. Without a calculator: Billy loves hot dogs and wants to buy as many as he can with his $10 bill. If each hot dog costs $1.75 how many hot dogs can Billy buy?

A)    3

B)    4

C)    5

D)    6

8. Without a calculator: Katy wants to buy a pair of shoes for $65 but has to pay a 6% sales tax. How much money will Katy need to buy those shoes?

A)    $61.10

B)    $65..06

C)    $68.90

D)    $71.00

## 2.1 Solutions to practice problems on multiplication and long division

1. (C)

$$
\begin{array}{r}
53 \\
\times 12 \\
\hline
106 \\
530 \\
\hline
636
\end{array}
$$

2. (C)

$$
\begin{array}{r}
23 \\
156\overline{)3588} \\
312\downarrow \\
\hline
468 \\
468 \\
\hline
0
\end{array}
$$

3. (D)

$$
\begin{array}{r}
256 \\
\times 36 \\
\hline
1536 \\
7680 \\
\hline
9210 \\
92.10
\end{array}
$$

The result must have two decimal places because the original numbers had a total of two decimal places.

4. (C)

$$\left(\frac{5244}{15.2}\right)\left(\frac{10}{10}\right) = \frac{52440}{152}$$

$$
\begin{array}{r}
345 \\
152\overline{)52440} \\
456\downarrow\downarrow \\
\hline
684 \\
608\downarrow \\
\hline
760 \\
760 \\
\hline
0
\end{array}
$$

5. (B)

$$\left(\frac{50}{12.5}\right)\left(\frac{10}{10}\right) = \frac{500}{125}$$

$$
\begin{array}{r}
4 \\
125\overline{)500} \\
500 \\
\hline
0
\end{array}
$$

6. (A)

$$
\begin{array}{r}
125 \\
\times 5 \\
\hline
625 \\
6.25
\end{array}
$$

The result must have two decimal places because the original numbers had a total of two decimal places.

7. (C)

$$\left(\frac{10}{1.75}\right)\left(\frac{10}{10}\right) = \frac{100}{17.5}\left(\frac{10}{10}\right) = \frac{1000}{175}$$

$$
\begin{array}{r}
5 \\
175\overline{)1000} \\
875 \\
\hline
125
\end{array}
$$

The answer is 5 with a remainder of 125. There is no need to complete the long division because Billy cannot buy a fraction of a hot dog.

8. (C)

$$
\begin{array}{r}
65 \\
\times 6 \\
\hline
390 \\
3.90
\end{array}
$$

Sales tax is $3.90.  $65.00 + $3.90 = $68.90

## 2.2    Order of operations

Although the syllabus for the SAT® does not list order of operations as a topic, it is not possible to get very far in math without this basic skill.  The SAT® may not have a question directed specifically at the order of operations but it is used in many algebra problems, especially equation solving, inequality solving, and working with exponents.  Many incorrect answer choices in the multiple choice problems are based on misunderstandings of order of operations.  Finally (in case you have not already been convinced), it is impossible to use a graphing calculator properly without knowing the order of operations because calculators follow its laws exactly.

The order of operations is best remembered by the acronym, PEMDAS:

**P** = parenthesis.  Always perform operations inside parentheses first.

**E** = exponents.  Next, raise terms to their powers (exponents).

**M** = multiplication.  Multiplication and division go together.

**D** = division.   Multiply and divide terms, from left to right.

**A** = addition.  Addition and subtraction go together and are the last step.

**S** = subtraction.  Last, add and subtract terms, left to right.


Like many things in math, examples are the best way to learn PEMDAS.  Start with

$$5 \cdot \left( 8 + 2^2 \right) \div 4 - 3^2$$

The first step is to simplify the expression within the parenthesis, giving us

$$5 \cdot (12) \div 4 - 3^2$$

Next, we clear the exponents

$$5 \cdot (12) \div 4 - 9$$

Next, we multiply and divide, left to right

$$60 \div 4 - 9$$
$$15 - 9$$

The last step is addition and subtraction, yielding an answer of 6.


PEMDAS does not only apply to numbers, it also applies to variables.  Consider

$$2x + \left( 2x + x \right)^2 - 6x^2 \div 2x - x$$

First simplify expressions inside parentheses

$$2x + \left( 3x \right)^2 - 6x^2 \div 2x - x$$

Next we clear out the exponents

$$2x + 9x^2 - 6x^2 \div 2x - x$$

Next divide

$$2x + 9x^2 - 3x - x$$

The last step is to add and subtract (combine like terms)

$$9x^2 - 2x$$

| 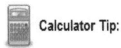 Calculator Tip: | PEMDAS errors often involve negative numbers. First of all, please remember that there is a negative key (labeled as "(-)" and located on the bottom right of the calculator) and a subtraction key (labeled as "-" and located on the far right of the calculator). These keys are different. The negative key is used to set the sign of a number, whereas the subtraction key is used to subtract one number from another (either number could be positive or negative).<br><br>The first screen shot below shows how to subtract negative 3 from 5. The key sequence is *5, -, (-), 3, Enter*. This gives you the correct result of 8. The calculator is following PEMDAS. It first multiplies -1 by 3. Then it subtracts -3 from 5.<br><br>The second screen shot below first shows how to calculate the square of negative 2, yielding the correct answer of positive 4. To get the correct result of positive 4 you must use parentheses. The correct key sequence is  *(, (-), 2, ), $x^2$, enter*. Then the second screen shot shows how students will often get the wrong answer of -4. This is because the calculator followed PEMDAS but the student did not. If you enter *(-), 2, $x^2$* the calculator will return -4. This is due to PEMDAS. The calculator deals with the <u>exponent first</u>, raising 2 to the second power, giving 4. Then it multiplies 4 by -1. |

| NORMAL FLOAT AUTO REAL DEGREE MP    ᐤ | NORMAL FLOAT AUTO REAL DEGREE MP    ᐤ |
|---|---|
| 5- -3<br><div style="text-align:right">8</div>■ | ( -2)²<br><div style="text-align:right">4</div>-2²<br><div style="text-align:right">-4</div> |

11

## 2.2 Practice problems on the order of operations

1.  Solve this by hand first and then verify on the calculator:  The expression $\dfrac{2-12\div 2}{-(-2)^2}$ simplifies to:

    A)      -5/4

    B)      -1

    C)      5/4

    D)      1

2.  Solve this by hand first and then verify on the calculator:  The expression
    $5-2^2+3(1+2)^2$ simplifies to:

    A)      10

    B)      28

    C)      36

    D)      108

3.  Solve this by hand first and then verify on the calculator:  The expression $\dfrac{-4}{2}-(-2)^3+1$ simplifies to:

    A)      -9

    B)      -7

    C)      7

    D)      9

4.  Solve this by hand first and then verify on the calculator:  The expression $3^2+\dfrac{2^3+1}{(1-2)^3}$ simplifies to:

    A)      -9

    B)      -1

    C)      0

    D)      9

5.  Solve this by hand first and then verify on the calculator:  The expression $\dfrac{8+(6-3)^2}{2^2-3^2-12}$ simplifies to:

    A)      -2

    B)      -1

    C)      1

    D)      2

6.  Without a calculator:  The expression $\dfrac{(3x)^3-x^3}{x^3}$ simplifies to

    A)      2

    B)      8

    C)      26

    D)      27

7.  Without a calculator:  The expression $-x^2-(-2x)^2-x+(-3)^3$ simplifies to:

    A)      $3x^2-x-27$

    B)      $7x^2-x+-27$

    C)      $-6x^2-27$

    D)      $-5x^2-x-27$

8.  Extra credit, without a calculator:  Tthe expression $\dfrac{(x^2)^2+2x^2-6x\div 2x}{x\cdot x\cdot x-x\cdot x+x+x+x-3}$ simplifies to

    A)      $x+1$

    B)      $x^2+3$

    C)      $x-1$

    D)      $x^2-3$

12

## 2.2 Solutions to practice problems on the order of operations

**1. (D)**

$$\frac{2-12\div 2}{-(-2)^2} = \frac{2-6}{-4} = \frac{-4}{-4} = 1$$

**2. (B)**

$$5-2^2+3(1+2)^2 = 5-2^2+3\cdot 3^2$$
$$= 5-4+3\cdot 9 = 5-4+27 = 28$$

**3. (C)**

$$\frac{-4}{2}-(-2)^3+1 = -2-(-8)+1 = -2+8+1 = 7$$

**4. (C)**

$$3^2+\frac{2^3+1}{(1-2)^3} = 9+\frac{8+1}{-1} = 9-9 = 0$$

**5. (B)**

$$\frac{8+(6-3)^2}{2^2-3^2-12} = \frac{8+3^2}{2^2-3^2-12} = \frac{8+9}{4-9-12} = \frac{17}{-17} = -1$$

**6. (C)**

$$\frac{(3x)^3-x^3}{x^3} = \frac{27x^3-x^3}{x^3} = \frac{26x^3}{x^3} = 26$$

**7. (D)**

$$-x^2-(-2x)^2-x+(-3)^3 = -x^2-4x^2-x-27$$
$$= -5x^2-x-27$$

**8. (A)**

$$\frac{(x^2)^2+2x^2-6x\div 2x}{x\cdot x\cdot x-x\cdot x+x+x+x-3} = \frac{x^4+2x^2-3}{x^3-x^2+3x-3}$$
$$= \frac{(x^2+3)(x^2-1)}{x^2(x-1)+3(x-1)}$$
$$= \frac{(x^2+3)(x+1)(x-1)}{(x^2+3)(x-1)}$$
$$= x+1$$

13

## 2.3    Percentages

Percentages are a fairly popular topic on the SAT® and they come in several forms. We start with a simple drill:  How many ways can we write five percent?  Three ways are possible:

$$5\%, .05 \text{ and } \frac{5}{100}.$$

The last way, as a fraction, is the most important to remember.

How many ways can we write x percent?  Two ways are possible:

$$x\% \text{ and } \frac{x}{100}.$$

The last way, as a fraction, is the only useful way to write x percent. It is critical to remember that because in word problems the phrase "what percent" is substituted by $\frac{x}{100}$ when we set up an equation.  Consider:

**What percent of 86 is 18?**

This is a relatively simple word problem.  To solve this problem we replace "what percent" with $\frac{x}{100}$, then we replace "is" with an equals sign, and set up an equation:

$$\frac{x}{100} = \frac{18}{86}$$

$$\left(\frac{x}{100}\right)86 = 18, \ 86x = 1800, \ x = \frac{1800}{86}, \ x = 20.93$$

The ratio approach is called "part is to whole" because the part portion is placed in the numerator and the whole portion is placed in the denominator.

Consider another simple word problem:

**28 is 16 percent of what number?**

To solve this problem we realize that 28 is part of a whole and the whole is the unknown. We take the ratio 28/x and replace "is" with an equals sign, and re-write 16 percent as 16/100.  When written as an equation we have:

$$\frac{28}{x} = \frac{16}{100}, \ 2800 = 16x, \ \frac{2800}{16} = x, \ 175 = x$$

If a calculator is allowed, it is faster (and better) to approach this problem directly, using decimal notation for the percentage rather than a ratio:

$$28 = 0.16x, \quad \frac{28}{.16} = x, \quad 175=x$$

Lastly we consider an even simpler word problem:

## What is 5% of 185?

If we were to set up an equation, we would have:

$$\left(\frac{5}{100}\right) = \frac{x}{185}, \quad 100x = 925, \quad x = 9.25$$

If a calculator is allowed, It is faster (and better) to solve using decimal notation for the percentage rather than a ratio:

$$(.05)185 = 9.25$$

With practice, you will gain insight into when it is better to use the decimal or fraction representations of percentage amounts. You should begin by understand how to use the fraction and then start using the decimal amounts to speed up calculations.

## Percentage change

A percentage change problem will give you a starting amount and an ending amount, and ask you to calculate the change. The formula for a percentage change is

$$\text{percentage change} = \left(\frac{ending - starting}{starting}\right)100$$

Note that if the percentage change is positive, that represents a percentage increase. If a store raises its price for a shirt from \$80 to \$90, the percentage increase is

$$\left(\frac{90-80}{80}\right)100 = \left(\frac{10}{80}\right)100 = \frac{1000}{80} = 12.5$$

Notice that in the example above, the percentage change is a positive 12.5 percent and therefore represents an increase.

If the percentage change is negative that represents a percentage decrease. If the total rainfall in Fargo was 30 inches last year and 24 inches this year, the percentage change is

$$\left(\frac{24-30}{30}\right)100 = \left(\frac{-6}{30}\right)100 = -20$$

Notice that in the example above, the percentage change is a negative 20 percent and therefore represents a decrease.

## Increasing or decreasing an amount by a percentage

In a problem where you are asked to increase or decrease an amount by a certain percentage, you will be given a starting value and the percentage to use. Your job is to calculate the ending amount. This calculation can be done using the percentage change formula but it is far better to use these formulas:

To increase a value by x percent, use the following:

$$\text{ending value} = \text{starting value}\left(1 + \frac{x}{100}\right)$$

For example, if a store decides to raise all of its prices by 5%, then a shirt that originally costs $80 will now cost

$$80\left(1 + \frac{5}{100}\right) = (1.05)80 = 84 \ .$$

To decrease a value by x percent, use the following:

$$\text{ending value} = \text{starting value}\left(1 - \frac{x}{100}\right)$$

If a store decides to reduce all of its prices by 5%, then a shirt that originally costs $80 will now cost

$$80\left(1 - \frac{5}{100}\right) = (0.95)80 = 76 \ .$$

## 2.3  Practice problems on percentages
### calculator permitted unless stated otherwise

1.  <u>Solve this by hand first and then verify on the calculator:</u>  What is 28% of 600?

A)     0.47

B)     21.42

C)     168

D)     2,142

2.  <u>Solve this by hand first and then verify on the calculator:</u>  15 is what percent of 500?

A)     0.03 %

B)     3 %

C)     33 %

D)     75 %

3.  <u>Solve this by hand first and then verify on the calculator:</u>  65 is 20 percent of what number?

A)     3.25

B)     13

C)     325

D)     1,300

4.  <u>Solve this by hand first and then verify on the calculator:</u> 300 is what percent of 15?

A)     4.5%

B)     20%

C)     45%

D)     450%

E)     2000%

5.  Some time ago, the price of a pound of sugar was 25 cents.  It is now $3.  How much has the price changed?

A)     0.9%

B)     11%

C)     91.6%

D)     1100%

**Questions 6 and 7 refer to the following information.**

The scatterplot below shows Mary's best long jump (measured in inches) when she was various ages.

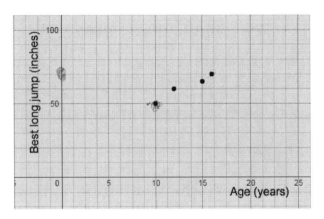

6.  What was Mary's percentage change in distance jumped from age 10 to age 16?

A)     60% decrease

B)     28% increase

C)     40% increase

D)     60% increase

7.  When Mary was 16 she got a different track coach, who set a new jumping target that was 20% higher than her best jump so far.  What was her new target?

A)     56 feet

B)     70 feet

C)     84 feet

D)     90 feet

8. Patty bought a shirt marked $120, and the store is having a sale of 20% off everything. How much will Patty pay for the shirt (excluding sales tax)?

- A) $24
- B) $96
- C) $114
- D) $144

9. 98% of Mr. Corn's students increase their math SAT score. Of those, 50% increase their score by at least 100 points. Overall, what percent of students increase their math SAT score by at least 100 points?

- A) 49
- B) 50
- C) 51
- D) 98
- E) 148

10. The difference between a certain number and 12 is equal to 85% of that number. What is the number?

- A) 6.49
- B) 12.85
- C) 14.11
- D) 80

11. 115% of what number is equal to 26.25?

- A) 3.9
- B) 22.3
- C) 22.8
- D) 30.2

12. The price of oil this year is $4.10 per gallon. If that represents a 30% increase over last year, what was the price of oil last year?

- A) 1.23
- B) 2.87
- C) 3.15
- D) 5.33

13. A store clerk was instructed to mark everything up by 15%. Instead he marked everything down by 15%. If a pair of shoes was originally marked $80, what is difference between the correct price and the incorrect price marked by the clerk?

- A) $8
- B) $12
- C) $24
- D) $68

14. Of the students who graduated from Main High School what percent were boys?

|  | Graduated | Did not graduate |
| --- | --- | --- |
| Girls | 110 | 5 |
| Boys | 85 | 28 |

- A) 37%
- B) 44%
- C) 77%
- D) 110%

15. Suppose your state charges 10% sales tax and you buy a hat from a discount store that always takes 10% off the price tag. If the amount that the store charges when you bought the hat (after the discount and tax are applied) is $29.70 what equation could you use to find the original price tag of the hat?

- A) $.90x + x = 29.7$
- B) $.90x + 1.1x = 29.7$
- C) $.1x + x + 1.1x = 29.7$
- D) $(1.1)(0.9)x = 29.7$

16. The hockey team has been great! In 20014, they won 20% more games than in 20013. In 2015 they won 50% more games than in 2014. What was their overall percentage change from 2013 through 2015?

- A) 70
- B) 80
- C) 90
- D) 170

# 2.3 Solutions to practice problems on percentages

1. (C)

$$\frac{28}{100} = \frac{x}{600}, \ 100x = 16,800, \ x = 168$$

```
NORMAL FLOAT AUTO REAL DEGREE MP
.28*600
                              168
```

2. (B)

$$\frac{15}{500} = \frac{x}{100}, \ 500x = 1500, \ x = 3$$

```
NORMAL FLOAT AUTO REAL DEGREE MP
(15/500)100
                               3.
```

3. (C)

$$\frac{20}{100} = \frac{65}{x}, \ 20x = 6500, \ x = 325$$

```
NORMAL FLOAT AUTO REAL DEGREE MP
65/.2
                             325.
```

4. (C)

$$\frac{300}{15} = \frac{x}{100}, \ 15x = 30,000, \ x = 2,000$$

```
NORMAL FLOAT AUTO REAL DEGREE MP
(300/15)*100
                             2000
```

5. (D)

$$\left(\frac{3.00 - .25}{.25}\right)100 = 1100$$

```
NORMAL FLOAT AUTO REAL DEGREE MP
((3-.25)/.25)100
                             1100
```

6. (C)

$$\left(\frac{70 - 50}{50}\right)100 = 40$$

7. (C)

$$70(1 + .20) = 84$$

8. (B)

$$120(1 - .20) = 96$$

9. (A)

Suppose there are 100 students in the class. So 98 of them increased their math score. Of the 98 who increased their math score, 49 had an increase of at least 100 points.

10. (D)

$$x - 12 = .85x, \ .15x = 12, \ x = 80$$

11. (C)

$$\left(\frac{115}{100}\right) = \frac{26.25}{x}, \ 115x = 2625, \ x = 22.83$$

12. (C)

$$4.10 = (1 + .30)x, \ 4.10 = 1.3x, \ 3.15 = x$$

13. (C)

The price should have marked $80(1 + .15) = 92$ but instead was marked $80(1 - .15) = 68$. The difference was $92 - 68 = 24$.

14. (A)

$$x = \left(\frac{85}{110 + 85}\right)100 = 37.3$$

15. (D)

First find the discount price of the hat $x(1 - .10) = .90x$. Then find the price after tax is applied $.90x(1 + .10) = (1.1)(0.9)x$.

16. (B)

Suppose they won 100 games in 2013. Then they won $100(1 + .20) = 120$ games in 2014. Then they won $120(1 + .50) = 180$ games in 2015. That would be a 80% increase.

## 2.4  Averages

Like many so-called simple things, the SAT® can take something simple like an average and stand it on its head.  We all know that

$$average = \frac{sum}{count} \; .$$

The average of 5 and 8 is $\frac{5+8}{2} = \frac{13}{2} = 6.5$ and the average of $x$ and $y$ would be $\frac{x+y}{2}$.

In general, when you see the word "average" on the SAT® you should think about the sum.  Many word problems involving averages are really about sums, and the following form of the equation for an average is <u>essential </u>to keep in mind:

$$sum = (average) \cdot (count)$$

Consider this word problem:

> Two people are on an elevator, and their average weight is 200 pounds.  The elevator has a capacity of 500 pounds.  The elevator comes to stop and a third person wants to get in.  What is the maximum amount that the third person can weigh?

The solution comes from thinking in terms of sums.  If the two people on the elevator have an average weight of 200 pounds, the sum of their weights must be 400 pounds.  They could each weigh 200 pounds, or one could weigh 50 pounds while the other weighs 350 pounds.  It does not matter what either weighs.  What matters is that together they weigh 400 pounds.  As the elevator has a capacity of 500 pounds, the third would-be passenger cannot weigh more than 100 pounds.

**Average rate of change**

Sometimes you will be asked to calculate an average rate of change.  The general formula for this is

$$average\ rate\ of\ change = \frac{ending\ value \text{ - } starting\ value}{number\ of\ changes}$$

For example, suppose the price of lettuce went from $1.50 to $2.50 over a period of four years.  The average change per year was

$$\frac{2.50-1.50}{4} = 0.25$$

Notice that the average rate of change is positive so this was an average increase of 25 cents per year, not an average decrease.

## Relationship between average rate of change and slope

By far, the most popular topic on the SAT® is "linear relationships." The test probes your understanding of lines in depth, and this theme is covered again and again throughout this book. The algebraic aspects of linear relations are covered in the algebra chapter, whereas the graphical aspects of linear relations are covered in the geometry chapter. But there are many inter-connections that are covered throughout the book, especially in the homework sets. One such connection is between average rate of change and slope.

In the sample problem above, you were told the starting value, ending value and number of time periods or changes in the price of lettuce. But what if the problem read like this: "Suppose the price of lettuce went from $1.50 in 2005 to $2.50 in 2009." You are now being given two coordinate pairs, the starting pair of (2005, 1.5) and the ending pair of (2009, 2.5). To calculate the average rate of change in the price of lettuce you can use a modified version of the average rate of change formula:

$$\text{average rate of change} = \frac{\text{ending value - starting value}}{\text{ending time or date - starting time or date}}$$

The average rate of change per year was

$$\frac{2.50-1.50}{2009-2005} = \frac{1}{4} = 0.25$$

This calculation is the exact same as the calculation of slope. If you were to graph the prices of lettuce from 2005 through 2009 and draw a line connecting the starting coordinates with the ending coordinates, the slope of that line would be the change in price (y) divided by the change in time (x), or the rise over the run. Note that it does not matter what happened to the price of lettuce between 2005 and 2009, only the endpoints matter.

## Average rate of change is unrelated to percentage change

Please take careful note that the average rate of change is different from the percentage change covered earlier.

The percentage change over the period of four years is

$$\left(\frac{2.50-1.50}{1.50}\right)100 = 67\%$$

In words, the price of lettuce increased by 67% over this four year period.

In the percentage increase, the number of years is irrelevant. In the average annual increase, the overall increase is divided by the number of years (or whatever the time unit or x-axis unit is).

## 2.4 Practice problems on averages
### calculator permitted unless stated otherwise

1. <u>Without a calculator</u>: If the average of x, y and z is 15, what is their sum?

   A)     5

   B)     15

   C)     30

   (D)     45

2. <u>Without a calculator</u>: If the average of x and y is 11 and the average of x, y and z is 5, what is the value of z?

   A)     -17

   (B)     -7

   C)     -6

   D)     6

3. An expression for the average of x, 2x, and 3y is

   A)     $3x + 3y$

   B)     $\dfrac{x+y}{3}$

   (C)     $x+y$

   D)     $\dfrac{3}{2}(x+y)$

4. If the average of $x^2$ and $x$ is ten, what is the value of $x$?

   (A)     -5.0

   B)     -3.7

   C)     -2.7

   D)     3.3

5. <u>Without a calculator</u>: If the average of x and y is 12 and z=6, what is the average of x, y, and z?.

   A)     6

   (B)     10

   C)     15

   D)     24

6. Twelve students took a test and their average score was 85. However, Bob was sick that day. After Bob took the test, the average score dropped to 82. What was Bob's score on the test?

   A)     3

   B)     36

   (C)     46

   D)     56

7. On a recent math test, the boys averaged 81 and the girls averaged 90. If there are twice as many boys in the class as girls, what was the overall average for the class?

   (A)     84

   (B)     84.5

   (C)     85

   (D)     85.5

8. The scatterplot below shows Mary's best long jump (measured in inches) when she was various ages.

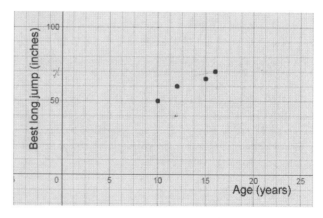

What was Mary's average change per year in the best distance jumped from age 10 to age 16?

   A)     0.3 inches per year

   B)     2.0 inches per year

   (C)     3.3 inches per year

   D)     11.6 inches per year

9. <u>Without a calculator</u>: If the average of 120 numbers is -20, what is their sum?
- A)      -0.17
- B)      -6
- C)      -24
- D)      -2400

10. In the graph below, what is the average rate of change in y from when x=1 to when x=4? .

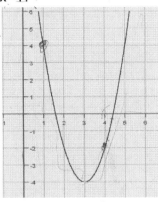

- A)      -6
- B)      -2
- C)      3
- D)      6

---

The table below pertains to problems 11-13. It shows hypothetical sales numbers for Mr. Corn's book.

| Year | Books Sold |
|------|------------|
| 2013 | 1,250 |
| 2014 | 2,350 |
| 2015 | 3,500 |
| 2016 | 4,750 |

11. What was the average number of books sold per year during the period of 2013 through 2015?
- A)      2,366
- B)      2,962
- C)      3,950
- D)      4,033

12. By what percent did sales increase from 2014 to 2016?
- A)      17
- B)      34
- C)      102
- D)      280

13. What was the average increase in annual sales from 2013 through 2016?
- A)      280
- B)      750
- C)      875
- D)      1167

---

14. The price of XYZ stock fluctuates widely. In January it closed at $3.50 but in February it closed at $2.25. However at the end of March it shot back up to $5.00. What was the average monthly change in the price of XYZ stock from January through March?

- A)      $0.50
- B)      $0.75
- C)      $1.00
- D)      $1.50

15. Each semester Kendall must achieve an average of 80 or more in order to keep her college scholarship. So far she has an average of 75 on the first three tests and there are two tests remaining in the semester. What is the minimum average that Kendall must attain on the next two tests to keep her scholarship?

- A)      $80 - 75$

- B)      $\dfrac{80 - 75}{2}$

- C)      $\dfrac{80(2) - 75(3)}{2}$

- D)      $\dfrac{80(5) - 75(3)}{2}$

# 2.4 Solutions to practice problems on averages

1. **(D)**

If $\dfrac{x+y+z}{3} = 15,$ then $x+y+z = 45$

2. **(B)**

$x + y = 22$

$x + y + z = 15$

So $z = 15 - 22 = -7$

3. **(C)**

The average is

$$\frac{x+2x+3y}{3} = \frac{3x+3y}{3} = x+y$$

4. **(A)**

$\dfrac{x^2+x}{2} = 10,\ x^2+x-20 = 0,\ (x+5)(x-4) = 0$

$x = 4$ or $x = -5$

5. **(B)**

If the average of x and y is 12, then the sum of x and y is 24. The sum of x, y and z is 24+6=30. The average of x, y, and z is 30/3 = 10.

6. **(C)**

Before Bob took the test, the class sum was $85 \cdot 12 = 1020$. After Bob took the test, the class sum was $82 \cdot 13 = 1066$. Therefore Bob's score on the test was $1066 - 1020 = 46$. Bob didn't do very well.

7. **(A)**

Let g be the number of girls in the class. Then the sum for the girls is $90g$ and the sum for the boys is $81(2g) = 162g$. So the sum for the entire class is 252g. There are a total of 3g students in the class so the class average is 252g/3g = 84.

8. **(C)**

Use the endpoints (10,50) and (16, 70)

$$\frac{70-50}{16-10} = \frac{20}{6} = 3.3$$

9. **(D)**

If the average of 120 numbers is -20 then their sum must be $120(-20) = -2400$

10. **(B)**

Find the slope:

$$\frac{-2-4}{4-1} = \frac{-6}{3} = -2$$

11. **(A)**

$$\frac{1250+2350+3500}{3} = 2366$$

12. **(C)**

$$\left( \frac{4750-2350}{2350} \right) 100 = 102.1$$

13. **(D)**

Use the endpoints (2013, 1250) and (2016, 4750).

$$\frac{4750-1250}{2016-2013} = \frac{3500}{3} = 1166.6$$

14. **(B)**

$$\frac{5.00-3.50}{2} = 0.75$$

15. **(D)**

Sum needed: 80(5)

Sum attained: 75(3)

Sum needed for next two tests: 80(5)-75(3)

# 3. Algebra

By far the bulk of the problems on the SAT® have to do with algebra and so the bulk of this book is concerned with algebra. The algebra chapter begins with some basic skills that are needed and then starts a thorough review of linear relations, the most popular topic on the test. Because the SAT® places emphasis on an integrated knowledge of math, the lessons are intended to be autonomous but some of the examples in the lessons and some of the practice problems require some knowledge from other lessons. This is intentional and it is because SAT® problems require students to make connections across lesson topics.

## 3.1 Distributing and common factors

In algebra, the skills of distributing and common factors are considered to be basic, similar to learning to tie your shoelaces. Many problems on the SAT® involve using the skills of distributing and common factors, and a few problems test these skills directly.

### Distributing

The simplest form of distributing involves multiplying a term across parentheses. For example:

$$3(2x-3y)=(3\cdot 2x)-(3\cdot 3y)=6x-9y$$

The term can be a constant, as in the example above, or it can contain variables. For example:

$$6xy(2x+3y)=(6xy\cdot 2x)+(6xy\cdot 3y)=12x^2y+18xy^2$$

A special case of distributing that frequently causes trouble is when you are required to distribute a negative. For example:

$$5x-(2x^2+3x-4)=5x-2x^2-3x+4=-2x^2+2x+4$$

### Finding the factors of a number

To find the factors of a number by hand, the most useful technique is to build a factor tree. The idea is that any integer (that is not itself a prime number) can be expressed as the product of prime numbers. What is a prime number? Well, a prime number is a positive integer that is divisible <u>only</u> by itself and 1. Note that 1 is **not** a prime number. The smallest prime number is 2 and all the other prime numbers are odd. Two is the smallest prime and the only even prime number. The prime numbers are: {2, 3, 5, 7, 11, 13, 17, 19, 23, ....}. A good exercise is to write down the first 20 or so prime numbers. Now back to our factor tree. Below is the factor tree for 210.

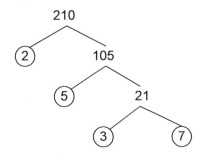

Notice that 210 is an even number. So we divide by two and get 105. The two is circled because two is prime. We notice that 105 is divisible by 5. So we divide by five and get 21. Five is circled because it is prime. The number 21 is divisible by three and seven, which are circled because they are prime.

The prime factorization of 210 is $210 = 2 \cdot 3 \cdot 5 \cdot 7$. The number 210 can be expressed as a product of primes because 210 is not itself prime.

We know that the <u>prime</u> factors of 210 are 2, 3, 5 and 7. But all the factors of 210 are combinations of the prime factors. In addition to 1 and 210, the factors of 210 are
$2 \cdot 3$, $2 \cdot 5$, $2 \cdot 7$, $3 \cdot 5$, $3 \cdot 7$, $5 \cdot 7$, $2 \cdot 3 \cdot 5$, etc. In other words, to find all the factors of 210 it is necessary to find all possible products of its prime factors. This can be very tedious to do by hand, so use the calculator tip below if you are working on a problem where a calculator is allowed.

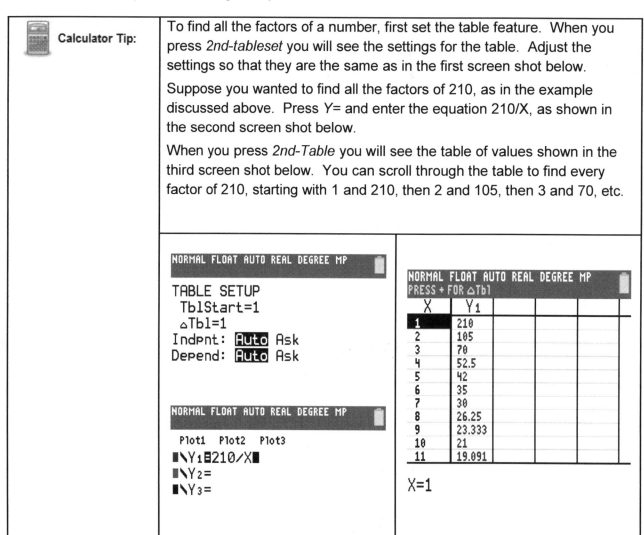

| | |
|---|---|
| **Calculator Tip:** | To find all the factors of a number, first set the table feature. When you press *2nd-tableset* you will see the settings for the table. Adjust the settings so that they are the same as in the first screen shot below. |
| | Suppose you wanted to find all the factors of 210, as in the example discussed above. Press *Y=* and enter the equation 210/X, as shown in the second screen shot below. |
| | When you press *2nd-Table* you will see the table of values shown in the third screen shot below. You can scroll through the table to find every factor of 210, starting with 1 and 210, then 2 and 105, then 3 and 70, etc. |

## Finding the greatest common factor (GCF)

When trying to simplify an expression a frequent first step is to pull out the greatest common factor (GCF). This is the opposite of distributing a single term across parentheses.

Suppose we want to factor the expression $6x - 9y$. Look for the factors that each term has in common:

$$6x = 2 \cdot 3 \cdot x \qquad 9y = 3 \cdot 3 \cdot y$$

The only factor in common to $6x$ and $9y$ is $3$. So now we take out the common factor:

$$6x - 9y = 3(2x - 3y).$$

Consider the expression $12x^2 y + 18xy^2 z$. Break each term into its factors and look for the factors that are common to both:

$$12x^2 y = 2^2 \cdot 3 \cdot x \cdot x \cdot y \qquad 18xy^2 z = 2 \cdot 3^2 \cdot x \cdot y \cdot y \cdot z$$

The common factors are $2 \cdot 3 \cdot x \cdot y$. We take these common factors out of the terms and get

$$12x^2 y + 18xy^2 z = 2 \cdot 3 \cdot xy(2x + 3yz) = 6xy(2x + 3yz).$$

In the example above, the constant terms we were dealing with were 12 and 18. We could have factored out 2, leaving 6 and 9. But 6 and 9 have a common factor of 3. We would then have to factor out the 3. It is far better to take out the greatest common factor (GCF) in one step.

Suppose we want to find the greatest common factor for 72 and 756. The greatest common factor can be found by following these steps:

1. Find the prime numbers that are factors for each term (see the calculator tip above).
2. Make a list of the prime factors that appear in every term.
3. Raise each of the prime factors to the smallest power that is used.

For the example of 72 and 756, we have the following:

1. $72 = 2^3 \cdot 3^2$ and $756 = 2^2 \cdot 3^3 \cdot 7$.
2. The common prime factors are 2 and 3.
3. The smallest power of 2 is 2, and the smallest power of 3 is 2.
4. The GCF is $2^2 \cdot 3^2 = 4 \cdot 9 = 36$.

| 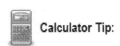  Calculator Tip: | The manual process above has the advantage of finding the GCF for any number of terms. However if you only need to find the GCF for two terms and the calculator is allowed, you may prefer this method. To find the GCF of 72 and 756 enter the following key sequence to locate the GCF *function: math-num-gcd* (note that this is labeled gcd on the calculator, not gcf). Then enter the 72 and 756 separated by a comma and press *enter*. |
| --- | --- |
| | NORMAL FLOAT AUTO REAL DEGREE MP |
| | gcd(72,756) |
| | 36 |

## Using common factors in division

So far we have looked at how to use common factors in multiplication. Using the constants from the GCF earlier example, we have

$$72xy - 756x = 36x(2y - 21).$$

But what if we were given a division problem? The process is much the same:

$$\frac{756x}{72xy} = \left(\frac{36x}{36x}\right)\left(\frac{21}{2y}\right) = \left(\frac{1}{1}\right)\frac{21}{2y} = \frac{21}{2y}$$

Whether multiplying or dividing, we pull out the GCF, which in this case is $36x$.

When doing division, many students find it easier to break the fraction into stacks. Using the same example as before, we break the fraction into a constant stack, an x-stack, and a y-stack. Then we simplify each stack. After that the stacks are combined to make a new fraction.

$$\frac{756x}{72xy} = \left(\frac{756}{72}\right)\left(\frac{x}{x}\right)\left(\frac{1}{y}\right) = \left(\frac{21}{2}\right)\left(\frac{1}{1}\right)\left(\frac{1}{y}\right) = \frac{21}{2y}$$

# 3.1 Practice problems on distributing and common factors
## calculator permitted unless stated otherwise

1. Without a calculator: The expression $3xy\left(2x^2+xy\right)$ is equivalent to:

A) $7x^3y$

B) $9x^2y$

C) $6x^3y+xy$

D) $6x^3y+3x^2y^2$

2. Without a calculator: The expression $648x^3y^6-162xyz$ is equivalent to:

A) $81xy(8x^2y^5-z)$

B) $81xyz(8x^2y^5-1)$

C) $162xy(4x^2y^5-z)$

D) $162xyz(4x^2y^5-1)$

3. Without a calculator: The simplest form of the expression

$360x^8y^5z^2-480x^3y^2z^3+540x^5y^7z^8$ is:

A) $15x^3y^2z\left(24x^5y^3z-32z^2+36x^2y^5z^5\right)$

B) $60x^3y^2z\left(6x^5y^3z-8z^2+9x^2y^5z^5\right)$

C) $15x^3y^2z^2\left(24x^5y^3-32z+36x^2y^5z^6\right)$

D) $60x^3y^2z^2\left(6x^5y^3-8z+9x^2y^5z^6\right)$

4. Without a calculator: The expression $5xy$ is equivalent to:

A) $\dfrac{50x^2y^2}{5xy}$

B) $\dfrac{30x^2y}{6x}$

C) $\dfrac{12x^3y}{60x^2}$

D) $\dfrac{15x^3y^8}{3x^4y^7}$

5. Without a calculator: The expression $\dfrac{120x^3y^2-136x^2z}{8x^2}$ can be simplified to:

A) $15xy^2-17z$

B) $15y^2-17z$

C) $-2xyz$

D) $-2(xy^2-17)$

6. Without a calculator: The expression $\dfrac{96xy^2z^3-36x^2yz^2}{12x^3yz^6}$ can be simplified to:

A) $\dfrac{8yz-3x}{xz^2}$

B) $8yz-3x$

C) $\dfrac{8y}{x^2}-\dfrac{3}{xz^4}$

D) $\dfrac{8yz-3x}{x^2z^4}$

7. If twice the sum of 13 and a number is equal to 15 times the difference of a number and 6, which equation could be used to solve for the number?

A) $2x+26=15x-6$

B) $26+x=15x-90$

C) $2(x+13)=15(x-6)$

D) $2(13+x)=15(6-x)$

8. Without a calculator: The expression $\dfrac{-x}{y}(x-y)$ is equivalent to:

A) $x-\dfrac{x^2}{y}$

B) $\dfrac{-x^2}{y}+1$

C) $\dfrac{x^2}{y}-x$

D) $xy-y^2$

## 3.1 Solutions to practice problems on distributing and factoring

1. (D)

$$3xy\left(2x^2 + xy\right) = 3xy \cdot 2x^2 + 3xy \cdot xy = 6x^3y + 3x^2y^2$$

2. (C)

Find GCF of 648 and 162:

$648 = 2^3 \cdot 3^4$ and $162 = 2 \cdot 3^4$ so GCF=$2 \cdot 3^4 = 162$

$648x^3y^6 - 162xyz = 162xy\left(4x^2y^5 - z\right)$

3. (D)

Use factor trees to find the GCF of 360 480 and 540

$360 = 2^3 \cdot 3^2 \cdot 5$ $\quad 480 = 2^5 \cdot 3 \cdot 5$ $\quad 540 = 2^2 \cdot 3^3 \cdot 5$

so GCF=$2^2 \cdot 3 \cdot 5 = 60$

$360x^8y^5z^2 - 480x^3y^2z^3 + 540x^5y^7z^8 =$

$\qquad 60x^3y^2z^2\left(6x^5y^3 - 8z + 9x^2y^5z^6\right)$

4. (B)

$$\frac{30x^2y}{6x} = \frac{6x\left(5xy\right)}{6x} = 5xy$$

5. (A)

Use factor trees to find the GCF of 120 and 136

$120 = 2^3 \cdot 3 \cdot 5$ and $136 = 2^3 \cdot 17$ so GCF=$2^3 = 8$

$$\frac{120x^3y^2 - 136x^2z}{8x^2} = \frac{8x^2\left(15xy^2 - 17z\right)}{8x^2} = 15xy^2 - 17z$$

6. (D)

Use factor trees to find the GCF of 96 and 36

$96 = 2^5 \cdot 3$ and $36 = 2^2 \cdot 3^2$ so GCF=$2^2 \cdot 3 = 12$

$$\frac{96xy^2z^3 - 36x^2yz^2}{12x^3yz^6} = \frac{12xyz^2\left(8yz - 3x\right)}{12x^3yz^6} = \frac{8yz - 3x}{x^2z^4}$$

7. (C)

8. (A)

$$\frac{-x}{y}(x - y) = \frac{-x^2}{y} + \frac{xy}{y} = x - \frac{x^2}{y}$$

## 3.2 Fractions and ratios

A fraction occurs when one value or expression is divided by another number or expression. Understanding how to perform operations on fractions is essential in a variety of situations. A ratio is just "a fraction in a context," where the numerator, denominator and overall ratio have physical meaning.

### Adding and subtracting fractions

Please remember that **fractions cannot be added or subtracted unless they have the same denominator**, called the common denominator.

Consider a simple case: $\frac{1}{2} + \frac{2}{7}$ . Hopefully you are not thinking that the answer is

$\frac{1}{2} + \frac{2}{7} = \frac{1+2}{2+7} = \frac{3}{9} = \frac{1}{3}$ !!!! That would be breaking just about every rule in math. (Believe it or not I have seen students do exactly that.) Remember to first convert each fraction so that both fractions have the same denominator, then add or subtract:

$$\frac{1}{2} + \frac{2}{7} = \left(\frac{1}{2}\right)\left(\frac{7}{7}\right) + \left(\frac{2}{7}\right)\left(\frac{2}{2}\right) = \frac{7}{14} + \frac{4}{14} = \frac{7+4}{14} = \frac{11}{14}$$

In this example the common denominator is 14. Although the product of the denominators can always be used, your work will be a bit simpler if you use the least common denominator (LCD). Consider the example of $\frac{7}{15} - \frac{2}{20}$ You could use 300 as the common denominator:

$$\frac{7}{15} - \frac{3}{20} = \left(\frac{7}{15}\right)\left(\frac{20}{20}\right) - \left(\frac{3}{20}\right)\left(\frac{15}{15}\right) = \frac{140}{300} - \frac{45}{300} = \frac{140-45}{300} = \frac{95}{300} = \left(\frac{19}{60}\right)\left(\frac{5}{5}\right) = \frac{19}{60}$$

The drawback to this approach is that you are working with larger numbers, and that causes you to have to simplify the fraction at the end. To simplify you have to realize that 5 goes into 19 _and_ 5 goes into 300, and that can be difficult to see. However the calculator tip below shows how to simplify a fraction on the calculator.

| Calculator Tip: | Simplifying fractions: Suppose you are working on the problem above and want to use the calculator to simplify 95/300. Just type *95/300* and press *enter*. Then type *math-Frac-enter*. |
|---|---|
| | NORMAL FLOAT AUTO REAL DEGREE MP<br><br>95/300<br>　　　　　　　　　　　.3166666667<br>Ans▶Frac<br>　　　　　　　　　　　　　　$\frac{19}{60}$ |

It is a little easier if you can find the LCD and use that instead. To find the LCD, calculate the prime factorization of each denominator: $15 = 3 \cdot 5$ and $20 = 2^2 \cdot 5$. Next, make a list of all of the prime factors found in either denominator, and then raise each prime factor to its largest power:

$$LCD = 2^2 \cdot 3^1 \cdot 5^1 = 60 .$$

Believe it or not, this technique for finding the LCD always works. But if you only have two fractions to deal with, it is much easier to use the graphing calculator as shown in the tip below.

| Calculator Tip: | Finding the LCD: Suppose you are working on the problem above and want to use the calculator to simplify find the LCD of 15 and 20. Just type *math-num-lcm(* and then enter *15,20)* . The result is shown in the screen shot below. |
| --- | --- |
| | 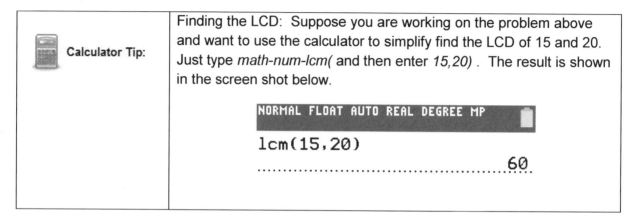 |

Now that we found the LCD is 60, we proceed with the subtraction:

$$\frac{7}{15} - \frac{3}{20} = \left(\frac{7}{15}\right)\left(\frac{4}{4}\right) - \left(\frac{3}{20}\right)\left(\frac{3}{3}\right) = \frac{28}{60} - \frac{9}{60} = \frac{19}{60} .$$

You may be wondering if this LCD stuff is worth all the effort. When you are only dealing with two fractions, it may not be. When you are dealing with several fractions the LCD is far easier, though the calculator can only handle two numbers at a time. There are multiple fraction problems at the end of this unit.

It is also necessary to add and subtract fractions involving variables. A simple example would be $\frac{3}{x} + \frac{y}{2}$ . The common denominator would be 2x, and this yields

$$\frac{3}{x} + \frac{y}{2} = \left(\frac{3}{x}\right)\left(\frac{2}{2}\right) + \left(\frac{y}{2}\right)\left(\frac{x}{x}\right) = \frac{6}{2x} + \frac{yx}{2x} = \frac{xy + 6}{2x} .$$

## Multiplying fractions

When multiplying fractions, multiply the numerators together to form the new numerator, and multiply the denominators together to form the new denominator. For example,

$$\left(\frac{2}{3}\right)\left(\frac{5}{7}\right) = \frac{2 \cdot 5}{3 \cdot 7} = \frac{10}{21}$$

The same rule applies to fractions with variables:

$$\left(\frac{x}{3y}\right)\left(\frac{4}{z}\right) = \frac{4x}{3yz}$$

## Dividing fractions

When two fractions are to be divided, multiply the fraction in the numerator by the reciprocal of the fraction in the denominator.  For example,

$$\left(\frac{2}{3}\right) \div \left(\frac{5}{7}\right) = \left(\frac{2}{3}\right)\left(\frac{7}{5}\right) = \frac{14}{15}$$

The same rule applies to fractions with variables:

$$\left(\frac{x}{3y}\right) \div \left(\frac{4x}{z}\right) = \left(\frac{x}{3y}\right)\left(\frac{z}{4x}\right) = \frac{z}{12y}$$

## When fractions (without variables) appear in equations

When a fraction without variables appears in one place in an equation, the best approach is to eliminate the fraction by multiplying both sides of the equation by the reciprocal of that fraction.  For example,

$$\frac{3}{5}x = 2, \ \left(\frac{5}{3}\right)\left(\frac{3}{5}x\right) = \left(\frac{5}{3}\right)(2), \ x = \frac{10}{3}$$

When different fractions without variables appear in different places in an equation, the best approach is to multiply both sides of the equation by the LCD of the fractions.  For example,

$$\frac{4}{15}x = \frac{2}{3}x + 2$$

$$15\left(\frac{4}{15}x\right) = 15\left(\frac{2}{3}x + 2\right)$$

$$4x = 10x + 30, \ -30 = 6x, \ -\frac{30}{6} = x, \ -5 = x$$

## When fractions (with variables) appear in equations

When solving an equation that has fractions with variables, a good approach is to cross-multiply.  For example:

$$\frac{2x}{7} = \frac{6}{35}, \ 70x = 42, \ x = \frac{42}{70} = \frac{3}{5}$$

Cross-multiplying works nicely even when fractions with variables appear on both sides of the equation.  For example,

$$\frac{2}{x-1} = \frac{x}{6}, \ 12 = x^2 - x, \ 0 = x^2 - x - 12, \ 0 = (x-4)(x+3), \ x = 4 \text{ or } x = -3$$

## Ratios, rates, and unit rates

A ratio is a fraction with a context. Let's consider the ratio of 3:2, give this a context, and pose a problem. "Suppose a recipe for biscuits calls for three parts flour and two parts milk. If we plan to use 21 ounces of flower how many ounces of milk should be used?" The solution lies in setting up an equation which is solved by cross-multiplying:

$$\frac{3}{2} = \frac{21}{x}, \ 3x = 42, \ x = 14$$

Let's consider the same biscuit problem, only now the problem asks: "Suppose that in the process of making dough for biscuits, three units of flour are used for every two units of milk. At that rate, how many ounces of milk will be consumed if 21 ounces of flour are used?" Notice the use of the word **rate**. This problem could be solved by setting up the same equation above (after all it is the exact same problem). But you could also think of this in terms of unit conversion. In this problem we are given a rate with two units (milk and flour) and we want to eliminate the flour units in order to solve for the milk units.

$$\left( \frac{2 \text{ milk}}{3 \text{ flour}} \right) (21 \text{ flour}) = \frac{42}{3} \text{milk} = 14 \text{ milk}$$

A special case of rate is called a **unit rate**, which is simply a rate that has the value of 1 in the numerator or denominator. Perhaps the most frequently used unit rate is the speed of an automobile which is measured in miles per hour (mph). But let's go back to the biscuit problem again with different wording. "Suppose that in the process of making dough for biscuits, 1.5 units of flour are consumed for every unit of milk. At that rate, if 21 ounces of flour are consumed, how many ounces of milk would be consumed?" In this problem we take the reciprocal of the unit rate stated in the problem so that the flour units cancel out, solving for milk.

$$\left( \frac{1 \text{ milk}}{1.5 \text{ flour}} \right) (21 \text{ flour}) = \frac{21}{1.5} \text{ milk} = 14 \text{ milk}$$

But the idea of rate or unit rate can also come up in tables and graphs. Going back to biscuits again, "Suppose the table below gives the amount of flour to be used for various amounts of milk. What is the average rate of change in flour?"

| Milk (x) | Flour (y) |
|----------|-----------|
| 0        | 0         |
| 2        | 3         |
| 4        | 6         |
| 6        | 9         |

In unit 2.4 we observed that the average rate of change is the same as slope, and that to compute an average rate of change we can use the (x,y) coordinates for two points. In this problem the average rate of change is constant, so we can use any pair of points. In the calculation below we use (2,3) and 6,9).

$$\text{average rate of change} = \text{slope} = \frac{\text{change in y}}{\text{change in x}} = \frac{9-3}{6-2} = \frac{6}{4} = \frac{3}{2}$$

34

If the problem with the table above stated "Suppose the table above gives the amount of flour to be used for various amounts of milk. If the relationship between flour and milk is linear, by how many units does flour change for each unit change in milk?" Now the problem is calling for a unit rate of change. We could start by finding the average rate of change (as shown above) and then converting it to a unit rate. The calculation would be:

$$\text{unit rate of change: } \frac{3}{2} = \frac{r}{1}, \ 2r = 3, \ r = \frac{3}{2} = 1.5$$

If the problem with the table stated: "Suppose the table above gives the amount of flour to be used for various amounts of milk. What equation could be used to model the linear relationship between flour and milk ?" We would note that every time milk increases by 2 units the flour increases by 3 units, indicating a slope of 3/2 or 1.5. We would note that when milk is zero the flour is also zero, indicating that the y-intercept is zero. That would mean the equation of the line is $y = 1.5x + 0$.

Finally, if the problem with the table stated " Suppose the table above gives the amount of flour to be used for various amounts of milk. What graph would show the linear relationship between flour and milk ?" The answer would be a graph that looks something like this:

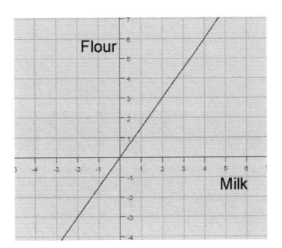

**Solving for a ratio**

Sometimes a problem will ask you to solve for the ratio of two or more variables. Your approach should be to solve for the variable being asked for in the numerator of the ratio, and then divide by the other variable to obtain the value of the ratio. For example, solving for x/y in the equation below:

$$\frac{x}{3} = \frac{y}{5}, \ 5x = 3y, \ x = \left(\frac{1}{5}\right)3y, \ \frac{x}{y} = \frac{3}{5}$$

**Direct and inverse variation**

This is a type of word problem that seems difficult until you see how to do it. We begin with two definitions:

The variables x and y vary **directly** if their relationship can be modeled as

$$y = kx$$

where k is a non-zero constant. If we suppose k to be positive, you can see that when the value of x increases, y increases. This is where the name "direct" variation comes from. The variables x and y move in the same direction.

The variables x and y vary **inversely** if their relationship can be modeled as

$$y = \frac{k}{x}$$

where k is a non-zero constant. If we suppose k to be positive, you can see that when the value of x increases, y decreases. This is where the name "indirect" or "inverse" variation comes from. The variables x and y move in opposite directions.

These problems usually take the same form. They begin by saying whether the relationship is direct or inverse and supply initial values of x and y. This enables you to evaluate k. Then the problem asks for a new value of y when the value of x changes. For example:

X and Y are inversely proportional, and when X=10 Y=20. What is the value of Y when X=5?

The problem is solved as follows:

$$y = \frac{k}{x}$$                    given

$$20 = \frac{k}{10}, \quad 200 = k$$                    substitute and solve for k

$$y = \frac{200}{x}$$                    new partial equation

$$y = \frac{200}{5} = 40$$                    substitute for X, solve for Y.

Note that Y increased when X decreased because X and Y are inversely related.

# 3.2 Practice problems on fractions and ratios
## calculator permitted unless stated otherwise

1. <u>Without a calculator</u>: What is the value of $\frac{7}{10} - \frac{5}{12}$ ?

    A)    -1

    B)    12/22

    C)    17/60

    D)    35/120

2. What is the value of $\frac{7}{10} + \frac{5}{12} - \frac{11}{42}$ ?

    A)    359/420

    B)    193/140

    C)    11/144

    D)    118/525

3. What is the value of $\left(\frac{-2}{3}\right) \cdot \left(\frac{6}{-11}\right) \cdot \left(\frac{3}{2}\right)$ ?

    A)    -7/6

    B)    6/11

    C)    36/55

    D)    7/6

4. <u>Without a calculator</u>: What is the value of $\left(\frac{3}{5}\right) \div \left(\frac{-5}{12}\right)$ ?

    A)    -1/4

    B)    -36/25

    C)    -4/1

    D)    -15/60

5. Simplify $\frac{2}{5x^2} - \frac{3}{25xy}$

    A)    $7/5x^2 y$

    B)    $-1/(5x(x-5y))$

    C)    $(10y-3x)/5x^2 y$

    D)    $(10y-3x)/25x^2 y$

6. Simplify $\frac{x}{1-x} - \frac{y}{1-y}$

    A)    $(x-y)/(x^2 -2xy+ y^2)$

    B)    $(x+y-2xy)/(2-x-y)$

    C)    $(y-x)/(x-y)$

    D)    $(x-y)/(xy-x-y+1)$

7. Simplify $\left(\frac{5x^2}{3y}\right) \cdot \left(\frac{6y^2}{8x}\right)$

    A)    $5x/4y$

    B)    $20xy/9$

    C)    $4y/5x$

    D)    $5xy/4$

8. Simplify $\left(\frac{5x^2}{3y}\right) \div \left(\frac{6y^2}{8x}\right)$

    A)    $5xy/4$

    B)    $20xy/9$

    C)    $4/5xy$

    D)    $20x^3 /9y^3$

9. Simplify $\frac{y}{x} - \frac{x}{y} + \frac{3}{xy}$

    A)    $\dfrac{y-x+3}{x+y+xy}$

    B)    $\dfrac{3}{xy}$

    C)    $\dfrac{y-x-3}{xy}$

    D)    $\dfrac{y^2 -x^2 +3}{xy}$

10. Simplify $\left(\dfrac{x}{y}\right) \cdot \left(\dfrac{xz}{y}\right) \cdot \left(\dfrac{yz}{x}\right)$

A)     $\dfrac{z}{xy^2}$

B)     $\left(\dfrac{xz}{y}\right)^2$

C)     $\dfrac{xz^2}{y}$

D)     $\dfrac{xz}{y}$

11. <u>Without a calculator</u>: simplify $\dfrac{\frac{3}{5}}{\frac{2}{2}}$

A)     6/5

B)     5/6

C)     2/15

D)     6/15

*(handwritten: $3/_1 \times 2/_5 = 6/_5$)*

12. Simplify $\dfrac{x^2-9}{x+1} \div \dfrac{x+3}{x^2-1}$

A)     $\dfrac{x-3}{x-1}$

B)     $\dfrac{x-1}{x-3}$

C)     $x^2-4x+3$

D)     $x^2+2x-3$

13. Simplify $\dfrac{x}{x-1} - \dfrac{x}{x+1}$

A)     $\dfrac{2x}{x^2-1}$

B)     $0$

C)     $\dfrac{-2x}{x^2-1}$

D)     $\dfrac{-2x}{x-1}$

14. <u>Without a calculator</u>: If $3x-15=2y-10$ and $y \neq 0$, then x/y is equal to:

A)     2/3

B)     $2y+5$

C)     $\dfrac{2y+5}{3}$

D)     $\dfrac{2y+5}{3y}$

15. <u>Without a calculator</u>: If $\dfrac{1}{2}xy = \dfrac{6}{5}y^2$ and $y \neq 0$, then what is the value of $\dfrac{x}{y}$?

A)     5/12

B)     6/10

C)     10/6

D)     12/5

16. <u>Without a calculator</u>: If $\dfrac{5}{6}x = \dfrac{2}{3}(x-5)+5$ then what is the value of x?

A)     0

B)     10

C)     20

D)     30

17. <u>Without a calculator</u>: If $\dfrac{x}{6} + \dfrac{x+1}{7} = \dfrac{5x}{12}$ then what is the value of x?

A)     3/4

B)     11/6

C)     4/3

D)     12/61

18. The football team had a pretty good season this year, with 2/3 of the games won and 1/9 of the games tied. What was their fraction of losses?

A)     1/9

B)     2/9

C)     3/9

D)     4/9

*(handwritten: $\frac{8}{3} - \frac{1}{9} = \frac{9}{9}$ ... $5/_9$)*

38

19. <u>Without a calculator</u>: If $\dfrac{5}{6x} = \dfrac{10}{7}$, and $x \neq 0$ then x equals

   A)        7/12

   B)        12/7

   C)        25/21

   D)        21/25

20. <u>Without a calculator</u>: If $\dfrac{x-5}{y-5} = \dfrac{2}{3}$, and $y \neq 0$ then x/y equals

   A)        (2y+5)/3

   B)        (2y-5)/3

   C)        (2y+5)/3y

   D)        (2y-5)/3y

21. If there are 16 ounces in a pound, how many pounds are in 80 ounces?

   A)        1/5

   B)        5

   C)        64

   D)        1280

22. A blueprint is drawn to scale, where two inches represents 25 feet. If a room is 70 feet long, how many inches long will it be on the blueprint?

   A)        0.2

   B)        0.7

   C)        1.4

   D)        5.6

23. Y varies directly with X. When X=5, Y=40. What is the value of Y when X increases to 7?

   A)        7/8

   B)        8/7

   C)        25

   D)        56

24. Y varies inversely with X. When X=5, Y=40. What is the value of Y when X increases to 7?

   A)        7/8

   B)        8/7

   C)        25

   D)        200/7

25. It takes Hayley 14 days to paint two rooms. At this rate, how many days would it take for her to paint five rooms?

   A)        1.4

   B)        12.5

   C)        17.5

   D)        35.0

26. A map is drawn to scale so that two inches is 70 miles. If two towns are 5 inches apart on the map, how far apart are they (in miles)?

   A)        7

   B)        35

   C)        175

   D)        350

27. Paul has played 10 lacrosse games and scored 3 goals. At this rate how many goals should he expect to score over the entire season if there are 14 games remaining in the season?

   A)        4

   B)        5

   C)        6

   D)        7

28. In general, SAT® scores are directly proportional to the amount of time spent studying. On average, when students spend 2 hours per week studying for the SAT®, their math score increases by 70 points. If Kelsey wants her score to increase by 105 points, how many hours per week should she study?

   A)        2

   B)        3

   C)        4

   D)        6

29. Suppose the strength of gravitational pull is inversely proportional to the square of the distance between two bodies. If the gravitational pull is 50 units when two bodies are 10 units apart, how strong is the pull when the two bodies are 100 units apart?

A) 0.05
B) 0.50
C) 5.00
D) 50.00

30. Lizzy planted a tree in her back yard and measured that it had grown 10 inches over the past six years. At that rate, how long will it take the tree to grow another 25 inches?

A) 15
B) 16
C) 35
D) 42

31. Fifty of this year's freshman class of 300 students tried out for the football team. If 250 freshman enroll in school next year, how many of them are expected to try out for football?

A) 42
B) 60
C) 550
D) 1500

**Questions 32 - 34 refer the to the following information:**

The Miller family live 1,000 miles from the Grand Canyon and they were on the road for 40 hours driving there. Their car gets 30 miles per gallon and the average cost of gas was $2.15 per gallon. Their gas tank holds 25 gallons.

32. What was their average speed?

A) 15 mph
B) 25 mph
C) 33 mph
D) 40 mph

33. How much money did the Millers spend on gas per mile travelled?

A) $0.02
B) $0.07
C) $0.33
D) $2.15

34. If the Millers had a quarter tank of gas when they started their drive, what is the fewest number of times they would have to stop for gas?

A) 0
B) 1
C) 2
D) 3

**Questions 35 and 36 refer to the table below, which shows the conversion rates between two currencies and the US dollar.**

|  | US dollars |
|---|---|
| 1 British pound | $1.42 |
| 1 Euro | $1.10 |

35. How many Euro can be purchased with 10 British pounds?

A) $6.40
B) $7.75
C) $12.91
D) $15.62

36. Jordan took 500 US dollars and converted them to British pounds. While in Britain she spent 50 of her British pounds and converted her remaining pounds into Euros. While visiting Europe she spent 100 Euros. Upon returning to the US she converted her remaining Euros to US dollars. How many US dollars did Jordan have left over from her trip?

A) $192
B) $203
C) $319
D) $429

40

# 3.2 Solutions to practice problems on fractions and ratios

1. (C)

$10 = 2 \cdot 5$ and $12 = 2^2 \cdot 3$. So the LCD is

$2^2 \cdot 3 \cdot 5 = 60$.  $\dfrac{7}{10} - \dfrac{5}{12} = \dfrac{42}{60} - \dfrac{25}{60} = \dfrac{17}{60}$

2. (A)

$10 = 2 \cdot 5$ and $12 = 2^2 \cdot 3$ and $42 = 2 \cdot 3 \cdot 7$. So the LCD is $2^2 \cdot 3 \cdot 5 \cdot 7 = 420$.

$\dfrac{7}{10} + \dfrac{5}{12} - \dfrac{11}{42} = \dfrac{7 \cdot 42}{420} + \dfrac{5 \cdot 35}{420} - \dfrac{11 \cdot 10}{420} = \dfrac{359}{420}$

3. (B)

$\left(\dfrac{-2}{3}\right) \cdot \left(\dfrac{6}{-11}\right) \cdot \left(\dfrac{3}{2}\right) = \dfrac{-36}{-66} = \dfrac{6}{11}$

4. (B)

$\left(\dfrac{3}{5}\right) \div \left(\dfrac{-5}{12}\right) = \left(\dfrac{3}{5}\right)\left(\dfrac{12}{-5}\right) = \dfrac{36}{-25} = -\dfrac{36}{25}$

5. (D)

$\dfrac{2}{5x^2} - \dfrac{3}{25xy} = \dfrac{2(5y)}{25x^2 y} - \dfrac{3x}{25x^2 y} = \dfrac{10y - 3x}{25x^2 y}$

6. (D)

$\dfrac{x}{1-x} - \dfrac{y}{1-y} = \dfrac{x(1-y) - y(1-x)}{(1-x)(1-y)} = \dfrac{x-y}{xy - x - y + 1}$

7. (D)

$\left(\dfrac{5x^2}{3y}\right)\left(\dfrac{6y^2}{8x}\right) = \dfrac{5 \cdot 6x^2 y^2}{3 \cdot 8xy} = \dfrac{30x^2 y^2}{24xy} = \dfrac{5xy}{4}$

8. (D)

$\left(\dfrac{5x^2}{3y}\right) \div \left(\dfrac{6y^2}{8x}\right) = \left(\dfrac{5x^2}{3y}\right)\left(\dfrac{8x}{6y^2}\right) = \dfrac{40x^3}{18y^3} = \dfrac{20x^3}{9y^3}$

9. (D)

$\dfrac{y}{x} - \dfrac{x}{y} + \dfrac{3}{xy} = \left(\dfrac{y}{x}\right)\left(\dfrac{y}{y}\right) - \left(\dfrac{x}{y}\right)\left(\dfrac{x}{x}\right) + \dfrac{3}{xy} = \dfrac{y^2 - x^2 + 3}{xy}$

10. (C)

$\left(\dfrac{x}{y}\right) \cdot \left(\dfrac{xz}{y}\right) \cdot \left(\dfrac{yz}{x}\right) = \dfrac{x^2 yz^2}{xy^2} = \dfrac{xz^2}{y}$

11. (A)

$\dfrac{\frac{3}{5}}{\frac{5}{2}} = \left(\dfrac{\frac{3}{1}}{\frac{5}{2}}\right)\left(\dfrac{\frac{2}{5}}{\frac{2}{5}}\right) = \dfrac{\frac{6}{5}}{\frac{5}{1}} = \dfrac{6}{5}$

12. (C)

$\dfrac{x^2 - 9}{x+1} \div \dfrac{x+3}{x^2 - 1} = \dfrac{(x+3)(x-3)}{x+1} \cdot \dfrac{(x+1)(x-1)}{x+3}$

$= (x-3)(x-1) = x^2 - 4x + 3$

13. (A)

$\dfrac{x}{x-1} - \dfrac{x}{x+1} = \left(\dfrac{x}{x-1}\right)\left(\dfrac{x+1}{x+1}\right) - \left(\dfrac{x}{x+1}\right)\left(\dfrac{x-1}{x-1}\right)$

$= \dfrac{x^2 + x - (x^2 - x)}{(x-1)(x+1)} = \dfrac{2x}{x^2 - 1}$

14. (D)

$3x - 15 = 2y - 10,\ 3x = 2y + 5,\ x = \dfrac{2y+5}{3},\ \dfrac{x}{y} = \dfrac{2y+5}{3y}$

15. (D)

$\dfrac{1}{2}xy = \dfrac{6}{5}y^2,\ x = \dfrac{12}{5}y,\ \dfrac{x}{y} = \dfrac{12}{5}$

16. (B)

$\dfrac{5}{6}x = \dfrac{2}{3}(x-5) + 5,\ \left(\dfrac{6}{5}\right)\left(\dfrac{5}{6}x\right) = \left(\dfrac{6}{5}\right)\left[\dfrac{2}{3}(x-5) + 5\right]$,

$x = \dfrac{4}{5}(x-5) + 6,\ x - \dfrac{4}{5}x = 2,\ \dfrac{1}{5}x = 2,\ x = 10$

17. (C)

$\dfrac{x}{6} + \dfrac{x+1}{7} = \dfrac{5x}{12},\ 84\left[\dfrac{x}{6} + \dfrac{x+1}{7}\right] = 84\left(\dfrac{5x}{12}\right)$,

$14x + 12x + 12 = 35x,\ 26x + 12 = 35x,\ 12 = 9x,\ 4/3 = x$

18. (B)

$\dfrac{2}{3} + \dfrac{1}{9} + x = 1,\ \dfrac{6}{9} + \dfrac{1}{9} + x = 1,\ x = \dfrac{2}{9}$

19. (A)

$\dfrac{5}{6x} = \dfrac{10}{7},\ 60x = 35,\ x = 35/60 = 7/12$

41

20. (C)

$\dfrac{x-5}{y-5} = \dfrac{2}{3}$, $3x - 15 = 2y - 10$, $3x = 2y + 5$,

$x = \dfrac{2y+5}{3}$, $\dfrac{x}{y} = \dfrac{2y+5}{3y}$

21. (B)

$\dfrac{16}{1} = \dfrac{80}{x}$, $16x = 80$, $x = 5$    OR

$80 \text{ oz} \left( \dfrac{1 \text{ pound}}{16 \text{ oz}} \right) = 5 \text{ pounds}$

22 ( D)

$\dfrac{2}{25} = \dfrac{x}{70}$,    $25x = 140$,    $x = 5.6 \text{ inches}$

23. (D)

$y = kx$

$40 = 5k$,    $k = 8$

$y = 8x$,    $y = 8 \cdot 7 = 56$

24. (D)

$y = \dfrac{k}{x}$

$40 = \dfrac{k}{5}$,    $k = 200$

$y = \dfrac{200}{x}$,    $y = \dfrac{200}{7}$

25. (D)

$\dfrac{14}{2} = \dfrac{x}{5}$, $2x = 70$, $x = 35$    OR

$5 \text{ rooms} \left( \dfrac{14 \text{ days}}{2 \text{ rooms}} \right) = 35 \text{ days}$

26. (C)

$\dfrac{2}{70} = \dfrac{5}{x}$, $2x = 350$, $x = 175$

27. (D)

$\left( \dfrac{3 \text{ goals}}{10 \text{ games}} \right) (24 \text{ games in the season}) = 7.2 \text{ games}$

28. (B)

$y = kx$, $70 = 2k$, $k = 35$

$y = 35x$, $105 = 35x$, $3 = x$

29. (B)

$y = \dfrac{k}{x^2}$, $50 = \dfrac{k}{10^2}$, $k = 5{,}000$

$y = \dfrac{5{,}000}{x^2} = \dfrac{5{,}000}{100^2} = 0.5$

30. (A)

$\left( \dfrac{6 \text{ years}}{10 \text{ inches}} \right) (25 \text{ inches}) = 15 \text{ years}$

31. (A)

$\left( \dfrac{50 \text{ try out}}{300 \text{ freshmen}} \right) (250 \text{ freshmen}) = 41.6 \text{ try out}$

32. (B)

$\left( \dfrac{1000 \text{ miles}}{40 \text{ hours}} \right) = 25 \text{ miles per hour (mph)}$

33. (B)

$\left( \dfrac{1 \text{ gallon}}{30 \text{ miles}} \right) \left( \dfrac{2.15 \text{ dollars}}{1 \text{ gallon}} \right) = 0.07 \dfrac{\text{dollars}}{\text{mile}}$

34. (C)

$(1000 \text{ miles}) \left( \dfrac{1 \text{ gallon}}{30 \text{ miles}} \right) \left( \dfrac{1 \text{ tank}}{25 \text{ gallons}} \right) = 1.33 \text{ tanks of gas}$

$1.33 - 0.25 = 1.08 \text{ tanks purchased}$

35. (D)

$(10 \text{ pounds}) \left( \dfrac{1.42 \text{ dollars}}{1 \text{ pound}} \right) \left( \dfrac{1.10 \text{ Euro}}{1 \text{ dollar}} \right) = 15.62 \text{ Euro}$

36. (C)

$(500 \text{ dollars}) \left( \dfrac{1 \text{ pound}}{1.42 \text{ dollars}} \right) = 352.11 \text{ pounds to start}$

$(302.11 \text{ pounds}) \left( \dfrac{1.42 \text{ dollars}}{1 \text{ pound}} \right) \left( \dfrac{1 \text{ Euro}}{1.10 \text{ dollars}} \right) = 390 \text{ Euro}$

$(290 \text{ Euro}) \left( \dfrac{1.10 \text{ dollars}}{1 \text{ Euro}} \right) = 319 \text{ dollars}$

## 3.3    Linear equations and systems

By far, linear relations is the single most popular math topic on the SAT®. The test requires a deep understanding of linear relations, from algebraic, graphical and statistical points of view. The focus of this chapter is the algebraic point of view but the chapters re-enforce and overlap each other in order to achieve an integrated understanding of this vital topic.

### Linear equations in one variable

Some of the problems on the test require you to solve a linear equation in one variable. For example:

> If three times a number is the same as five less than twice that number, what is the value of the number?

This requires you to set up the equation $3n = 2n - 5$ and solve, yielding the answer of negative five.

Linear equations in one variable require you to handle word problems, scanning for keywords. Many of these keywords are shown below. Linear equations might also involve fractions (see Section 3.2 if you need more review of equations involving fractions).

| Operation | Keywords or phrases |
|---|---|
| Addition | sum |
| | a certain amount greater than another amount |
| | a certain amount more than another amount |
| Subtraction | difference |
| | a certain amount less than another amount |
| Multiplication | product |
| | times |
| | double, triple, etc. |
| Division | quotient |
| | ratio |
| | half, one half, one-third, etc. |
| Powers | squared, cubed, etc. |
| | raised to a power |
| Roots | square root, cube root, etc. |
| Equality | is |
| | is equal to |
| | is the same as |

### Linear equations in two variables

Perhaps the best known linear equation is y=mx+b, which is called the slope-intercept form of the line. It gets its name because graphically, m is the slope of the line (slope is the way we measure how quickly the line rises or falls), and (0,b) is the point where the line crosses the y-axis (called the y-intercept). In the algebraic context, the slope is the amount that the y-value changes every time the x-value changes by one unit. The y-intercept is the starting value for y in situations where x represents time.

Suppose you want a mathematical model of how much money it costs to ride in a taxi. You could write an equation in the slope-intercept form:

$$\text{cost} = 2.50m + 3.00$$

where the y-variable represents the cost of the taxi ride and $m$ represents the number of miles driven. In this context, the y-intercept of 3.00 is the amount of money it costs to enter the taxi (it has not yet driven anywhere because the cost is $3 when $m$ is zero) and the slope of 2.50 is the amount of money that will be added to your total cost for every mile driven.

Graphical point of view

The graphical view of the taxi equation is illustrated below. Notice that the line crosses the y-axis at 3.00. The meaning of the y-intercept is that $3.00 is the amount of money required to step into the taxi (where the number of miles driven is zero). The additional cost of $2.50 per mile is represented by the slope of the line. Choose two points on the line (in this case we chose (0,3) and (2,8)) and find the slope by measuring the rise (in this case 5 units) over the run (in this case 2 units). The slope is 5/2 or 2.50.

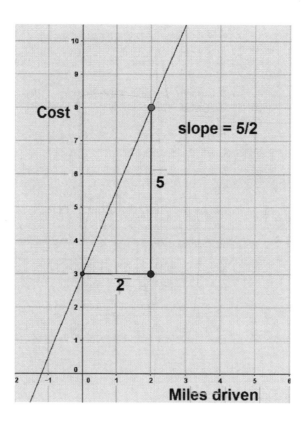

## Function and data points of view

The function point of view of the taxi equation is to think of the cost of the taxi ride as a function of the miles driven. We could re-write the taxi equation as:

$$c(m) = 2.50m + 3.00$$

and populate a data table with miles and cost values.

| $m$ | $c(m)$ |
|-----|--------|
| 0 | 3.00 |
| 1 | 5.50 |
| 2 | 8.00 |
| 3 | 10.50 |
| 4 | 13.00 |

## Solving for one variable in terms of the other variable

A common situation on the test is where you are asked to express one variable in terms of another variable (or multiple other variables). In the taxi equation above we already express cost in terms of miles driven with the equation $c = 2.50m + 3.00$. But what if we were asked to express miles in terms of cost? This might sound like a strange thing to do but consider this situation. Suppose the taxi driver tells you that the cost of your taxi ride was $25.50. You probably would want to have some idea of whether that price is reasonable or not by figuring out how many miles had been driven. To do this with the proper math, we solve for $m$ in terms of $c$:

$c = 2.50m + 3.00$         the original equation

$c - 3.00 = 2.50m$         subtract 3.00 from both sides

$\dfrac{c - 3.00}{2.50} = m$         divide both sides by 2.50

In the example above, a taxi ride that cost $25.50 means that the taxi drove 9 miles because

$$\frac{25.50 - 3.00}{2.50} = \frac{22.50}{2.50} = 9$$

## Systems of linear equations

Some algebra problems and many word problems require you to solve a pair of linear equations in two variables. When you are given two equations the first step is to stack the equations so that the variables are on one side of the equation and the constants are on the other side. That will enable you to decide whether to use the substitution method or the elimination method.

## Substitution

Substitution is a very simple way to do the job. When given a pair of equations, re-write one of the equations to isolate one of the variables. Then substitute that variable into the second equation. For example, consider the pair of equations:

$$x + 2y = 10$$
$$2x + 3y = 500$$

Substitution for this pair of equations is simple because the first equation can be re-written as $x = 10 - 2y$. Next replace $x$ with $10 - 2y$ in the second equation:

$$2x + 3y = 500$$
$$2(10 - 2y) + 3y = 500$$
$$20 - 4y + 3y = 500$$
$$y = -480$$

Finish the problem by finding the value of $x$:

$$x = 10 - 2y = 10 - 2(-480) = 10 + 960 = 970$$

## Elimination

The other method of solving a pair of equations is elimination. First, one or both equations are multiplied by constants. Next, the equations are added to one another or subtracted from one another. In our example above, we could have first multiplied the top equation by two, yielding:

$$2x + 4y = 20$$
$$2x + 3y = 500$$

Next we can subtract the second equation from the first equation, giving

$$2x - 2x + 4y - 3y = 20 - 500$$
$$y = -480$$

In general, elimination is faster than substitution, but more prone to error.

Sometimes it is necessary to multiply both equations by constants, as you can see in the next example.

$$3x + 2y = 255$$
$$2x + 5y = 500$$

Multiply the top equation by two and the bottom equation by three. This yields

$$6x + 4y = 510$$
$$6x + 15y = 1500$$

Subtracting the bottom equation gives

$$4y - 15y = 510 - 1500$$
$$-11y = -990, \quad y = 90$$

Substituting 90 for y in the first equation gives

$$3x + 2 \cdot 90 = 255, \quad 3x = 75, \quad x = 25 .$$

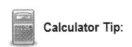
Pairs of equations may also be solved on the calculator. First, on paper, you must put each equation into the slope-intercept format (y= format), isolating the y variable. In the example above we started with two equations, $x + 2y = 10$ and $2x + 3y = 500$. Putting these into slope-intercept format yields $y = \dfrac{-x}{2} + 5$ and $y = \dfrac{-2x}{3} + \dfrac{500}{3}$. The first screen shot below shows the two equations once they have been entered into the equation editor (the *Y=* button of the graphing calculator).

If you press the *graph* key right away you may get a window range error. Press the *window* key and change the window settings to get a proper view of the two lines, including where they intersect. The window settings that were used are shown as the second screen shot below (Xmin = -100, etc.). Other methods are to use the zoom-in and zoom-out options on the zoom menu, or have the calculator set the window for you by pressing *zoom-0:ZoomFit*. You will have to toggle down the zoom menu to find the zoom to fit option.

Each equation is represented by a line on the graph. The intersection of the lines represents the solution. To have the calculator find the solution, type *2ⁿᵈ-calc* to see the calculate menu. Choose option *5:intersect.*to start the calculation dialog. When prompted for the first curve, toggle the cursor onto one of the lines and press *enter*. When prompted for the second curve, toggle the cursor onto the other line and press *enter*. When prompted *guess?* toggle the cursor to the vicinity where the intersection occurs and press *enter*.

At this point you should have a screen that looks like the screen shot below. One of the equations will be shown at the top of the screen. The x and y coordinates of the solution will be shown at the bottom of the screen.

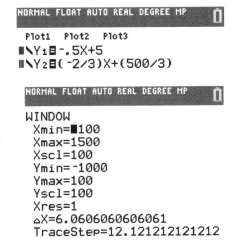

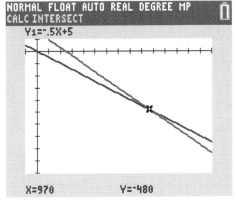

## Possible Outcomes

When you are given two equations with two variables, there can be three possible outcomes: one solution, no solution and an infinite number of solutions. So far we have only been concerned with using substitution or elimination to find the one solution, but some problems will specifically ask about which type of outcome will occur with a given pair of equations. Other problems will tell you the desired outcome and ask you to modify the system to obtain that outcome.

The various outcomes and the conditions under which those outcomes occur are organized into the table below.

| Outcome | Conditions | Example | Graph |
|---|---|---|---|
| One solution | Occurs when the slopes are different. | $y = x + 2$<br>$y = 2x + 1$<br>solution $= (1,3)$ | |
| No solution | Occurs when the slopes are the same but the y-intercepts are different. | $y = x + 2$<br>$y = x - 1$<br>no solution<br>lines are parallel | |
| Infinite solutions | Occurs when the slopes are the same and the y-intercepts are the same. | $y = x + 1$<br>$2y = 2x + 2$<br>infinite solutions<br>(same line) | |

## 3.3 Practice problems on linear equations and systems
### calculator permitted unless stated otherwise

1. <u>Without a calculator</u>: The solution to the equation $4(x+2)=3(5-x)$ is:

    A)    $x=7/15$

    B)    $x=1$

    C)    $x=13/7$

    D)    $x=7$

2. <u>Without a calculator</u>: The solution to the equation $\dfrac{3(x-6)}{5}=x$ is:

    A)    $x=-9$

    B)    $x=-3$

    C)    $x=-9/4$

    D)    $x=9$

3. <u>Without a calculator</u>: If $\dfrac{4x}{3}=2(x+9)$ then $x$ must be equal to:

    A)    -54

    B)    -27

    C)    -6.75

    D)    -4.5

4. <u>Without a calculator</u>: If $\dfrac{2x+k}{5}=30$ and $k=10$ then what is the value of $x$?

    A)    50

    B)    60

    C)    70

    D)    80

5. <u>Without a calculator</u>: If $3x-5=20$, then what is the value of $2x-\dfrac{10}{3}$?

    A)    20

    B)    $\dfrac{25}{3}$

    C)    25

    D)    $\dfrac{40}{3}$

6. Amy's weight this year is 50 pounds less than twice her weight from last year. If she weighs 120 pounds this year, what equation can be used to find her weight from last year?

    A)    $x=60+25$

    B)    $x=60+50$

    C)    $x=2(120)+50$

    D)    $x=2(120+100)$

7. <u>Without a calculator</u>: If the cost of manufacturing mobile phones is $10,000 for the factory time plus $80 per phone and the each phone sells for $100, how many phones must be manufactured for the mobile phone manufacturer to break even (when costs equal revenue)?

    A)    50.0

    B)    50.5

    C)    500.0

    D)    550.0

8. <u>Without a calculator</u>: All together, Michael and his two friends have exactly $30 to spend on lunch. Hot dogs cost $3.50 and drinks cost $1.50. If they each get two hot dogs, how many drinks can they buy?

    A)    4

    B)    6

    C)    7

    D)    8

9. <u>Without a calculator</u>: The velocity $(v)$ of an object is equal to its initial velocity $(v_0)$ plus the product of its acceleration $(a)$ and the elapsed time $(t)$. Which of the choices below expresses elapsed time in terms of the other variables.

    A)    $t=av-v_0$

    B)    $v=av-av_0$

    C)    $t=\dfrac{v-v_0}{a}$

    D)    $t=\dfrac{v+v_0}{a}$

10. Mr. Corn's monthly profit from his book is a function of the number of reviews on Amazon. The function is $P(r) = 5(71 + 3r)$. How many reviews must he have in order to obtain a monthly profit of $1,000?

A) 43

B) 62

C) 215

D) 310

11. If a triangle has a base of 18 and an area of 216, how long is its altitude (height)?

A) 6

B) 12

C) 24

D) 48

12. <u>Without a calculator</u>: If a rectangle has a length that is five less than triple its width, which choice below expresses the <u>perimeter</u> of the rectangle?

A) $4w - 5$

B) $8w - 5$

C) $8w - 10$

D) $3w^2 - 5w$

13. <u>Without a calculator</u>: Katy received a gift card for $100 toward her mobile phone plan. If her plan charges $0.75 per minute for phone calls, which function $R(m)$ below could be used to predict how much money will remain on her gift card after $m$ minutes of phone calls?

A) $R(m) = .75m + 100$

B) $R(m) = 100 - .75m$

C) $R(m) = 100m + .75$

D) $R(m) = 100m - .75$

**Questions 14,15 and 16 refer to the data in the table below.**

The table displays data which illustrate a linear relationship between the hours spent per day studying and the grade point average (GPA).

| Study hours per day | Grade point average (GPA) |
|---|---|
| 2 | 2.3 |
| 4 | 2.6 |
| 8 | 3.2 |
| 10 | $y$ |
| $x$ | 4.0 |

14. Which of the following equations models the relationship between the GPA ($g$) and hours studied ($h$)?

A) $g(h) = .15h + 2$

B) $g(h) = .15h + 2.3$

C) $g(h) = .30h + 2$

D) $g(h) = .30h + 2.3$

15. What is the value of $.15x + y$?

A) -0.50

B) 0.15

C) 5.50

D) 9.83

16. If the linear relationship holds, which of the following must be true?

I. If a student wants a 4.0 GPA, s/he should study $x$ hours per week.

II. If a student studies 10 hours every day s/he can expect a GPA of $y$.

III. $\dfrac{4 - y}{x - 10}$ represents the improvement in GPA for every extra hour spent studying.

A)      I only
B)      I and II only
C)      I and III only
D)      II and III only

___

17. Water is being drained out of a swimming pool. $V$ represents the volume (in gallons) of water remaining in the pool after it has drained for $h$ hours. The relationship between $V$ and $h$ can be modeled by the equation $V = 777 - 25h$. What does 25 mean in this equation?

A) It takes 25 hours to drain the pool

B) After the pool is drained there will be 25 gallons of water left in it.

C) As each hour passes, there will be 25 fewer gallons of water in the pool.

D) It will take $\dfrac{25}{777}$ hours to drain the pool.

18. Mr. Corn participates in a raffle at the local grocery store. When he signs up to participate he gets 20 raffle tickets for free. When he buys groceries he receives 2 tickets for every $10 that he spends at the store. Which of the equations below can be used to calculate the number of tickets that Mr. Corn will accumulate after spending $d$ dollars at the grocery store?

A)      $.2d + 20$

B)      $.2d - 20$

C)      $2d + 20$

D)      $20d + 2$

19. Without a calculator: The volume of a pyramid is given by the equation $V = \dfrac{1}{3}lwh$, where $l$ is the length of the base, $w$ is the width of the base, and $h$ is the height of the pyramid. If the area of the base of the pyramid is 40 square inches and the volume of the pyramid is 124 cubic inches, how tall is the pyramid?

A)      3.1 inches
B)      9.3 inches
C)      27.9 inches
D)      14,880 inches

___

**Questions 20 and 21 pertain to the graph below, which shows the relationship between height and weight for teenage boys.**

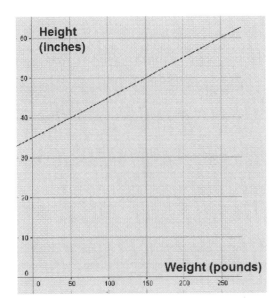

20.. Which of the following statements is true about the relationship between height and weight for teenage boys?

I. Boys typically weigh about 35 pounds when they are born.

II. On average, a boy grows 10 inches for every 100 pounds that he gains.

III. Heavier boys tend to be taller than lighter boys.

A)      I only
B)      II only
C)      I and III only
D)      II and III only

21. Suppose the equation of the line above is $10y - x = 350$. What weight would be predicted for a teenage boy who is 7 feet tall (one foot equals 12 inches)?
- A)   280 pounds
- B)   390 pounds
- C)   420 pounds
- D)   490 pounds

22. 1. If $x + y = 3$ and $3x + 5y = 13$, then $x - y$ is equal to:
- A)   -2
- B)   -1
- C)   1
- D)   2

23. Tickets to a show cost $3 for students and $7 for adults. If 250 tickets were sold and ticket sales totaled $1102, how many adult tickets were sold?
- A)   35
- B)   88
- C)   111
- D)   162

24. If $3x + 5y = 13$ and $6x + 7y = 20$, find the value of $\dfrac{y}{x}$.
- A)   0.5
- B)   1
- C)   1.5
- D)   2

25. If $5x + 2y = 8$ and $3x - 7y = 13$, find the value of $x - y$.
- A)   -1
- B)   1
- C)   2
- D)   3

26. Joanna saves nickels and quarters in a jar. If she saved five times as many nickels as quarters, and her coin collection is worth $390, how many quarters has she saved?
- A)   195
- B)   300
- C)   780
- D)   3900

27. Lizzy's cell phone plan charges 5 cents per message for in-network text messages and 10 cents per message for out-of-network text messages. If she sent a total of 1500 messages and her bill was $80, how many out-of-network messages did she send?
- A)   50
- B)   60
- C)   100
- D)   1400

28. If $2x + by = 8$ and $ax + y = 4$, what values of $a$ and $b$ would cause this pair of equations to have infinitely many solutions?
- A)   $a = 1,\ b = 1$
- B)   $a = 1,\ b = 2$
- C)   $a = 2,\ b = 1$
- D)   $a = 2,\ b = 2$

29. Suppose $ax + by = c$ and $dx + ey = f$, and that $ce \neq bf$, which of the conditions below would cause this system of equations to have no solution?
- A)   $a = d$
- B)   $b = e$
- C)   $ae = bd$
- D)   $ad = be$

# 3.3 Solutions to practice problems on linear equations and systems

**1. (B)**

$4(x+2)=3(5-x),\ 4x+8=15-3x,$

$7x=15-8,\ 7x=7,\ x=1$

**2. (A)**

$\dfrac{3(x-6)}{5}=x,\ 3(x-6)=5x,$

$3x-18=5x,\ -18=2x,\ -9=x$

**3. (B)**

$\dfrac{4x}{3}=2(x+9),\ 4x=6(x+9),$

$4x=6x+54,\ -2x=54,\ x=-27$

**4. (C)**

$\dfrac{2x+k}{5}=30,\ 2x+10=150,$

$2x=140,\ x=70$

**5. (D)**

$3x-5=20,\ \dfrac{2}{3}(3x-5)=\dfrac{2}{3}(20),$

$2x-\dfrac{10}{3}=\dfrac{40}{3}$

**6. (A)**

$120=2x-50,\ 120+50=2x,$

$\dfrac{120+50}{2}=x,\ 60+25=x$

**7. (C)**

$10,000+80n=100n,\ 10,000=20n,\ 500=n$

**8. (B)**

After they pay $21 for hot dogs, they will have $9 left.

Drinks cost $1.50 each, so they can buy six drinks.

**9. (C)**

$v=v_0+at,\ v-v_0=at,\ \dfrac{v-v_0}{a}=t$

**10. (A)**

$1000=5(71+3r),\ 200=71+3r,\ 129=3r,\ 43=r$

**11. (C)**

$216=\dfrac{1}{2}(18)h,\ 216=9h,\ 24=h$

**12. (C)**

$l=3w-5,\ p=2l+2w=6w-10+2w=8w-10$

**13. (B)**

**14. (A)**

$\text{slope}=\dfrac{2.6-2.3}{4-2}=\dfrac{.3}{2}=.15,\ y=.15x+b$

at $(2,\ 2.3)$ $2.3=.15(2)+b,\ 2=b,\ y=.15x+2$

**15. (C)**

In problem 14 we found the slope to be .15.

$\dfrac{4-y}{x-10}=.15,\ 4-y=.15x-1.5,\ 5.5=.15x+y$

**16. (D)**

I. false because the units are hours per day, not per week (sorry but this is a common "trick" on standardized tests).

II. true

III. true because $\dfrac{4-y}{x-10}$ is the slope

**17. (C)**

**18. (A)**

The rate at which tickets accumulate is two tickets per 10 dollars, 2/10, or 0.2 per dollar.

**19. (B)**

$V=\dfrac{1}{3}lwh,\ 124=\dfrac{1}{3}40h,\ 372=40h,\ 9.3=h$

**20. (D)**

I. false. The graph has nothing to do with age.
II. true. Using the points (50,40) and (150,50)
we can see that the slope is
$$\frac{50-40}{150-50}=\frac{10}{100}=\frac{1}{10}$$
III. true. The slope of the line is positive.

**21. (D)**

$10y-x=350,\ 10(84)-x=350,\ 490=x$

**22. (B)**

Use substitution:

$3x+5y=13$

$3(3-y)+5y=13$
$9-3y+5y=13,\ y=2,\ x=3-2=1$
$x-y=1-2=-1$

**23. (B)**

Use substitution:

$S+A=250$
$3S+7A=1102$
$3(250-A)+7A=1102$
$750+4A=1102,\ A=88$

**24. (D)**

Multiplying the first equation by 2 gives
$6x+10y=26$
$6x+7y=20$

Subtracting the equations gives
$3y=6,\ y=2,\ x=1,\ \dfrac{y}{x}=2$

**25. (D)**

Multiplying the first equation by 3 and the
second equation by 5 gives

$15x+6y=24$
$15x-35y=65$

Then subtract
$6y+35y=24-65,\ 41y=-41,\ y=-1,\ x=2$

$x-y=2--1=3$

**26. (C**

$5Q=N$
$.25Q+.05N=390$

Use substitution:

$.25Q+.05(5Q)=390$
$.50Q=390,\ Q=780$

**27. (C)**

$5x+10y=8000$
$x+y=1500,\ x=1500-y$
$5(1500-y)+10y=8000$
$7500-5y+10y=8000$
$5y=500,\ y=100$

**28. (B)**

Put each equation into slope-intercept form:

$$y=\frac{-2}{b}x+\frac{8}{b}\ \text{ and }\ y=-ax+4$$

Slopes and intercepts must be the same

$$\frac{-2}{b}=-a,\ ab=2\ \text{ and }\ \frac{8}{b}=4,\ \text{ therefore }b=2,\ a=1$$

**29. (C)**

Put each equation into slope-intercept form:

$$y=\frac{-a}{b}x+\frac{c}{b}\ \text{ and }\ y=\frac{-d}{e}x+\frac{f}{e}$$

For there to be no solution the slopes must be
the same $\dfrac{-a}{b}=\dfrac{-d}{e},\ ae=bd$

54

## 3.4    Linear inequalities and systems of inequalities

In linear equations, the solution (if there is one) is a point (x,y). In linear inequalities, the solution (if there is one) is a region. If the linear inequality has only one variable, the solution can be graphed as a portion of a number line or a section of the x-y plane. If the linear inequality has two variables, the solution is a region within the x-y plane.

### Linear inequalities in one variable

Some of the problems on the test require you to solve a linear inequalities in one variable. For example, this word problem:

> If Paige has $5.00 to spend on apples and each apple costs 35 cents, what is the greatest number of apples that can she buy?

This requires you to set up the inequality $.35x \leq 5.00$ and solve (divide each side of the inequality by .35), yielding the answer of $x \leq 14.3$, which defines a region of the number line. Because it is not possible to buy a portion of an apple the answer to this problem is the largest integer that lies in the solution region, 14 apples. The answers to this word problem could be multiple choice options like 13, 14, 15, or 16. If you choose anything other than 14 your choice is incorrect because the problem is asking for the greatest number of apples that Paige can buy.

Linear inequalities are solved using the same techniques used to solve linear equalities, namely adding, subtracting, multiplying and dividing as needed, collecting like terms along the way. But there is a key difference: **if you multiply or divide by a negative value, you must change the direction of the inequality**. Consider this example:

$-2(x-8) \leq 4$    original inequality

$-2x + 16 \leq 4$    distribute the -2

$-2x \leq -12$    combine like terms (add 16 to both sides)

$x \geq 6$    isolate the variable (divide both sides by -2, change direction)

The last step isolates the variable by dividing by a negative value, so the direction of the inequality is changed. Remember to change the direction of the inequality whenever you multiply or divide both sides ot the inequality by a negative value.

When graphed on a number line, the solution looks like:

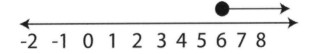

-2  -1  0  1  2  3  4  5  6  7  8

Other examples of number line solution regions are shown below. Notice the relationship between the inequality and the endpoints of the graph. When the inequality contains an equal sign ($\leq$ or $\geq$) then the endpoint is a closed dot. When the inequality does not contain an equal sign ($<$ or $>$) then the endpoint is an open dot.

| Algebraic inequality | Graphical number line |
|---|---|
| $x \geq 1$ | ![number line with closed dot at 1, arrow pointing right; -4 -3 -2 -1 0 1 2 3 4] |
| $x < -2$ | ![number line with open dot at -2, arrow pointing left; -4 -3 -2 -1 0 1 2 3 4] |
| $-3 \leq x < 3$ | ![number line with closed dot at -3, open dot at 3, line between; -4 -3 -2 -1 0 1 2 3 4] |

The solution to the problem where $x \geq 6$ could also be graphed as a region of the x-y plane, as shown below: Notice that the solution region is bounded on the left by a solid line. That is because $x$ is greater than or equal to six. Solid lines are used with greater than or equal to ($\geq$) and with less than or equal to ($\leq$). If the inequality is strictly greater than ($>$) or strictly less than ($<$), the line demarcating the solution region will be dashed rather than solid. This convention is consistent with whether the end points on a number line are filled (when an equals sign is involved) or not filled (when an equals sign is not involved).

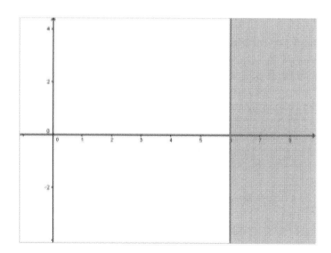

Compound inequalities

There are some problems where a compound inequality is used. For example, suppose the length of a screw has to be within one-tenth of an inch of exactly two inches long. That means that the length ($l$) must satisfy the compound inequality $-.1 < l - 2 < .1$. The screw cannot be more than .1 above exactly two inches or more than .1 below exactly two inches. We solve the inequality just as before, but instead of performing an operation on two sides of the inequality, we perform the same operation on three sides of the inequality, as shown below:

$$-.1 < l - 2 < .1$$  original compound inequality

$$2 + -.1 < 2 + l - 2 < 2 + .1$$  add 2 to all three sides of the compound inequality

$$1.9 < l < 2.1$$  simplify

The same steps and rules of solving inequalities apply to solving compound inequalities.


## Linear inequalities in two variables

The solution to a linear inequality is a region of the x-y plane. To find the solution region:

1. Graph the equation of the line. Use a dashed line if the inequality is < or >. Use a solid line if the inequality is ≤ or ≥.

2. If the line does not go through the origin plug (0,0) into the inequality. If the inequality is true then the origin lies in the solution region. If the inequality is false then the origin lies outside the solution region. Shade the solution region as appropriate.

3. If the line goes through the origin, plug a different point, say (1,1) into the inequality. Then follow the instructions in step 2 above.

For example, consider the inequality $y > 2x - 3$. First we graph the line using the y-intercept of (0,-3) and the slope of 2. We make the line dashed (not solid) because the inequality is strictly greater than. Next we plug (0,0) into the inequality, which gives us $0 > 0 - 3$. This inequality is true so the origin lies in the solution region. Then we shade the region of the x-y plane that contains the origin, as shown below.

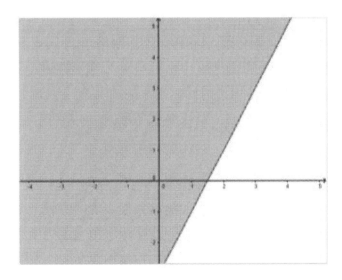

| 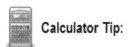| The graphing calculator can be used to find the solution region of an inequality with two variables. It will even do the shading for you.

Begin by pressing the key Y= to get into the equation editor. Then enter the inequality that you wish to graph, say $y > 2x - 3$. Initially the equation editor will look like the first screen shot below.

Next move the cursor all the way to the left, where the color (if your calculator supports color) and the line symbol are shown. Press enter. You will be brought into a dialog where you can choose a different line symbol. Continue through the dialog (unfortunately the dialog differs with the exact model of calculator that you own) until you have changed the solid line symbol to the greater than symbol as shown in the second screen shot below.

Next, press the graph key to display the solution region, as shown below in the third screen shot.

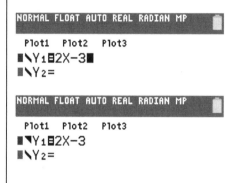 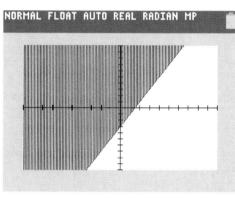 |

## Systems of linear inequalities in two variables

A system of linear inequalities involves finding the solution region to two or more inequalities. To illustrate we will stick with the earlier inequality of $y > 2x - 3$. Systems of linear inequalities often result from word problems.

Suppose Emma is using red and green apples to bake in a pie. She wants the pie to be sweet so the number of red apples (y) must be at least three less than twice the number of green apples (x), that gives us the first inequality $y > 2x - 3$. The pan she uses for pies cannot handle more than 6 apples total, which gives us the inequality $x + y \leq 6$. So far we have a system with two inequalities but let's make this interesting. Suppose that to get the right flavor Emma also must use a mixture of red and green apples, that means that $x > 1$ and $y > 1$. Now we will build the solution region step by step.

| | |
|---|---|
| Let's begin with the easy parts first, namely $x > 1$ and $y > 1$. That gives us the rectangular solution region bounded on the bottom left corner at (1,1). Notice that dashed lines are used. | 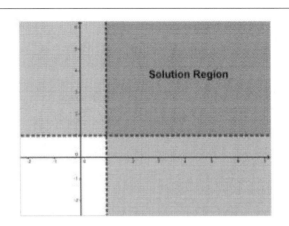 |
| Now we repeat the work on graphing the inequality $y > 2x - 3$, following the exact same steps discussed earlier, shading above the line and using a dashed line.<br><br>Shading above the line gives us a solution region that is the upper part of a kind of U-shaped area, above the diagonal line but inside the box bounded by (1,1). | 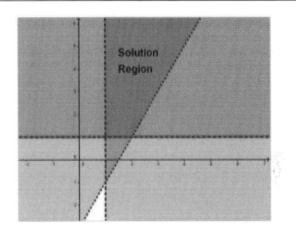 |
| Lastly we graph the line $x + y \leq 6$, using a solid line because of the $\leq$. Testing (0,0) produces a result that is true because $0 + 0 \leq 6$. That means we shade below this line because (0,0) is a part of this line's solution region.<br><br>Notice that the final solution region forms an odd looking quadrilateral (four sided) area, below the solid diagonal line, above the dashed diagonal line, but inside the box bounded by (1,1.) | 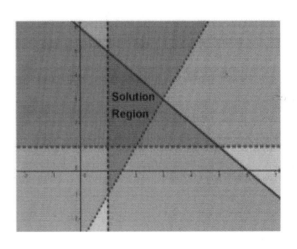 |

59

## 3.4 Practice problems on linear inequalities and systems of inequalities
### calculator permitted unless stated otherwise

1. <u>Without a calculator</u>: What is the solution to the following inequality: $3x + 17 > 5$?

A)     x>-4

B)     x<-4

C)     x>4

D)     x<4

2. <u>Without a calculator</u>: What is the solution to the following inequality: $3x - 10x < -14$?

A)     x>-2

B)     x<-2

C)     x>2

D)     x<2

3. <u>Without a calculator</u>: What is the solution to the following inequality: $0 < 8x + 6 < 30$?

A)     .75>x>-3

B)     -.75<x<3

C)     .75>x>-4.5

D)     .75<x<4.5

4. <u>Without a calculator</u>: If $2x - 18 \leq 3$, then what is the largest possible value of $5x + 1$?

A)     10.5

B)     52.5

C)     53.5

D)     54

5. <u>Without a calculator</u>: Morgan is trying to decide where to rent a car. EZ Rentals rents cars for $50 per day plus $.35 per mile, whereas Friendly Rentals rents cars for $40 per day plus $.40 per mile. How many miles does Morgan have to drive to make EZ Rentals less expensive than Friendly Rentals?

A)     50

B)     51

C)     200

D)     201

6. <u>Without a calculator</u>: Mary and Jordan are playing a game where Mary has 10 points and Jordan has 7 points. If Jordan earns $x$ additional points and $x > 3$, what is the fewest additional points Mary must earn in order to have at least as many points as Jordan?

A)     x-3

B)     x+3

C)     x-7

D)     x+7

7. <u>Without a calculator</u>: Which of the number lines below shows the solution region for $-2(4x + 5) > 30$ ?

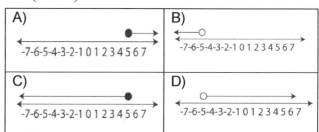

8. <u>Without a calculator</u>: Which of the graphs below shows a shaded solution region for the inequality $y \geq -2$?

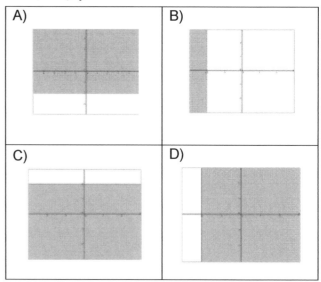

9. Grace bought a book of 20 tickets for rides at an amusement park. Her favorite ride, which she will save for last, requires 3 tickets. If Grace uses an average of 9 tickets per hour, which of the inequalities below can be used to calculate how many _minutes_ she can spend on other rides before she has to stop, in order to still have enough tickets for her favorite ride?

A) $20 - 9x \geq 3$

B) $9x + 17 < 0$

C) $20 - \dfrac{3x}{20} \geq 3$

D) $\dfrac{3x}{20} + 17 > 0$

10. Michael decides to start up a web site to sell baseball cards. The average price that he will charge per card is $5. The cost of starting up the web site is $100 and it costs $50 per month to keep the web site running. After a period of 8 months go by Michael will shut the web site down if he has not made a profit. In order to justify keeping the web site running how many cards does Michael have to have sold by the end of the 8 month period?

A) 33

B) 34

C) 166

D) 167

---

**Questions 11 and 12 refer to the following information:**

Charlie's restaurant has small tables for two people and big tables for five people. Charlie wants to have at least 40 large tables so that he can handle larger parties. The license for the restaurant limits occupancy to 300 people.

11. Which of the following systems of equations could be used to find the solutions to the number of large and small tables that Charlie could put in his restaurant?

A) $2x + 5y \geq 300,\ y \geq 40$

B) $2x + 5y \leq 300,\ x \geq 40$

C) $2x + 5y \leq 300,\ y \geq 40$

D) $2x + 5y \geq 300,\ x \geq 40$

12. Which of the following (small, big) table combinations would Charlie be <u>unable</u> to use in his restaurant?

A) (0, 60)

B) (15, 54)

C) (40, 50)

D) (50, 40)

---

13. <u>Without a calculator</u>: Which system of equations results in the solution region shown below?

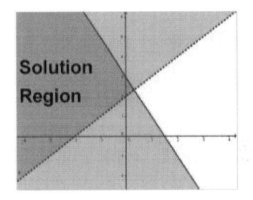

A) $y > x + 2,\ y < -2x + 3$

B) $y < 5x + 2,\ y \geq -2x + 3$ y

C) $y \leq 5x + 2,\ y \leq -2x + 3$

D) $y > 5x + 2,\ y \leq -2x + 3$

14. James is mixing a concentrate of lemon juice with 500 ounces of water. If the mixture must be no more than 1.5% lemon juice, what is the most lemon juice that he can add to the water?

A) 5 ounces

B) 6 ounces

C) 7 ounces

D) 8 ounces

15. The solution region to the system of inequalities $y < -3x - 1$ and $y < 2x + 4$ does not lie in which of the following quadrants?

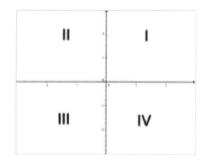

A)      I
B)      II
C)      III
D)      IV

16. Which of the following graphs shows the solution region for the system of inequalities: $y > x + 1$ and $y > -x - 2$?

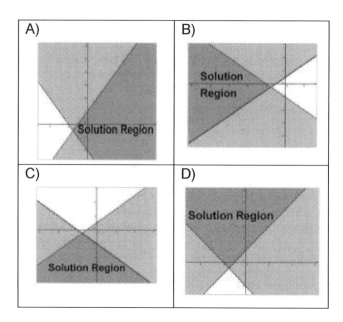

17. If $2x + 5y < 100$ and $x \geq 10$ which of the following statement must be true about $y$?

A)      $y < 16$

B)      $y > 16$

C)      $y \leq 16$

D)      $y \geq 16$

18. Nikki is planning a birthday party for her sister but her apartment only can accommodate 20 people and she cannot decide who to invite. Nikki wants to have twice as many friends $(f)$ as relatives $(r)$, but she has to invite her mother, her father and of course her cousin Carlie. Which of the systems of inequalities could Nikki use to model her situation?

A)      $f + r \leq 20, \ f = 2r, \ r \geq 3$

B)      $f + r \leq 18, \ f = 2r, \ r \geq 3$

C)      $f + r \leq 20, \ 2f = r, \ r \geq 3$

D)      $f + r \leq 18, \ 2f = r, \ r \geq 3$

19. Suppose the amount of oil a certain furnace burns can be as few as 1.5 gallons per hour and as many as 2.0 gallons per hour, and that oil costs $3.50 per gallon. What would be the range in the cost of running that furnace for a 24 hour period?

A)      $36 < c < 48$

B)      $36 \leq c \leq 48$

C)      $126 < c < 168$

D)      $126 \leq c \leq 168$

20. What are the coordinates of the vertices of the solution region for the following set of equations?

$$x + y > 4$$
$$x > -1$$
$$y > 3$$

A)      (-1,5) and (1,3)

B)      (0,6) and (1,4)

C)      (3,3) and (4,4)

D)      (2,4) and (3,5)

# 3.4 Solutions to practice problems on linear inequalities and systems of inequalities

1. (A)
$3x + 17 > 5$, $3x > -12$, $x > -4$
2. (C)
$3x - 10x < -14$, $-7x < -14$, $x > 2$

3. (B)
$0 < 8x + 6 < 30$, $-6 < 8x < 24$, $-.75 < x < 3$
4. (C)
$2x - 18 \le 3$, $2x \le 21$, $x \le 10.5$
$5x \le 52.5$, $5x + 1 \le 53.5$

5. (D)
$50 + .35x < 40 + .40x$, $10 < .05x$, $200 < x$
6. (A)
Let y represent the number of points that Mary must earn. Then $10 + y \ge 7 + x$, or $y \ge x - 3$.
7. (B)
$-2(4x + 5) > 30$, $4x + 5 < -15$, $4x < -20$, $x < -5$

8. (A)
The height of the region must be above -2.

9. (C)
3/20 is the average number of tickets per minute that Grace will use.

10. (D)
revenue=3x, cost = 100 +8(50) = 500
profit = revenue-cost = $3x - 500 > 0$
$3x > 500$, $x > \dfrac{500}{3}$, $x > 166.\overline{6}$
11. (C)
The number of people in the restaurant cannot be more than 300, so $2x + 5y \le 300$. The variable $y$ represents the large five-person table, of which there must be at least 40.
12. (C)
$(40, 50)$ would result in 40(2)+50(5) people (too many)

13. (D)
The line with the positive slope is dotted and therefore must be greater than. The line with the negative slope is solid and therefore must be less than or equal to.

14. (C)
$\dfrac{x}{500 + x} \le .015$, $x \le 7.5 + .015x$, $.985x \le 7.5$, $x \le 7.6$

15. (A)
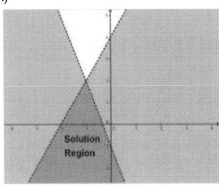

16. (D)
Each region must be shaded above the line.

17. (A)
$x \ge 10$ means that $2x \ge 20$ means that 5y<80 or $y < 16$. Y cannot equal 16 because if x were 10 then $2x + 5y = 100$.

18. (B)
Nikki can only invite 18 people because her apartment can only accommodate 20 people total, counting herself and her sister. She must invite at least 3 relatives.

19. (D)
gallons per day: $1.5 \le g \le 2.0$, $36 \le 24g \le 48$
cost per day:
$(3.50)(36) \le c \le (3.50)(48)$, $126 \le c \le 168$

20. (A)

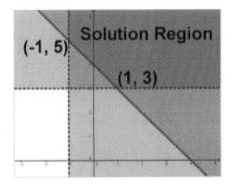

## 3.5    FOILing and factoring

Distributing was covered in earlier in unit 3.1.  A special case of distributing involves multiplying a pair of terms by another pair of terms.  For example:

$$(a+b)(c+d) = a(c+d) + b(c+d) = ac + ad + bc + bd$$

Some students find this to be a bit intimidating and prefer to make use of an acronym for this process: The acronym comes from:

F         = first (the first terms are a and c)

O         = outer (the outer terms are a and d)

I         = inner (the inner terms are b and c)

L         = last (the last terms are b and d)

That's all there is to it!  For example

$$(2x+3)(x-y) = 2x^2 - 2xy + 3x - 3y$$

First     $2x \cdot x = 2x^2$

Outer   $2x(-y) = -2xy$

Inner    $3 \cdot x = 3x$

Last     $3(-y) = -3y$

## Factoring

Factoring is just FOILing in reverse.  In fact, one of my students used to call factoring "reverse FOILing."  The general problem is that we want to factor the expression

$$ax^2 + bx + c .$$

There are two cases to consider.  The easy case is where a=1, so let's start there.

## Factoring when $a = 1$

We are using what I call the diamond method to factor, though the rest of the world refers to this as the "ac method".  But whatever you call it, all that matters is that it works!

If a=1, the expression that we want to factor looks like this

$$x^2 + bx + c$$

There are four steps to factoring this:

| | |
|---|---|
| Place the middle coefficient, $b$, into the top portion of the diamond. | 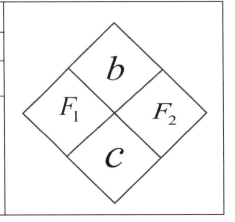 |
| Place the constant term, $c$, into the bottom portion of the diamond. | |
| Find two factors, $F_1$ and $F_2$ that multiply to $c$ but also sum to $b$. | |
| Now you are finished! $x^2 + bx + c = (x + F_1)(x + F_2)$ | |

Consider the following example:

$$x^2 - 9x - 10$$

| | |
|---|---|
| Place the middle coefficient, -9, into the top portion of the diamond. | 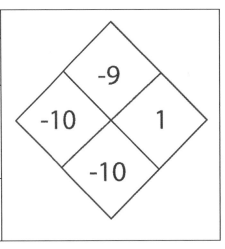 |
| Place the constant term, -10, into the bottom portion of the diamond. | |
| Find two factors, $F_1$ and $F_2$ that multiply to -10 but also sum to -9. The factors of 10 are 1 and 10, and 2 and 5. We cannot use 2 and 5 because there is no way they could add or subtract to -9. But we can use 1 and 10 because -10+1 is equal to -9. | |
| Now you are finished! $x^2 - 9x - 10 = (x - 10)(x + 1)$ | |

<u>Always confirm your answer by FOILING</u>:

$$(x+1)(x-10) = x^2 - 10x + x - 10 = x^2 - 9x - 10.$$

| | | |
|---|---|---|
|  | **Calculator Tip:** | Finding the factors of a number can be tedious, but the calculator can help. See the calculator tip in Unit 3.1 to learn how to find the factors of a number using the graphing calculator. |

**Factoring when** $a \neq 1$

Now consider the more difficult case of

$$ax^2 + bx + c .$$

The first few steps are very similar:

| | |
|---|---|
| Place the middle coefficient, $b$, into the top portion of the diamond. | 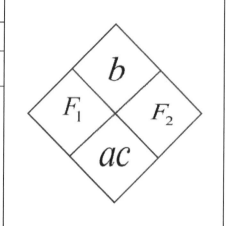 |
| Place the product, $ac$, into the bottom portion of the diamond. | |
| Find two factors, $F_1$ and $F_2$ that multiply to $ac$ but also sum to $b$. | |
| Take the original expression: $ax^2 + bx + c$ <br><br> Rewrite the middle term.  $ax^2 + F_1 x + F_2 x + c$ <br><br> Group the pairs of terms together:  $(ax^2 + F_1 x) + (F_2 x + c)$ <br><br> Pull any common factors out for each term and then factor completely by grouping.  This sounds more complicated than it actually is, so please see the example below. | |

Consider factoring the following:

$$4x^2 + 5x - 6$$

| | |
|---|---|
| Place the middle coefficient, 5, into the top portion of the diamond. | 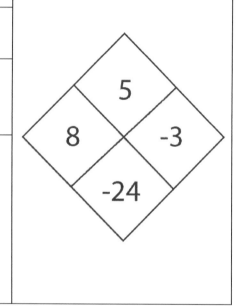 |
| Place the product, $4(-6) = -24$, into the bottom portion of the diamond. | |
| Find two factors, $F_1$ and $F_2$ that multiply to -24 but also sum to 5. The factors of 24 are 1 and 24, and 2 and 12, and 3 and 8, and 4 and 6.  3 and 8 work well because $8 - 3 = 5$ and 8(-3)=-24. | |
| Take the original expression: $4x^2 + 5x - 6$ <br><br> Rewrite the middle term.  $4x^2 + 8x - 3x - 6$ <br><br> Group the pairs of terms together:  $(4x^2 + 8x) + (-3x - 6)$ <br><br> Pull any common factors out for each term: $4x(x+2) -3(x+2)$. We are hoping for a common term and there is one, $(x+2)$. <br><br> Factor by grouping: $(4x - 3)(x + 2)$ | |

$$4x^2 + 5x - 6 = \left(4x - 3\right)\left(x + 2\right) .$$

Always confirm your answer by FOILING:

$$\left(4x - 3\right)\left(x + 2\right) = 4x^2 - 3x + 8x - 6 = 4x^2 + 5x - 6$$

## Special cases (perfect squares)

There are three patterns of factoring and FOILing that you must memorize and be able to recognize on the test. These pertain to perfect squares:

$$(x+y)^2 = x^2 + 2xy + y^2$$
$$(x-y)^2 = x^2 - 2xy + y^2$$
$$(x+y)(x-y) = x^2 - y^2$$

It is not good enough to be able to FOIL or factor these from scratch when you encounter them on the test. This sample problem illustrates why.

Suppose $(x+y)^2 = 100$, $x^2 = 20$, and $y^2 = 30$. Find the value of $xy$. If you do not recognize the pattern you will not know what to do. However recognizing the pattern enables the problem to be solved easily.

$$(x+y)^2 = x^2 + 2xy + y^2$$
$$100 = 20 + 2xy + 30$$
$$50 = 2xy$$
$$25 = xy$$

## Factoring in Division

Factoring is often used to simplify an expression that is being divided. This is illustrated below:

$$\frac{x^2 - 9}{x^2 + 5x + 6} = \frac{(x+3)(x-3)}{(x+3)((x+2)} = \left(\frac{x+3}{x+3}\right)\left(\frac{x-3}{x+2}\right) = \frac{x-3}{x+2}$$

First the the numerator and denominator are factored completely. Then the factor $(x+3)$ is isolated in the numerator and the denominator. Then they cancel out.

## 3.5 Practice problems on FOILing and factoring
### calculator permitted unless stated otherwise

1. <u>Without a calculator</u>: The expression $(2x-3)(5x+7)$ is equivalent to:

A) $\quad 7x+4$

B) $\quad 10x^2+14$

C) $\quad 10x^2-x-21$

D) $\quad 10x^2+29-21$

2. <u>Without a calculator</u>: The expression $(x+8)^2$ is equivalent to:

A) $\quad 2x+16$

B) $\quad x^2+8x+64$

C) $\quad x^2+64$

D) $\quad x^2+16x+64$

3. <u>Without a calculator</u>: The expression $x^2-6x+8$ is equivalent to:

A) $\quad (x+8)(x-1)$

B) $\quad (x-8)(x+1)$

C) $\quad (x-4)(x-2)$

D) $\quad (x+4)(x-2)$

4. <u>Without a calculator</u>: The expression $x^2-5xy-176y^2$ is equivalent to:

A) $\quad (x-16y)(x+11y)$

B) $\quad (x-8y)(x-22y)$

C) $\quad (x-8y)(x+22y)$

D) $\quad (x+8y)(x-22y)$

5. <u>Without a calculator</u>:The expression $3x^2-19x+20$ is equivalent to:

A) $\quad (3x-5)(x-4)$

B) $\quad (3x-5)(x+40)$

C) $\quad (3x-4)(x-5)$

D) $\quad (3x-4)(x+5)$

6. <u>Without a calculator</u>: The expression $20x^2-36xy+16y^2$ is equivalent to:

A) $\quad (5x+8y)(4x+8y)$

B) $\quad (5x-8y)(4x+2y)$

C) $\quad (2x+y)(10x-16y)$

D) $\quad 4(x-y)(5x-4y)$

7. <u>Without a calculator</u>: The expression $\dfrac{2x^2-6x-8}{x^2-1}$ is equivalent to:

A) $\quad -8$

B $\quad \dfrac{2x-8}{x-1}$

C) $\quad \dfrac{2x+8}{x+1}$

D) $\quad \dfrac{2x-8}{x+1}$

8. <u>Without a calculator</u>: If $x^2-y^2=50$ and $x+y=20$, what is the value of $x-y$?

A) $\quad 0$

B) $\quad 1$

C) $\quad 2$

D) $\quad 2.5$

9. <u>Without a calculator</u>: Which of the following are equivalent?

I. $(x-y)^2$

II. $(y-x)^2$

III. $-(x-y)^2$

A) $\quad$ I and II only

B) $\quad$ I and III only

C) $\quad$ II and III only

D) $\quad$ none are equivalent

10. <u>Without a calculator</u>: If $(x+y)^2 = 50$ and $x^2 + y^2 = 30$, what is the value of $xy$?

A)          10
B)          20
C)          30
D)          40

11. <u>Without a calculator</u>:  The expression $\dfrac{x^2-4}{4x}$ is equivalent to:

A)          1
B)          $x-4$
C)          $x-1$
D)          $\dfrac{x}{4} - \dfrac{1}{x}$

12. <u>Without a calculator</u>:  Simplify

$\dfrac{x^2+x-6}{2x^2+6x} \div \dfrac{x-2}{x}$

A)          $\dfrac{1}{2}$
B)          1
C)          2
D)          $\dfrac{(x-2)^2}{2x^2}$

13.  If the difference between the area of a circle and the circumference of that same circle is $35\pi$, how long is the radius of the circle?

A)          1
B)          2
C)          5
D)          7

14. <u>Without a calculator</u>:  When the difference of two less than a number is divided by the difference of four less than the square of the same number, the result is:

A)          $x+2$
B)          $\dfrac{1}{x+2}$
C)          $x-2$
D)          $\dfrac{1}{x-2}$

15.  The length of a rectangle is two units longer than its width.  If the area of the rectangle is 32 square units, what is the length of the rectangle?

A)          4
B)          6
C)          8
D)          10

16. <u>Without a calculator</u>:  If the sides of a triangle are $x^2$, $(x+1)^2$, and $(x-1)^2$ and the perimeter of the triangle is 77 units long, what is the length of the longest side?

A)          5
B)          16
C)          25
D)          36

17.  Drew needs exactly 600 feet of fencing to enclose his rectangular yard.  If the area of his yard is 12,500 square feet, what is the length (in feet) of his yard?

A)          75
B)          100
C)          200
D)          250

18.  Brooke has a large protective case on her cell phone as shown below.  If her case is three inches all around her cell phone, and the dimensions of the case are $x$ inches by $x+3$ inches, what is the area of the case?

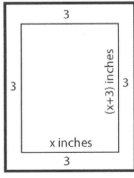

A)          $12x+54$
B)          $x^2+3x$
C)          $x^2+9x+18$
D)          $x^2+6x+9$

# 3.5 Solutions to practice problems on FOILING and factoring

**1 (C)**

$$(2x-3)(5x+7) = 10x^2 + 14x - 15x - 21$$
$$= 10x^2 - x - 21$$

**2. (D)**

$$(x+8)^2 = (x+8)(x+8) = x^2 + 8x + 8x + 64$$
$$= x^2 + 16x + 64$$

**3. (C)**

$$x^2 - 6x + 8 = x^2 - 4x - 2x + 8 = (x^2 - 4x) - (2x - 8) =$$
$$x(x-4) - 2(x-4) = (x-2)(x-4)$$

**4. (A)**

$$x^2 - 5xy - 176y^2 = x^2 - 16xy + 11xy - 176y^2$$
$$= (x^2 - 16xy) + (11xy - 176y^2)$$
$$= x(x-16y) + 11y(x-16y) = (x+11y)(x-16y)$$

**5. (C)**

$$3x^2 - 19x + 20 = 3x^2 - 15x - 4x + 20$$
$$= (3x^2 - 15x) - (4x - 20)$$
$$= 3x(x-5) - 4(x-5) = (3x-4)(x-5)$$

**6. (D)**

$$20x^2 - 36xy + 16y^2 = 4(5x^2 - 9xy + 4y^2)$$
$$= 4(5x^2 - 5xy - 4xy + 4y^2) = 4[(5x^2 - 5xy) - (4xy - 4y^2)]$$
$$= 4[5x(x-y) - 4y(x-y)] = 4(5x - 4y)(x-y)$$

**7. (B)**

$$\frac{2x^2 - 6x - 8}{x^2 - 1} = \frac{2(x^2 - 3x - 4)}{(x+1)(x-1)} = \frac{2(x+1)(x-4)}{(x+1)(x-1)}$$
$$= \frac{2(x-4)}{x-1} = \frac{2x-8}{x-1}$$

**8. (D)**

$$x^2 - y^2 = (x+y)(x-y)$$
$$50 = 20(x-y)$$
$$2.5 = x - y$$

**9. (A)**

$$(x-y)^2 = (x-y)(x-y) = x^2 - 2xy + y^2$$
$$(y-x)^2 = (y-x)(y-x) = y^2 - 2xy + x^2$$
$$-(x-y)^2 = -(x-y)(x-y) = -(x^2 - 2xy + y^2)$$

**10. (A)**

$$(x+y)^2 = x^2 + 2xy + y^2 = 50$$
$$2xy + 30 = 50, \ 2xy = 20, \ xy = 10$$

**11. (D)**

$$\frac{x^2 - 4}{4x} = \frac{x^2}{4x} - \frac{4}{4x} = \frac{x}{4} - \frac{1}{x}$$

**12. (A)**

$$\frac{x^2 + x - 6}{2x^2 + 6x} \div \frac{x-2}{x} = \frac{(x+3)(x-2)}{2x(x+3)} \left( \frac{x}{x-2} \right) = \frac{1}{2}$$

**13. (D)**

$$\pi r^2 - 2\pi r = 35\pi$$
$$r^2 - 2r - 35 = 0$$
$$(r-7)(r+5) = 0, \ r = 7$$

**14. (B)**

$$\frac{x-2}{x^2 - 4} = \frac{x-2}{(x-2)(x+2)} = \frac{1}{x+2}$$

**15. (B)**

$$x(x+2) = 32, \ x^2 + 2x - 32 = 0, \ (x+8)(x-4) = 0$$
$$x = 4, \ 2x = 8$$

**16. (D)**

$$x^2 + (x+1)^2 + (x-1)^2 =$$
$$x^2 + (x^2 + 2x + 1) + (x^2 - 2x + 1) = 3x^2 + 2$$

$$3x^2 + 2 = 77, \ 3x^2 = 75, \ x^2 = 25, \ x = 5$$
$$(5+1)^2 = 36$$

**17. (D)**

If 600 is the perimeter of the yard, then

$$600 = 2l + 2w, \ 300 = l + w$$

If the area of the yard is 12,500 then
$lw = 12,500$.

$$l(300 - l) = 12,500 \quad l^2 - 300l + 12,500 = 0$$
$$(l-250)(l-50) = 0, \quad l = 250 \text{ or } l = 50$$

**18. (A)**

total area $= (x+6)(x+3+6) = x^2 + 15x + 54$
cell phone area $= x(x+3) = x^2 + 3x$
difference $= (x^2 + 15x + 54) - (x^2 + 3x) = 12x + 54$

## 3.6    Complex numbers

The phrase "complex numbers" is often misused.  It turns out that all numbers are complex numbers because all numbers can be written in the form $a + bi$, where $i = \sqrt{-1}$ (it is often better to remember that $i^2 = -1$).  The constant $i$ is called <u>the</u> imaginary number because all other imaginary numbers can be written in terms of $i$.  When you think of it, $i$ cannot be a real number because you cannot take the square root of a negative number.  Another way of thinking of it is that the square of any real number is positive, whereas the square of $i$ is negative.

The $a$ is the real portion of the complex number and the $bi$ is the imaginary portion of the complex number ($a$ and $b$ are real constants -- also note that they do not have to be integers).  If $b = 0$ then the complex number is called real, and if $b \neq 0$ then the complex number is called imaginary.  The diagram below illustrates the relationships among complex, real, and imaginary numbers.

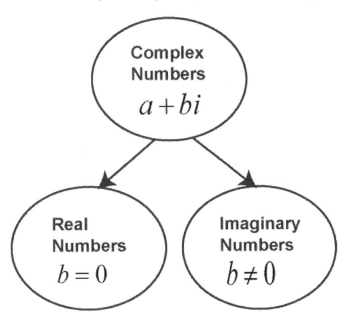

## Imaginary Numbers
Suppose we want to solve the equation

$$x^2 + 9 = 0 \ .$$

We would perform two steps and then be stuck:

$$x^2 = \text{-}9$$

$$x = \pm\sqrt{\text{-}9}$$

We are stuck because a negative number cannot have a real square root.  So to get around this, mathematicians invented $i$, the imaginary number.  By definition, $i = \sqrt{\text{-}1}$ and $i^2 = \text{-}1$.  So now we can finish the problem by writing:

$$x = \pm\sqrt{\text{-}9} = \pm\sqrt{9} \cdot \sqrt{\text{-}1} = \pm 3i$$

The expression $3i$ is an imaginary number because $b$ is three, not zero.

## Addition, subtraction and multiplication of imaginary numbers

Now that you understand what imaginary numbers are and one of the reasons why they were invented, you need to be able to perform three operations: addition, subtraction, and multiplication.

Suppose we have two imaginary numbers, $a+bi$ and $c+di$. Then:

$$(a+bi)+(c+di)=(a+c)+(b+d)i$$
$$(a+bi)-(c+di)=(a-c)+(b-d)i$$

For example

$$(2+i)+(3-2i)=2+3+i-2i=5-i$$
$$(2+i)-(3-2i)=2-3+i+2i=-1+3i$$

As you can see above, addition and subtraction are what you would expect. Treat $i$ as though it were a variable. The same applies to multiplication—the imaginary numbers are FOILed:

$$(a+bi)(c+di)=ac+adi+bci+bdi^2=(ac-bd)+(ad+bc)i$$

For example:

$$(2+i)(3-2i)=2\cdot3-4i+3i-2i^2=6-i-2(-1)=8-i$$

## Division of imaginary numbers (the use of conjugates)

You must know how to simplify expressions with imaginary numbers in the denominator. This is done using conjugates. The conjugate of $a+bi$ is $a-bi$. In other words, to find the conjugate of an imaginary number just change the sign of the imaginary portion of the number.

For example, the conjugate of $3-5i$ is $3+5i$. We use this fact to simplify fractions, as in the following

$$\frac{2}{3-5i}=\left(\frac{2}{3-5i}\right)\left(\frac{3+5i}{3+5i}\right)=\frac{2(3+5i)}{9-15i+15i-25i^2}=\frac{2(3+5i)}{9+25}=\frac{2(3+5i)}{34}=\frac{3+5i}{17}$$

## Powers of $i$

A favorite type of problem involves powers of $i$. These follow a pattern that is easy to see, once you get the hang of it.

$$i=i$$
$$i^2=-1$$
$$i^3=i\cdot i^2=-i$$
$$i^4=\left(i^2\right)^2=(-1)^2=1$$

Powers of $i$ will always equal 1 or -1 when the power is even; and $i$ or $-i$ when the power is odd. Some examples:

$$i^{18} = \left(i^2\right)^9 = \left(-1\right)^9 = -1$$

$$i^{52} = \left(i^2\right)^{26} = \left(-1\right)^{26} = 1$$

$$i^{17} = i^{16} \cdot i = \left(i^2\right)^8 \cdot i = \left(-1\right)^8 \cdot i = i$$

$$i^{51} = i^{50} \cdot i = \left(i^2\right)^{25} \cdot i = \left(-1\right)^{25} \cdot i = -i$$

 **Calculator Tip:**

You will be happy to know that all of the calculations shown above that involve imaginary numbers can be done on the graphing calculator, and some of these are shown below.

To find $i$ the imaginary number on the calculator, just press 2$^{nd}$ and then press the decimal point key on the bottom row of the calculator.

| | |
|---|---|
| `NORMAL FLOAT AUTO REAL RADIAN MP`<br><br>`(2+i)+(3-2i)`<br>`                    5-i` | Addition<br>$\left(2+i\right)+\left(3-2i\right)=5-i$ |
| `NORMAL FLOAT AUTO REAL RADIAN MP`<br><br>`(2+i)-(3-2i)`<br>`                  -1+3i` | Subtraction<br>$\left(2+i\right)-\left(3-2i\right)=-1+3i$ |
| `NORMAL FLOAT AUTO REAL RADIAN MP`<br><br>`(2+i)(3-2i)`<br>`                    8-i` | Multiplication $\left(2+i\right)\left(3-2i\right)=8-i$ |
| `NORMAL FLOAT AUTO REAL RADIAN MP`<br><br>`2/(3-5i)`<br>`  .1764705882+.2941176471i` | Division<br>$\dfrac{2}{3-5i} = \dfrac{3+5i}{17}$ |
| `NORMAL FLOAT AUTO REAL RADIAN MP`<br>`i--`<br>`               -1+2E-13i`<br>`i^52`<br>`                1+2E-13i`<br>`i^17`<br>`                 3E-13+i`<br>`i^51`<br>`                 1E-13-i` | Powers of $i$<br>$i^{18} = \left(i^2\right)^9 = \left(-1\right)^9 = -1$<br>$i^{52} = \left(i^2\right)^{26} = \left(-1\right)^{26} = 1$<br>$i^{17} = i^{16} \cdot i = \left(i^2\right)^8 \cdot i = \left(-1\right)^8 \cdot i = i$<br>$i^{51} = i^{50} \cdot i = \left(i^2\right)^{25} \cdot i = \left(-1\right)^{25} \cdot i = -i$ |

You probably noticed that the calculator always produces answers using decimals rather than fractions. If needed, you can convert a decimal value to a fraction by using *math-frac*. Also the calculator estimates the value of zero which sometimes causes zero to appear in scientific notation as a number with a very small power. For example $2 \times 10^{-13}$ is as close to zero as you can get.

## 3.6 Practice problems on complex numbers

**Solve these problems by hand first and then verify on the calculator (NOTE: $i = \sqrt{-1}$ )**

1. The sum $(3-2i)+(-1+3i)$ simplifies to:
A)    $3-i$
B)    $3+i$
C)    $2-i$
D)    $2+i$

2. The difference $(3-2i)-(-1+3i)$ simplifies to:
A)    $2-i$
B)    $2+i$
C)    $4-5i$
D)    $4+i$

3. The sum of $2-3i$ and its conjugate is:
A)    $4$
B)    $4-6i$
C)    $4+6i$
D)    $-6i$

4. The product of $2-3i$ and its conjugate is:
A)    $13$
B)    $14$
C)    $4+6i$
D)    $4+9i$

5. The expression $(2-5i)^2$ simplifies to:
A)        $-21$
B)        $29$
C)      $-1-20i$
D)      $-21-20i$

6. The expression $\dfrac{3}{3+2i}$ simplifies to:
A)    $(9-2i)/13$
B)    $(9-6i)/13$
C)    $(9-2i)/6$
D)    $(3-2i)/2$

7. The expression $\dfrac{8-3i}{2-5i}$ simplifies to:
A)    $-(31+34i)/21$
B)    $(1-34i)/29$
C)    $(1+34i)/29$
D)    $(31+34i)/29$

8. The value of $i^8$ is:
A)    $-1$
B)    $1$
C)    $-i$
D)    $i$

9..The value of $i^{886}$ is:
A)    $-1$
B)    $1$
C)    $-i$
D)    $i$

10. The value of $i^{355}$ is:
A)    $-1$
B)    $1$
C)    $-i$
D)    $i$

11. The expression $4i^3+6i^2+7i-8$ simplifies to
A)    $3i-2$
B)    $3i-14$
C)    $11i-2$
D)    $11i-14$

12. If $(8i+3)(mi-n)=a+bi$ then $a+b$ must be equal to:
A)    $-5m-5n$
B)    $-5m-11n$
C)    $11m-5n$
D)    $11m-11n$

# 3.6 Solutions to practice problems on complex numbers

### 1. (D)

$(3-2i)+(-1+3i) = 3-1-2i+3i = 2+i$

```
NORMAL FLOAT AUTO REAL RADIAN MP
(3-2i)+( -1+3i)
                            2+i
```

### 2. (C)

$(3-2i)-(-1+3i) = 3+1-2i-3i = 4-5i$

```
NORMAL FLOAT AUTO REAL RADIAN MP
(3-2i)-( -1+3i)
                            4-5i
```

### 3. (A)

$(2-3i)+(2+3i) = 2+2-3i+3i = 4$

```
NORMAL FLOAT AUTO REAL RADIAN MP
(2-3i)+(2+3i)
                              4
```

### 4. (A)

$(2-3i)(2+3i) = 4+6i-6i-9i^2$
$= 4-9(-1) = 13$

```
NORMAL FLOAT AUTO REAL RADIAN MP
(2-3i)(2+3i)
                             13
```

### 5. (D)

$(2-5i)^2 = (2-5i)(2-5i)$
$= 4-10i-10i+25i^2 = -21-20i$

```
NORMAL FLOAT AUTO REAL RADIAN MP
(2-5i)²
                         -21-20i
```

### 6. (B)

$\dfrac{3}{3+2i} = \left(\dfrac{3}{3+2i}\right)\left(\dfrac{3-2i}{3-2i}\right) = \dfrac{9-6i}{9-4i^2} = \dfrac{9-6i}{13}$

```
NORMAL FLOAT AUTO REAL RADIAN MP
3/(3+2i)
  .6923076923-.4615384615i
```

### 7. (D)

$\dfrac{8-3i}{2-5i} = \left(\dfrac{8-3i}{2-5i}\right)\left(\dfrac{2+5i}{2+5i}\right) = \dfrac{16-6i+40i-15i^2}{4-25i^2}$

$= \dfrac{31+34i}{29}$

```
NORMAL FLOAT AUTO REAL RADIAN MP
(8-3i)/(2-5i)
   1.068965517+1.172413793i
```

### 8. (B)

$i^8 = \left(i^2\right)^4 = (-1)^4 = 1$

```
NORMAL FLOAT AUTO REAL RADIAN MP
i⁸
                        1-2ᴇ⁻13i
```

### 9. (A)

$i^{886} = \left(i^2\right)^{443} = (-1)^{443} = -1$

```
NORMAL FLOAT AUTO REAL RADIAN MP
i⁸⁸⁶
                  -1-1.86ᴇ⁻11i
```

### 10. (C)

$i^{355} = i^{354} \cdot i = \left(i^2\right)^{177} i = -i$

```
NORMAL FLOAT AUTO REAL RADIAN MP
i³⁵⁵
                       5ᴇ⁻13-i
```

### 11. (B)

$4i^3 + 6i^2 + 7i - 8 = -4i - 6 + 7i - 8 = 3i - 14$

```
NORMAL FLOAT AUTO REAL RADIAN MP
4i³+6i²+7i-8
                          -14+3i
```

### 12. (B)

$(8i+3)(mi-n) = a+bi$
$8mi^2 - 8ni + 3mi - 3n = a+bi$
$(-8m-3n) + (-8n+3m)i = a+bi$
$a = -8m-3n$
$b = 3m-8n$
$a+b = -5m-11n$

## 3.7  Quadratic equations and their graphs

Quadratic equations contain a squared term, such as $x^2$, but no higher order terms (terms raised to a power greater than two).  Another name for a quadratic equation is a second degree polynomial.  The graph of a quadratic equation is called a parabola.  The height of the graph, usually represented by the variable y, is set equal to an expression involving a squared term.  You need to be able to recognize quadratic equations, find the y-intercept of the parabola if there is one, find the vertex of the parabola, find the x-intercepts of the parabola (also called the zeros or roots of the equation) if there are any,  understand the symmetry of the parabola, and graph the parabola by hand.

### Equations in standard form

A quadratic equation in standard form is $y = ax^2 + bx + c$.

The graph of a quadratic equation is a parabola.  The parabola opens up if $a > 0$ and the parabola opens down if $a < 0$.  The parabola is symmetric about its axis of symmetry, which is an invisible line running vertically through the vertex.  The equation for the axis of symmetry is $x = -b/2a$.  This is illustrated in the figures below.

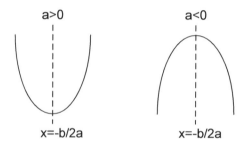

Finding the y-intercept: set x equal to zero and then solve for y.  This will give you the y-intercept if there is one.

Finding the vertex:  First find the axis of symmetry using the formula –b/2a as shown above.  This gives you the x-coordinate of the vertex.  Next find the y-coordinate of the vertex by plugging the x-coordinate into the equation of the parabola.

Finding the x-intercepts (also called zeroes and roots)

There are several methods to find the roots.  One method is to factor  the quadratic expression and then set each factor to zero (see unit 3.5 and/or see the intercept form below).  Another method is to use the quadratic formula, which you are expected to memorize:

$$x = \frac{-b \pm \sqrt{b^2 - 4ac}}{2a}.$$

You are also expected to memorize that the sum of the two roots is $\dfrac{-b}{a}$ and that the product of the roots is $\dfrac{c}{a}$.

You can see what kind of roots exist by graphing the equation. If the parabola never crosses the x-axis then the equation has two imaginary roots. If the parabola crosses the x-axis at two points, then the equation has two real roots. If the vertex of the parabola lies on the x-axis (is tangent to the x-axis) then the equation has one real root (also called a double root).

## The discriminant

Instead of graphing, you can get information about the roots or x-intercepts of the parabola by finding the sign of the discriminant, $b^2 - 4ac$. When the discriminant is positive, there are two real roots (the parabola intersects the x-axis at two points). When the discriminant is negative, there are two imaginary roots (the parabola never crosses the x-axis). When the discriminant is zero there is one real double root (the parabola touches the x-axis at one point). You are expected to be able to determine the number and type of roots by using the discriminant, rather than solve the quadratic equation or graph the parabola to see its roots.

## Example of a quadratic equation in standard form

Suppose you need to analyze and graph the equation $y = 2x^2 - 3x - 2$ by hand (the calculator approach is shown in the tip below). First find the y-intercept by setting x to zero, giving you the point (0,-2) for the y-intercept. Next find the vertex by finding the axis of symmetry. $x = -b/2a = 3/4$. Plug 3/4 into the x-value for the quadratic equation in order to find the y-value of the vertex: $y = 2(3/4)^2 - 3(3/4) - 2 = (18/16) - (9/4) - 2 = (9/8) - (18/8) - (16/8) = -25/8$. We now have the coordinates of the vertex as (.75, -3.125). To find the x-intercepts (also called roots or zeroes of the equation), use the quadratic formula:

$$x = \frac{-b \pm \sqrt{b^2 - 4ac}}{2a} = \frac{3 \pm \sqrt{9 - 4(2)(-2)}}{4} = \frac{3 \pm \sqrt{25}}{4}$$

Because the discriminant is positive we know there will be two real roots.

$$x = \frac{3 \pm 5}{4} = \frac{8}{4} \text{ and } \frac{-2}{4} \qquad (2,0) \text{ and } (-.5,0)$$

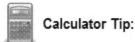

| **Calculator Tip:** | Using the example above, enter the quadratic equation into the *Y=* equation editor. Then press *graph*. If you cannot see the graph, try adjusting the window by pressing *zoom-ZStandard*. If that does not help, press *window* and adjust the size of the graphing window. | 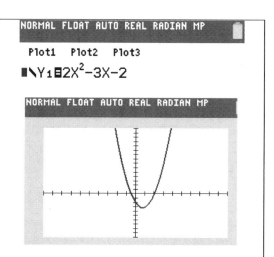 |
| --- | --- | --- |
| | To find the y-intercept use *2ⁿᵈ-calc-value*. Type 0 for your x-value and press *enter*. Notice the x-y coordinates are shown on the bottom of the screen and the cursor is placed on the y-intercept. | 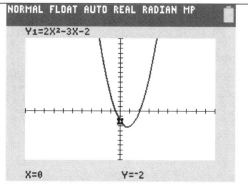 |
| | To find the vertex, use *2ⁿᵈ-calc-minimum* (or *2ⁿᵈ- calc-maximum* if the parabola opens down). The dialog will ask you to position the cursor to the left of the vertex, to the right of the vertex, and then approximately on the vertex. Coordinates of the vertex are shown on the bottom of the screen and the cursor is positioned on the vertex. | 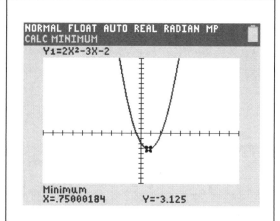 |
| | To find the x-intercepts, use *2ⁿᵈ- calc-zero*. For each intercept, the dialog will ask for a point to the left of the intercept, to the right of the intercept, and then approximately on the intercept. Coordinates of the zero are shown on the bottom of the screen and the cursor is positioned on the zero. | 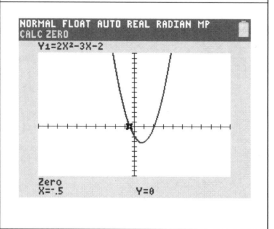 |

## Equations in vertex form

If the goal is to graph the parabola by hand, it is easier to do so when the equation is written in vertex form rather than standard form. The vertex form of the equation is

$$y = a(x-h)^2 + k$$

The vertex is at $(h,k)$ and the axis of symmetry is the equation $x=h$. This is illustrated in the figures below.

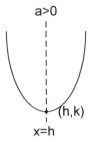 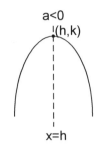

Finding the y-intercept: set x equal to zero and then solve for y. This will give you the y-intercept if there is one.

Finding the vertex: Simply read the values of h and k from the equation of the parabola. The coordinates of the vertex are (h, k).

Finding the x-intercepts (also called zeroes and roots): If $k \leq 0$ the set y to zero and solve for $x$:

$$0 = (x-h)^2 + k, \quad -k = (x-h)^2, \quad x = h \pm \sqrt{-k}$$

## Converting from standard form to vertex form

You should be prepared to see quadratic equations in either standard form or vertex form. Remember how to convert an equation from standard form to vertex form using the technique called "**completing the square**?" This technique is illustrated below.

Suppose we wanted to re-write the equation $y = x^2 - 12x + 46$ into vertex form:

| | |
|---|---|
| $y = x^2 - 12x + 46$ | the original equation |
| $y - 46 = x^2 - 12x$ | isolate the x-terms |
| $y - 46 + 36 = x^2 - 12x + 36$ | add the constant $\left(\dfrac{b}{2}\right)^2 = \left(\dfrac{-12}{2}\right)^2 = (-6)^2 = 36$ |
| $y = (x-6)^2 - 10$ | simplify to get the **vertex form of the equation** |
| $(6, -10)$ | coordinates of the vertex |

That was an easy example because $a = 1$. Now we will take the equation where $a = 2$ in standard form $2x^2 - 3x - 2 = y$ and **complete the square** to place it in vertex form.

:

$$2x^2 - 3x - 2 = y \qquad \text{the original equation}$$

$$2x^2 - 3x = y + 2 \qquad \text{isolate the x-terms}$$

$$x^2 - \frac{3}{2}x = \frac{y}{2} + 1 \qquad \text{divide both sides of the equation by 2}$$

$$x^2 - \frac{3}{2}x + \frac{9}{16} = \frac{y}{2} + \frac{25}{16} \qquad \text{add the constant } \left(\frac{b}{2}\right)^2 = \left(\frac{-3}{4}\right)^2 = \frac{9}{16} \text{ to both sides}$$

$$\left(x - \frac{3}{4}\right)^2 = \frac{y}{2} + \frac{25}{16} \qquad \text{factor the left side}$$

$$2\left(x - \frac{3}{4}\right)^2 - \frac{25}{8} = y \qquad \text{simplify to get the \textbf{vertex form of the equation}}$$

$$\left(\frac{3}{4}, \frac{-25}{8}\right) \qquad \text{coordinates of the vertex}$$

Continuing this problem by hand, we plug zero in for x to find the y-coordinate of the y-intercept:

$$y = 2\left(\frac{3}{4}\right)^2 - \frac{25}{8} = \frac{18}{16} - \frac{28}{8} = \frac{-10}{8} = -2.$$ The coordinates of the vertex can be found by simply reading

the vertex form of the equation as shown above. To find the x-intercepts, set y to zero and solve:

$$2\left(x - \frac{3}{4}\right)^2 - \frac{25}{8} = 0, \ \left(x - \frac{3}{4}\right)^2 = \frac{25}{16}, \ x - \frac{3}{4} = \pm\frac{5}{4}, \ x = \frac{3}{4} \pm \frac{5}{4}, \ x = 2 \text{ and } x = \frac{-1}{2}$$

|  Calculator Tip: | Regardless of which form the quadratic equation is in, the calculator steps are the same. Start by plugging the equation into the Y= equation editor and then follow the steps given earlier for the standard form. You will get exactly the same graph and same answers. | 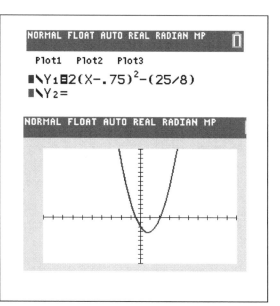 |
|---|---|---|

**Equations in intercept form**

The intercept form of the quadratic equation is

$$y = a(x - z_1)(x - z_2)$$

What is so convenient about the intercept form is that we can see that the parabola crosses the x-axis at $(z_1, 0)$ and $(z_2, 0)$. Another convenient feature of the vertex form is that we can use symmetry to get the x-coordinate of the vertex.

For example, let's take the quadratic equation we have been using, $y = 2x^2 - 3x - 2$. We can convert this to intercept form by factoring:

$$y = 2x^2 - 3x - 2, \; y = 2x^2 - 4x + x - 2, \; y = (2x^2 - 4x) + (x - 2)$$
$$y = 2x(x - 2) + 1(x - 2), \; y = (2x + 1)(x - 2)$$
$$y = (2x + 1)(x - 2) \text{ is the intercept form of the equation.}$$

<u>Finding the y-intercept</u>: set x equal to zero and then solve for y. This gives us $y = (1)(-2) = -2$. So the y-intercept is (0,-2).

<u>Finding the x-intercepts (also called zeroes and roots)</u>: Setting y to zero gives two equations to be solved: $2x + 1 = 0$ and $x - 2 = 0$. So the parabola crosses the x-axis at $\left(\dfrac{-1}{2}, 0\right)$ and $(2, 0)$

<u>Finding the vertex</u>: A very convenient feature of the intercept form is that we can find the x-coordinate of the vertex by using symmetry. The x-coordinate must lay on the midpoint between the two zeros on the x-axis. In this example the axis of symmetry must lie halfway between -0.5 and 2.0, which is 0.75. This symmetry is illustrated below. The y-coordinate of the vertex is found by plugging 0.75 in for x.

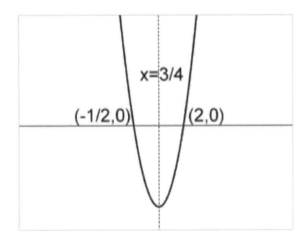

Any time you have the coordinates of two points on a parabola and those two points are at the same height (they have the same y-coordinate) you can find the x-coordinate of the axis of symmetry by taking the midpoint of the two x-coordinates.

**Equating quadratic equations (and higher order polynomials)**

A certain kind of problem shows up on standardized tests with some frequency, so it is worth giving it your attention. If you have an equation that looks like this:

$$ax^2 + bx + c = dx^2 + ex + f$$

then the corresponding coefficients are equal to each other, in this case $a = d$, $b = e$, and $c = f$. For example, if

$$ax^2 + 5x + 4 = x^2 + (k+1)x + k$$

then $a = 1$, and $k = 4$.

This same principle can be extended to any pair of polynomials provided they have the same degree (the degree of a polynomial is the size of the highest power). For example, if

$$ax^4 + 3x^2 + bx + c = 8x^4 + dx^2 + 4x + d + 5$$

then $a = 8$, $3 = d$, $b = 4$, and $c = d + 5 = 8$.

## 3.7 Practice problems on quadratic equations and their graphs
### Solve these problems by hand first and then verify on the calculator.

1. Which of these parabolas opens up?

    I.   $y = 2x^2 - 5x - 3$

    II.  $y = -2x^2 - 5x - 5$

    III. $y = 2x^2 + 5x + 3$

A)    I only

B)    II only

C)    III only

D)    I and III only

2. The vertex of the parabola $y = 3x^2 - 6x + 8$ is located at:

A)    (-2, 32)

B)    (-1, 17)

C)    (0, 8)

D)    (1, 5)

3. If a parabola crosses the x-axis at (-5,0) and (3,0) then its axis of symmetry must be:

A)    $x = -3$

B)    $x = -1$

C)    $x = 1$

D)    $x = 3$

4. The vertex of the parabola $y + 16 = (x - 1)^2$ is located at:

A)    (-1, -16)

B)    (-1, 16)

C)    (1, -16)

D)    (1, 16)

---

**Questions 5-6 refer to the following information.**

A parabola has the equation: $y = 2x^2 + x - 6$.

5. Find the axis of symmetry:

A)    $x = -0.5$

B)    $x = -0.25$

C)    $x = 0.25$

D)    $x = 0.5$

6. Find the roots (zeros):

A)    $x = -1, 3$

B)    $x = 1, 3$

C)    $x = 1.5, -2$

D)    $x = -1.5, 2$

---

7. In the parabola below, the coordinates (a, b) are:

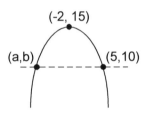

A)    (-5, 10)

B)    (-5, 15)

C)    (-9, 10)

D)    (-9, 15)

8. If the roots of a parabola are -3 and 5, then the equation of the parabola could be:

A)    $y = x^2 - 2x - 15$

B)    $y = x^2 + 2x - 15$

C)    $y = x^2 + 8x + 15$

D)    $y = x^2 - 8x + 15$

9. If the parabola $2x^2 + bx + 4$ passes through the point (2,18) then the value of $b$ must be:

(A)    3

(B)    4

(C)    5

(D)    6

---

**Questions 10-11 refer to the following information.**

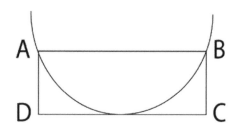

10. If ABCD is a rectangle, DC is 4 units long, and the equation of the parabola is $y = (x-3)^2 + 1$, then how long is BC?

A)    2

B)    3

C)    4

D)    5

11. If the coordinates of point A are (0,5) and the equation of the parabola is $y = (x-3)^2 + 1$, what is the area of rectangle ABCD?

A)    6

B)    12

C)    18

D)    24

---

12. If $4x^2 + bx + c = (ax+1)^2$ and $a > 0$, then $a+b+c$ is equal to:

A)    4

B)    5

C)    6

D)    7

13. If $ax^2 + bx - 9 = (x-k)(2x+k)$ and $b > 0$ then $k$ is equal to:

A)    $-3$

B)    $-1$

C)    1

D)    3

14. If $2x^2 + bx + 36 = ax^2 + (k+a)(k+x) + 1$ and $k < 0$ then $b$ is equal to:

A)    $-7$

B)    $-5$

C)    5

D)    7

15. If the height of a ball at time (t) is given by $h(t) = -5t^2 + 20t + 8$, at what point in time will the ball hit the ground?

A)    2

B)    $\dfrac{-2 + 2\sqrt{35}}{-5}$

C)    $\dfrac{-10 + 2\sqrt{35}}{-5}$

D)    $\dfrac{-10 + 2\sqrt{15}}{-5}$

16. Which of the points below lies on the axis of symmetry for the parabola with the equation of $y = 3x^2 + 12x - 15$?

A)        (-4,3)

B)        (-2,2)

C)        (2,5)

D)        (4,4)

17. For which of the equations below is the value of the discriminant equal to -23?

A)        $y = x^2 - x - 3$

B)        $y = -3x^2 - 2x + 7$

C)        $y = x^2 - 3x + 2.25$

D)        $y = 3x^2 - 5x + 4$

18. A parabola never crosses the x-axis if its discriminant is:

A)        positive

B)        negative

C)        zero

D)        zero or negative

19. One of the solutions to the equation $x^2 - 3x + 2.25 = 0$ is:

A)        0.5

B)        1.0

C)        1.5

D)        2.5

20. When the equation $y = x^2 - 6x - 3$ is written in vertex form, it becomes:

A)        $y = (x+3)^2 - 12$

B)        $y = (x+3)^2 + 12$

C)        $y = (x-3)^2 - 12$

D)        $y = (x-3)^2 + 12$

21. If a parabola intersects the x-axis at the points (-3,0) and (3,0), then the equation of the parabola could be:

I.    $y = x^2 - 9$

II.   $y = -x^2 + 9$

III.  $y = (x+3)^2$

(A)        I only

(B)        II only

(C)        III only

(D)        I and II only

22. Suppose the cost of manufacturing a bottle of shampoo is given by $c(x) = 2x^2 - 30x + 130$, where $x$ is the number of bottles manufactured (in thousands). How many units should be manufactured in order to minimize the cost per bottle?

A)        7,500

B)        15,000

C)        17,500

D)        30,000

23. If
$3x^5 + ax^3 + bx^2 - (a+b+c-5k) = cx^5 - 2x^3 + kx^2 + 11$
then $k$ must be equal to

A)        2.0

B)        2.5

C)        3.0

D)        3.5

24. What values of $k$ would make it possible for the difference between the area of a circle and the circumference of that same circle to be equal to $k$?

A)        $k > 0$

B)        $k < 0$

C)        $k > \pi$

D)        $k < \pi$

# 3.7 Solutions to practice problems on quadratic equations and their graphs

1 (D)  A parabola opens up if the coefficient of the $x^2$ term is positive.  That coefficient is positive in the first and third equations.

2. (D)  Start by finding the axis of symmetry: $(-b)/(2a) = 6/6 = 1$.  Then substitute x=1 into the equation of the parabola:

$$f(1) = 3\cdot 1^2 - 6\cdot 1 + 8 = 3 - 6 + 8 = 5$$

3. (B)  The x-intercepts are equidistant from the axis of symmetry.  The value of -1 is 4 units from -5 and 4 units from +3.

4. (C)  Rewrite the equation:

$$y + 16 = (x-1)^2$$
$$y = (x-1)^2 - 16 = (x-h)^2 + k$$

The vertex is at (h, k) = (1, -16).

5. (B)  The axis of symmetry is
$x = -b/2a = -1/2(2) = -.25$.

6. (C)  Factor $y = 2x^2 + x - 6 = (2x-3)(x+2)$.

To find the roots, set each factor to zero.
$2x - 3 = 0$, $x = 1.5$ and $x + 2 = 0$, $x = -2$

Note that the roots are equidistant from the axis of symmetry, x=-0.25.

7. (C)  This problem uses symmetry.  The axis of symmetry is x=-2.  If the point (5, 10) is 7 units from the axis of symmetry then the point (a, 10) must also be 7 units from the axis of symmetry, or (-9, 10).

8. (A)
$(x+3)(x-5) = 0$, $x^2 + 3x - 5x - 15 = 0$

9. (A)
$18 = 2(2^2) + b(2) + 4$, $6 = 2b$, $3 = b$

10. (C)  The coordinates of the vertex are (3,1).  Because DC=4, the coordinates of point C are (5,1).  Therefore the y-coordinate of point B is
$y = (5-3)^2 + 1 = 5$, and BC is 5-1=4.

11. (D)  The coordinates of the vertex are (3,1).  Therefore the coordinates of point D must be (0,1).  So AD is 4 units.  CD is 6 units because the vertex is at the midpoint of CD.  The area is 4(6)=24 units.

12. (D)
$$4x^2 + bx + c = (ax+1)^2 = a^2x^2 + 2ax + 1$$
$a^2 = 4$ or $a = 2$, $b = 2\cdot 2 = 4$, and $c = 1$. So $a + b + c = 7$

13. (A)
$$ax^2 + bx - 9 = (x-k)(2x+k) = 2x^2 - kx - k^2$$
$k^2 = 9$, $k = \pm 3$

But k must be -3 because b>0 and b = -k.

14. (B)
$$a = 2 \text{ so } ax^2 + (k+a)(k+x) + 1 = 2x^2 + (k+2)(k+x) + 1$$
$$= 2x^2 + (k+2)x + (k^2 + 2k + 1) = 2x^2 + (k+2)x + (k+1)^2$$
$(k+1)^2 = 36$, but $k < 0$ so $k + 1 = -6$, and $k = -7$.
If $k = -7$ and $b = k + 2$, then $b = -7 + 2 = -5$.

15. (C)
$$x = \frac{-20 \pm \sqrt{(-20)^2 - 4(-5)(8)}}{-10} = \frac{-20 \pm \sqrt{400 + 160}}{-10}$$
$$= \frac{-20 \pm \sqrt{560}}{-10} = \frac{-20 \pm 4\sqrt{35}}{-10} = \frac{-10 \pm 2\sqrt{35}}{-5}$$

16. (B)  In the equation $y = 3x^2 + 12x - 15$, a=3 and b=12.  So the axis of symmetry is –b/2a=-12/6 = -2.  Any point with an x-coordinate of -2 could lie on the axis of symmetry.

17. (D)  Calculate the discriminant for each equation.
    A. D=1-4(-3)=13
    B. D=4-4(-21)=88
    C. D=9-4(2.25)=0
    D. D=25-4(12)=-23

18. (B)  If the discriminant is negative, there are no real roots and the parabola never crosses the x-axis.

19. (C)  Use the quadratic formula.  For
$$x^2 - 3x + 2.25 = 0$$
$$x = \frac{3 \pm \sqrt{9 - 4(2.25)}}{2} = \frac{3 \pm \sqrt{9-9}}{2} = \frac{3}{2}$$

20. (C)  Complete the square.
$$y = x^2 - 6x - 3, \ y + 3 = x^2 - 6x,$$
$$y + 3 + 9 = x^2 - 6x + 9, \ y + 12 = (x-3)^2$$

21. (D)  The first two equations cross the x-axis at the points indicated, whereas the third equation crosses the x-axis at only one point (-3,0)

22. (A)  The minimum cost will occur at the vertex, which is $-b/2a = 30/4 = 7.5$

23. (C)
$a = -2$, $b = k$, $c = 3$, $-(a+b+c-5k) = 11$
$-(-2+k+3-5k) = 11$, $4k - 1 = 11$, $k = 3$

24. (D)
$$\pi r^2 - 2\pi r = k, \ \pi r^2 - 2\pi r - k = 0$$
discriminant: $(-2\pi)^2 - 4\pi k > 0$
$4\pi^2 - 4\pi k > 0$, $4\pi(\pi - k) > 0$, $\pi > k$

## 3.8    Systems involving quadratic equations and inequalities

A system of equations can be solved algebraically or graphically, whereas a system of inequalities must be solved graphically.  We begin with systems of equations.

### Systems of equations

A typical system of equations will involve a line and a parabola.  The goal is to find the point or points of intersection, if any.

<u>Two points of intersection</u>:  Suppose the parabola has the equation $y = 2x^2 - 3x - 2$ and the line has the equation $y = x + 4$.  Shown below are the algebraic and graphical solutions that are used to find the points of intersection.

| Algebraic solution | Graphical solution |
|---|---|
| Equate the expressions for the line and parabola and solve for $x$ $$x + 4 = 2x^2 - 3x - 2$$ $$0 = 2x^2 - 4x - 6$$ $$0 = x^2 - 2x - 3$$ $$0 = (x-3)(x+1)$$ $$x = -1, x = 3$$ Plug each x-value into the equation of the line to find the y-values of the points of intersection: (-1, 3) and (3,7). | Carefully graph each equation and find the points of intersection. 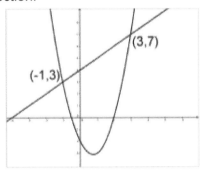 |

| | | |
|---|---|---|
|  Calculator Tip: | Enter the equations into the *Y=* equation editor.  Then press *graph*. If you cannot see the graph, try adjusting the window by pressing *zoom-ZStandard*.  If that does not help, press *window* and adjust the size of the graphing window. Press $2^{nd}$-*calc-intersect*.  Follow the dialog, choosing one graph, then the other graph.  Then position the cursor near the intersection of interest and press *enter*.  The exact coordinates of the intersection of interest are shown at the bottom of the screen and the cursor is placed at the intersection. | 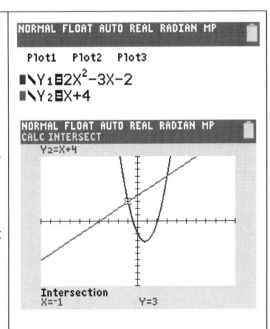 |

<u>One point of intersection</u>: Consider the same parabola $y = 2x^2 - 3x - 2$ and the equation $y = -25/8$. These will have a single point of intersection and the point of intersection will be the vertex of the parabola. The algebraic and graphical solutions are shown below.

| Algebraic solution | Graphical solution |
|---|---|
| Equate the expressions for the line and parabola and solve for $x$<br><br>$-(25/8) = 2x^2 - 3x - 2$<br>$0 = 2x^2 - 3x + (9/8)$<br>$0 = 16x^2 - 24x + 9$<br>$0 = (4x - 3)(4x - 3)$<br>$x = 3/4 = 0.75$ | Carefully graph each equation and find the points of intersection.<br><br>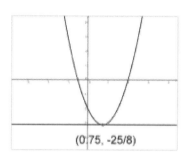<br>(0.75, -25/8) |

<u>No points of intersection</u>: Of course the line may never intersect with the parabola. Consider the same parabola $y = 2x^2 - 3x - 2$ and the equation $y = x - 6$

| Algebraic solution | Graphical solution |
|---|---|
| Equate the expressions for the line and parabola and solve for $x$<br><br>$-6 = 2x^2 - 3x - 2$<br>$0 = 2x^2 - 3x + 4$<br>$x = \dfrac{3 \pm \sqrt{9 - 4(2)(4)}}{4} = \dfrac{3 \pm \sqrt{-27}}{4}$<br><br>No real solution | Carefully graph each equation and determine that there are no points of intersection.<br><br>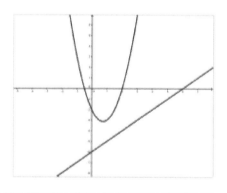 |

<u>General case -- use the discriminant</u>: Sometimes you will not be given the equations of interest, but will be asked to find equations that produce a certain outcome: two intersections, one intersection, or no intersections. This can be done with the discriminant (see Unit 3.7). The discriminant is the expression under the radical when using the quadratic formula, $b^2 - 4ac$.

Consider the completely general case of a parabola $y = ax^2 + bx + c$ and a line $y = mx + k$. Set them equal to each other to get $ax^2 + bx + c = mx + k$. Set to zero to get $ax^2 + (b - m)x + (c - k) = 0$. Now you have a quadratic equation that is set to zero and you can use the discriminant to find values of a, b, c, m and k that produce two solutions (discriminant is positive), one solution (discriminant is zero) and no solutions (discriminant is negative). A few examples of this approach appear in the homework problems at the end of this unit.

## Systems of inequalities

An inequality involving a parabola requires you to shade either inside or outside the parabola. For example, consider the inequality $y \geq 2x^2 - 3x - 2$. First we graph the equation of the parabola using a solid line because the inequality involves an equals sign (otherwise we would use a dotted line). Then we test a convenient point, in this case we are using (0,0). Because the inequality $0 \geq 0 - 0 - 2$ is true we shade inside the parabola because the point (0,0) lies inside the parabola and is part of the solution region (see Unit 3.4 to refresh your skills at graphing inequalities). The graph of the solution region is shown on the left, below:

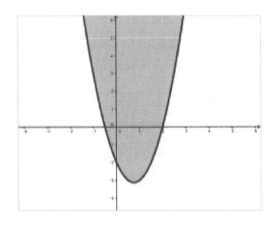

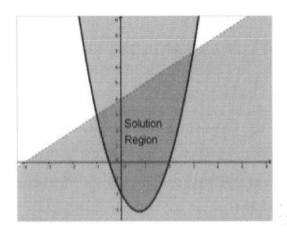

Now we will combine this parabola inequality with the linear inequality $y < x + 4$ to form a system of inequalities. First we plot the graph of the line using a dotted line because the inequality does not involve an equals sign. To decide whether to shade above the line or below the line, we test the point (0,0). Because the inequality $0 < 0 + 4$ is true, we will shade the region that contains the point (0,0) which in this case happens to be below the line. The graph of the solution region of the system of inequalities is shown above, on the right.

| 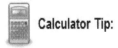 Calculator Tip: | To obtain a graph similar to the example above, enter the quadratic and linear equations into the $Y=$ equation editor. For the quadratic equation, toggle the cursor until it is on top of the box on the far left of the screen, and press *enter*. Scroll through the line choices to find the greater than symbol and press *enter*. Do the same for the second equation, but for that equation scroll through the line choices to find the less than and then press enter. Your screen should look like the one on the top. When you press the *graph* key you should see a graph like that shown on the bottom. | 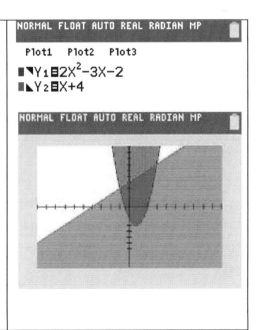 |
|---|---|---|

## 3.8 Practice problems on systems involving quadratic equations and inequalities
### Solve these problems by hand first and then verify on the calculator.

1. What are the solution(s) to the system $y = 2(2x-1)(x-5)$ and $y - 14x = -62$ ?

A)     (3,0) and (6,0)

B)     (3, -20) and (6, 22)

C)     (-3, 112) and (-6, 286)

D)     (2.25, -19.25)

2. What are the solution(s) to the system $y = 2x^2 + 20$ and $y = 0.5x^2 - 5x + 48.5$ ?

A)     (3, 38)

B)     (3, 38) and $\left( \dfrac{-19}{3}, 300\dfrac{2}{3} \right)$

C)     (3, 38) and $\left( \dfrac{-19}{3}, 100\dfrac{2}{9} \right)$

D)     No real solution

3. How many ordered pairs (x, y) satisfy this system of equations: $y = x^2 + 2x + 1$ and $y = 2x + 4$ ?

A)     0

B)     1

C)     2

D)     Infinitely many

4. What values of $k$ would cause the following system of equations to have no real solutions:

$y = 3x^2 + 2x + 1$ and $y = -2x + k$ ?

A)     $k < \dfrac{-4}{3}$

B)     $k < \dfrac{-1}{3}$

C)     $k < \dfrac{1}{3}$

D)     $k < \dfrac{4}{3}$

5. The graph below shows the solution region to which of the following systems of inequalities?

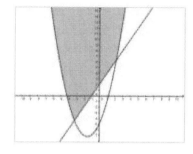

A)     $y > x^2 + 3x - 5$ and $y < 2x + 2$

B)     $y > x^2 + 3x + 2$ and $y > 2x + 2$

C)     $y < x^2 + 3x - 5$ and $y > 2x + 2$

D)     $y > x^2 + 3x - 5$ and $y > 2x + 2$

6. The graph below shows the solution region to which of the following systems of inequalities?

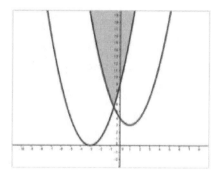

A)     $y \le (x-1)^2 + 3$ and $y \le (x+3)^2$

B)     $y \le (x-1)^2 + 3$ and $y \ge (x+3)^2$

C)     $y \ge (x-1)^2 + 3$ and $y \le (x+3)^2$

D)     $y \ge (x-1)^2 + 3$ and $y \ge (x+3)^2$

7. What relationship between $c$ and $k$ would cause the graphs of these two equations to intersect at two points

$y = 2x^2 + 3x + (c - k)$ and $y = 3x + k$ ?

A)     $c < k$

B)     $c < 2k$

C)     $c > k$

D)     $c > 2k$

### 3.8 Solutions to practice problems on systems involving quadratic equations and inequalities

**1 (B)**

$$y = 14x - 62 = 2(2x-1)(x-5)$$
$$7x - 31 = 2x^2 - 18x + 36$$
$$0 = x^2 - 9x + 18, \quad 0 = (x-6)(x-3)$$
When $x = 3$, $y = 14(3) - 62 = -20$
When $x = 6$, $y = 14(6) - 62 = 22$

**2. (C)**

$$2y = 4x^2 + 40 = x^2 - 10x + 97$$
$$0 = 3x^2 + 10x - 57 = 3x^2 + 19x - 10x - 57$$
$$0 = (3x^2 + 19x) - (10x + 57) = x(3x+19) - 3(3x+19)$$
$$0 = (x-3)(3x+19)$$
When $x = 3$, $y = 2(9) + 20 = 38$
When $x = \dfrac{-19}{3}$, $y = 2\left(\dfrac{-19}{3}\right)^2 + 20 = 100\dfrac{2}{3}$

**3. (B)**

$$y = 2x + 4 = x^2 + 4x + 5$$
$$0 = x^2 + 2x + 1$$
Solve by factoring: $0 = (x+1)(x+1)$
Solve with discriminant $= 4 - 4(1)(1) = 0$

**4. (B)**

$$y = -2x + k = 3x^2 + 2x + 1$$
$$0 = 3x^2 + 4x + (1-k)$$
Discriminant $= 16 - 4(3)(1-k) < 0$
$16 - 12 + 12k < 0$, $12k < -4$, $k < -1/3$

**5. (D)**

The solution region is above the line so (0,0) lies outside the solution region. Eliminate (A).

The parabola has a y-intercept that is negative. Eliminate (B).

The solution region lies inside the parabola. Eliminate (C).

**6. (D)**

The solution region is inside both parabolas and the point (0,0) is outside both parabolas.

Test the first parabola, $y = (x-1)^2 + 3$. At (0,0) we get $0 < 1 + 4$ so we will look for a greater than. Eilminate (A) and (B).

Test the second parabola, $y = (x+3)^2$. At (0,0) we get $0 < 9$ so we will look for a greater than. Eliminate (C).

**7. (B)**

$$y = 3x + k = 2x^2 + 3x + (c-k)$$
$$0 = 2x^2 + (c - 2k)$$
Discriminant $= 0 - 4(2)(c - 2k) > 0$
$-8c + 16k > 0$, $16k > 8c$, $2k > c$

## 3.9 Higher order polynomials

In Unit 3.7 we covered second degree polynomials (called quadratic equations) and their graphs (called parabolas). In this unit we cover general $n^{th}$ degree polynomials that take the form

$$p(x) = c_n x^n + c_{n-1} x^{n-1} + ... + c_1 x + c_0$$

### 3.9.1 Operations on two (or more) polynomials

In the sections below we will discuss the operations of addition, subtraction, and multiplication using the example polynomials

$$p(x) = x^4 + x^3 - 6x^2 - 5x - 1$$

$$q(x) = x^2 - 2x - 1$$

### Addition and Subtraction

To add or subtract polynomials, it is simply a matter of combining like terms, that is terms that have the same power. In the examples we are using:

$$p(x) + q(x) = x^4 + x^3 + (-6+1)x^2 + (-5-2)x + (-1-1)$$

$$p(x) + q(x) = x^4 + x^3 - 5x^2 - 7x - 2$$

$$p(x) - q(x) = x^4 + x^3 + (-6-1)x^2 + (-5+2)x + (-1+1)$$

$$p(x) - q(x) = x^4 + x^3 - 7x^2 - 3x$$

### Multiplication

To multiply two polynomials we take each term of one polynomial and distribute these across all the terms of the other polynomial. In our example:

$$q(x) \cdot p(x) = x^2(x^4 + x^3 - 6x^2 - 5x - 1) - 2x(x^4 + x^3 - 6x^2 - 5x - 1) - 1(x^4 + x^3 - 6x^2 - 5x - 1)$$

$$= (x^6 + x^5 - 6x^4 - 5x^3 - x^2) + (-2x^5 - 2x^4 + 12x^3 + 10x^2 + 2x) + (-x^4 - x^3 + 6x^2 + 5x + 1)$$

$$= x^6 - x^5 - 9x^4 + 6x^3 + 15x^2 + 7x + 1$$

### 3.9.2 Graphing rational functions (ratios of polynomials)

Some problems involve rational functions, which are a ratio of two polynomials $\dfrac{p(x)}{q(x)}$, but division is not what is indicated. Instead the question is asking about the graph of the ratio.

In this situation the first step is to replace x with zero to find the y-intercepts. Then factor p(x) and q(x) fully and simplify the ratio by cancelling out the factors that are common to p(x) and q(x). If a common factor, say (x+5), is cancelled, it means that the graph has a hole at x=-5. Factors remaining in the numerator create x-intercepts. Factors remaining in the denominator create vertical asymptotes. Horizontal asymptotes are determined by using this chart:

| Condition | Equation of the horizontal asymptote |
|---|---|
| degree of p(x) > degree of q(x) | There is no horizontal asymptote. |
| degree of p(x) = degree of q(x) | y = the ratio of the leading coefficients of p(x) and q(x). |
| degree of p(x) < degree of q(x) | y=0 |

The following will illustrate the process of examining a rational function.  Suppose

$$\frac{p(x)}{q(x)} = \frac{x^2 + 3x + 2}{x^2 - x - 2} = \frac{(x+1)(x+2)}{(x+1)(x-2)} = \frac{x+2}{x-2}, \ x \neq -1$$

The y-intercept is found to be (0, -1) by replacing x with zero.  Simplification of the ratio tells us that the graph has a hole at x=-1.  Plugging zero into the numerator tells us that the graph has x-intercept at y=-1.  The factor in the numerator tells us that there is an x-intercept at x=-2.  The factor in the denominator tells us that there is a vertical asymptote at x=2.  The numerator and denominator both have the same degree (two), so the equation of the horizontal asymptote is y=1/1, or y=1 (each leading coefficient is equal to 1).  A graph of p(x)/q(x) is :

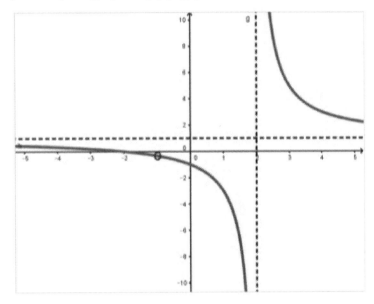

Note:  Limitations of the graphing utility prevent displaying an empty hole in the graph shown above, but an empty hole exists.  The ratio is not defined at x=-1.

### 3.9.3        Dividing polynomials

**Polynomial long division**

One of the skills that you are expected to have is the ability to divide two polynomials using long division.  Continuing with the example from above, suppose

$$\frac{p(x)}{q(x)} = \frac{x^4 + x^3 - 6x^2 - 5x - 1}{x^2 - 2x - 1}.$$

Sometimes you get lucky and $p(x)$ and/or $q(x)$ factors. When that happens, just factor each polynomial and simplify. In this example, the polynomials do not factor so the only thing left to do is polynomial long division.

Step 1. Set up the long division

$$x^2 - 2x - 1 \overline{\smash{\big)}\,x^4 + x^3 - 6x^2 - 5x - 1}$$

Step 2. Multiply by $x^2$

$$\begin{array}{r} x^2 \phantom{+x^3-6x^2-5x-1} \\ x^2 - 2x - 1 \overline{\smash{\big)}\,x^4 + x^3 - 6x^2 - 5x - 1} \\ x^4 - 2x^3 - x^2 \phantom{-5x-1} \end{array}$$

Step 3. Subtract

$$\begin{array}{r} x^2 \phantom{+x^3-6x^2-5x-1} \\ x^2 - 2x - 1 \overline{\smash{\big)}\,x^4 + x^3 - 6x^2 - 5x - 1} \\ \underline{x^4 - 2x^3 - x^2} \phantom{-5x-1} \\ 3x^3 - 5x^2 - 5x - 1 \end{array}$$

Step 4. Multiply by $3x$

$$\begin{array}{r} x^2 + 3x \phantom{-6x^2-5x-1} \\ x^2 - 2x - 1 \overline{\smash{\big)}\,x^4 + x^3 - 6x^2 - 5x - 1} \\ \underline{x^4 - 2x^3 - x^2} \phantom{-5x-1} \\ 3x^3 - 5x^2 - 5x - 1 \\ 3x^3 - 6x^2 - 3x \phantom{-1} \end{array}$$

Step 5. Subtract

$$\begin{array}{r} x^2 + 3x \phantom{-6x^2-5x-1} \\ x^2 - 2x - 1 \overline{\smash{\big)}\,x^4 + x^3 - 6x^2 - 5x - 1} \\ \underline{x^4 - 2x^3 - x^2} \phantom{-5x-1} \\ 3x^3 - 5x^2 - 5x - 1 \\ \underline{3x^3 - 6x^2 - 3x} \phantom{-1} \\ x^2 - 2x - 1 \end{array}$$

Step 6. Multiply by $1$

$$\begin{array}{r} x^2 + 3x + 1 \\ x^2 - 2x - 1 \overline{\smash{\big)}\,x^4 + x^3 - 6x^2 - 5x - 1} \\ \underline{x^4 - 2x^3 - x^2} \phantom{-5x-1} \\ 3x^3 - 5x^2 - 5x - 1 \\ \underline{3x^3 - 6x^2 - 3x} \phantom{-1} \\ x^2 - 2x - 1 \\ x^2 - 2x - 1 \end{array}$$

Step 7. Subtract to find the remainder is zero

$$\begin{array}{r} x^2 + 3x + 1 \\ x^2 - 2x - 1 \overline{\smash{\big)}\,x^4 + x^3 - 6x^2 - 5x - 1} \\ \underline{x^4 - 2x^3 - x^2} \phantom{-5x-1} \\ 3x^3 - 5x^2 - 5x - 1 \\ \underline{3x^3 - 6x^2 - 3x} \phantom{-1} \\ x^2 - 2x - 1 \\ \underline{x^2 - 2x - 1} \\ 0 \end{array}$$

In this problem the remainder is zero, and we can write that

$$p(x) = x^4 + x^3 - 6x^2 - 5x - 1 = (x^2 + 3x + 1)(x^2 - 2x - 1) + \frac{0}{x^2 - 2x - 1}$$

Because the remainder is zero we can say that $x^2 + 3x + 1$ and $x^2 - 2x - 1$ are factors of $x^4 + x^3 - 6x^2 - 5x - 1$. If we wanted to find the zeros or roots of $x^4 + x^3 - 6x^2 - 5x - 1$ we would find the values of $x$ for which either of its factors are equal to zero. This is the same process that we followed in Unit 3.7 with quadratic equations, though polynomial long division was not needed because if the quadratic did not factor we could use the quadratic formula.

**Special case where $q(x) = x - c$ (synthetic division)**

Sometimes the denominator q(x) is equal to x plus or minus a constant. When that occurs you could still use polynomial long division. For example

$$\frac{p(x)}{q(x)} = \frac{x^3 + 7x^2 + 13x + 15}{x + 5}.$$

The solution using long division looks like this:

$$
\begin{array}{r}
x^2 + 2x + 3 \\
x+5\overline{)x^3 + 7x^2 + 13x + 15} \\
\underline{x^3 + 5x^2} \\
2x^2 + 13x + 15 \\
\underline{2x^2 + 10x} \\
3x + 15 \\
\underline{3x + 15} \\
0
\end{array}
$$

But there is a much faster way to get the same result, and that is called synthetic division. The steps are as follows:

Step 1.  Set up the synthetic division

$$-5 \,\begin{array}{|cccc} 1 & 7 & 13 & 15 \\ \hline & & & \end{array}$$

Step 2.  Bring down the first coefficient

$$-5 \,\begin{array}{|cccc} 1 & 7 & 13 & 15 \\ \hline 1 & & & \end{array}$$

Step 3.  Multiply $(-5)(1)$

$$-5 \,\begin{array}{|cccc} 1 & 7 & 13 & 15 \\ & -5 & & \\ \hline 1 & & & \end{array}$$

Step 4.  Add $7 + (-5)$

$$-5 \,\big|\, \begin{array}{cccc} 1 & 7 & 13 & 15 \\ & -5 & & \\ \hline 1 & 2 & & \end{array}$$

Steps 5+.  Continue multiplying and adding

$$-5 \,\big|\, \begin{array}{cccc} 1 & 7 & 13 & 15 \\ & -5 & -10 & -15 \\ \hline 1 & 2 & 3 & 0 \end{array}$$

From the coefficients in the bottom row, we can see that the answer is $1x^2 + 2x + 3$ with no remainder. Thus we conclude that $x + 5$ and $1x^2 + 2x + 3$ are factors of $x^3 + 7x^2 + 13x + 15$ and that $-5$ is a zero or root of $x^3 + 7x^2 + 13x + 15$.

### 3.9.4   The remainder theorem

A general way to consider remainders is illustrated by the equation $\dfrac{p(x)}{h(x)} = q(x) + \dfrac{R(x)}{h(x)}$. The polynomial $q(x)$ is called the quotient and the polynomial $R(x)$ is called the remainder. An equivalent form of the above equation is sometimes more useful, namely $p(x) = q(x)h(x) + R(x)$.

**Special case where** $h(x) = x - c$

An interesting thing happens when $h(x) = x - c$, where $c$ is a constant. When that is the case, $p(c) = R(c)$. So if you want to evaluate $p(x)$ at some point where $x = c$, instead of plugging the value of $c$ into the expression for p(x), you can plug the value of c into the expression for the remainder $R(x)$, which can be much simpler than the original expression for p(x). Another way to think of this is that if you know the value of $R(c)$ then you know the value of $p(c)$.

In an earlier example we used synthetic division to show that when $p(x) = x^3 + 7x^2 + 13x + 15$ was divided by $q(x) = x + 5$, the remainder was always zero. If we wanted to find the value of $p(-5)$ the long route would be to find $p(-5) = (-5)^3 + 7(-5)^2 + 13(-5) + 15 = 0$, but the shorter route is to see that $p(-5)$ must be zero because $R(-5) = 0$.

Really amazing things happen if when p(x) is divided by h(x) the remainder is zero **AND** if $h(x) = x - c$. Under those circumstances the following statements are true:

        a)   c is a zero of the polynomial p(x)
        b)   c is a root of the polynomial p(x)
        c)   p(c) = 0
        d)   (c,0) is an x-intercept of the polynomial p(x)
        e)   The graph of p(x) goes through the point (c,0)
        f)    (x-c) is a factor of the polynomial p(x)
        g)   $p(c) = q(x) \cdot (x - c) + 0$
        h)   $R(x) = 0$ for all values of $x$
        i)    The polynomial p(x) is divisible by (x-c)

Believe it or not, it is necessary to be familiar with the many different ways the same meaning is conveyed in the list above. Problems can use a variety of phrases to indicate that c is a zero. Take some time to familiarize yourself with the equivalent statements above.

### 3.9.5    Finding the zeros (roots) of a polynomial by hand

In Unit 3.7, we found the zeros of a second-degree polynomial by factoring and setting each factor to zero. If the quadratic polynomial could not be factored, we used the quadratic formula to find them.

The process for finding the zeros for a higher order polynomial is a little bit different, and it will depend on whether you are allowed to use a calculator.

<u>Finding the zeros when a calculator is not allowed</u>

Chances are that if you are asked to find the zeros of a polynomial, the polynomial you are given will have at least one real zero, that is it will cross the x-axis at least once. (If it does not then all the zeros are imaginary.) Recall the general form of the polynomial is: $p(x) = c_n x^n + c_{n-1} x^{n-1} + ... + c_1 x + c_0$. If there is a real zero that is also rational (irrational numbers are quantities like $\pi$ and $\sqrt{2}$) then the zeros must be $\dfrac{\text{factors of } c_0}{\text{factors of } c_n}$.

The best way to understand this is by example. Suppose you want to find the zeros of $x^4 + 3x^3 - x^2 - 13x - 10$. All possible rational real zeros are factors of 10 divided by factors of 1. You would have to test $\pm 10, \pm 5, \pm 2, \pm 1$ to determine whether any of these values are zeros, either by plugging them back into $p(x) = x^4 + 3x^3 - x^2 - 13x - 10$ or by using synthetic division to find a value that produces a zero remainder. Eventually you would discover that $p(2) = 2^4 + 3(2^3) - 4 - 13(2) - 10 = 0$. The synthetic division is:

$$
\begin{array}{r|rrrrr}
 & 1 & 3 & -1 & -13 & -10 \\
2 & & 2 & 10 & 18 & 10 \\
\hline
 & 1 & 5 & 9 & 5 & 0
\end{array}
$$

Next we examine the reduced polynomial $x^3 + 5x^2 + 9x + 5$ that is found on the last row of the synthetic division. All possible rational real zeros of this reduced polynomial are $\pm 5, \pm 1$. After some trial and error we discover that -1 is a zero. That synthetic division is:

$$
\begin{array}{r|rrrr}
 & 1 & 5 & 9 & 5 \\
-1 & & -1 & -4 & -5 \\
\hline
 & 1 & 4 & 5 & 0
\end{array}
$$

Finally we have a reduced polynomial that is a quadratic! It is $x^2 + 4x + 5$. At first it looks like it might factor but it does not. So we use the quadratic formula to find the other two zeros:

97

$$x = \frac{-4 \pm \sqrt{16-20}}{2} = \frac{-4 \pm 2i}{2} = -2 \pm i$$

We can now say that the zeros (roots) of $x^4 + 3x^3 - x^2 - 13x - 10$ are $2, -1, -2+i$, and $-2-i$. Note that imaginary zeros always come in conjugate pairs. An equivalent statement is that

$$x^4 + 3x^3 - x^2 - 13x - 10 = (x-2)(x+1)(x-(-2+i))(x-(-2-i))$$

### Finding the zeros when a calculator is allowed

Finding the zeros when a calculator is allowed is much easier, but the calculator can only be used to find real zeros, that is the places where the graph of the polynomial crosses the x-axis. The imaginary zeros need to be found by hand. But first we do the easy part by following the calculator tip below.

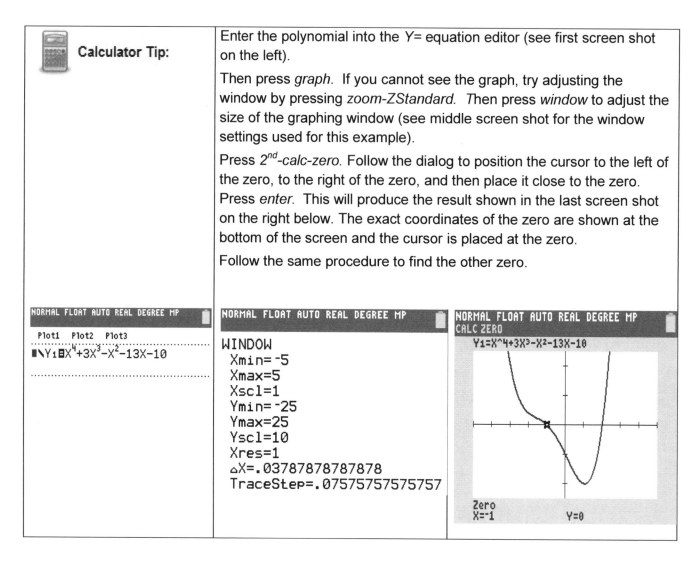

| **Calculator Tip:** | Enter the polynomial into the *Y=* equation editor (see first screen shot on the left). |
| --- | --- |
| | Then press *graph*. If you cannot see the graph, try adjusting the window by pressing *zoom-ZStandard*. Then press *window* to adjust the size of the graphing window (see middle screen shot for the window settings used for this example). |
| | Press *2ⁿᵈ-calc-zero*. Follow the dialog to position the cursor to the left of the zero, to the right of the zero, and then place it close to the zero. Press *enter*. This will produce the result shown in the last screen shot on the right below. The exact coordinates of the zero are shown at the bottom of the screen and the cursor is placed at the zero. |
| | Follow the same procedure to find the other zero. |

If at this point you need to find the imaginary zeros you would use synthetic division to confirm the two zeros you found on the calculator and then use the quadratic formula on the reduced quadratic, as shown in the above no calculator version of the solution.

### 3.9.6    Graphing polynomials by hand

There can be situations on the SAT® where you must know how to graph a polynomial by hand. Even when you are in the section where a calculator is allowed it sometimes is easier/faster to answer the problem by hand. To sketch a rough graph by hand, there are just a few things you need to know.

#### Y-intercept

The y-intercept is easy and quick to find. Take a look at the general form of the polynomial above and note that $p(0) = c_0$. In other words, the polynomial will always travel through $(0, c_0)$, where $c_0$ is the constant term of the polynomial.

#### X-intercepts and tangents

The easiest way to find the x-intercepts is to factor the polynomial. In the no calculator section the polynomial will typically factor. If you cannot see how to factor the polynomial then you can find the zeros by following the procedure described above.

When you find the factors you have found the real zeros. The multiplicity of the factor tells you whether the zero is a point where the curve crosses the x-axis (multiplicity is odd) or whether the zero is a point where the curve is tangent to the x-axis (multiplicity is even). Multiplicity is the power to which the factor is raised. See the example below.

#### End behavior

End behavior describes the direction in which the graph is moving as the x-values become very small or very large. It is easy to remember end behavior by considering the chart below which uses graphs of the relatively simple parent functions of $y = x^2$ and $y = x^3$ to illustrate end behavior. Note that when the degree is even, the curve starts and ends the same way, up-up or down-down. But when the degree is odd, the curve starts and ends in opposite ways.

| | | Leading coefficient >0 | Leading coefficient <0 | |
|---|---|---|---|---|
| **Degree even** | Starts high<br><br>Ends high | | Starts low<br><br>Ends low | |
| **Degree odd** | Starts low<br><br>Ends high | | Starts high<br><br>Ends low | |

Examples

Consider the mother of all parabolas $y = x^2$. The equation can be written in factored form as $y = (x-0)^2$. The factor tells you that the x-intercept is at (0,0). Because the multiplicity is even, you know that the curve is tangent to the x-axis at (0,0); it does not cross over the x-axis. Because the degree is even and the leading coefficient is positive, end behavior tells you that the curve starts high and ends high. Check the curve of $y = x^2$ shown in the top left box of the figure on the previous page.

Consider the equation $y = x^3$. The equation can be written in factored form as $y = (x-0)^3$. That tells you that the x-intercept is at (0,0). Because the multiplicity is odd, you know that the curve passes through the x-axis at that point. Because the degree is odd and the leading coefficient is positive, end behavior tells you that the curve starts low and ends high. Check the curve of $y = x^3$ shown in the bottom left box.

Lastly, consider a more complicated polynomial $y = -(x-1)^2(x+1)$. The factors and their multiplicities tell you that there is a tangent at (1,0) and that the curve crosses the x-axis at (-1,0). If you were to FOIL the factored polynomial, the leading term would be $-x^3$. End behavior tells you that the curve will start high and end low because the degree is odd and the leading coefficient is negative. The curve of $y = -(x-1)^2(x+1)$ is shown below.

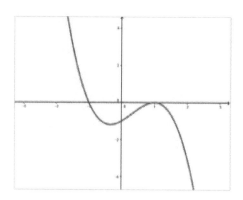

### 3.9 Practice problems on higher order polynomials
### Solve these problems by hand first and then verify on the calculator

1. Which of the following are zeros (roots) of the polynomial $p(x) = x^3 + 2x^2 - 3x$ ?

   I.  $-3$

   II.  $0$

   III  $1$

A)    I only
B)    II only
C)    I and III only
D)    I, II and III

2. If 5 is a zero (root) of $x^3 - 5x^2 - x + 5$ then another zero (root) is:

A)    $-i$
B)    $i$
C)    -5
D)    -1

3. If when $x^3 + x^2 - bx + 2$ is divided by $x + 1$ the remainder is 3, what must be the value of $b$ ?

A)    -1
B)    0
C)    1
D)    2

4. What is the remainder when $x^3 + x^2 - x + 2$ is divided by $x^2 - x - 1$ ?

A)    $2x + 4$
B)    $x + 2$
C)    $2x$
D)    $x$

5. How many times does the graph of $p(x) = x^3 + x^2 - x + 2$ cross the x-axis?

A)    0
B)    1
C)    2
D)    3

6. If $x - 2$ and $x + 2$ are factors of $p(x) = x^4 + 5x^2 - 36$, which of the following is <u>NOT</u> a zero (root) of $p(x)$?

A)    $-3i$
B)    $1$
C)    $2$
D)    $3i$

7. If $2x - 1$ is a factor of $8x^5 - bx^2 + 6x - 10$ then what is the value of $b$ ?

A)    -27
B)    -3
C)    3
D)    27

8. Which of the following is equivalent to
$$\frac{3x^4 + x^3 - 2x^2 + x + 8}{x^2 + 2x + 1} ?$$

A)    $3x^2 - 5x - 15 + \dfrac{36x + 23}{x^2 + 2x + 1}$

B)    $3x^2 - 5x - 5 + \dfrac{16x + 3}{x^2 + 2x + 1}$

C)    $3x^2 - 5x + 5 + \dfrac{16x + 13}{x^2 + 2x + 1}$

D)    $3x^2 - 5x + 5 + \dfrac{-4x + 3}{x^2 + 2x + 1}$

9. What is the difference of $x^8 - 3x^5 + 6x^3 - 8$ and $-3x^8 - 2x^7 + 3x^3$ ?

A)    $-2x^8 + 2x^7 - 3x^5 - 9x^3 - 8$
B)    $-2x^8 - 2x^7 - 3x^5 + 9x^3 - 8$
C)    $4x^8 + 2x^7 - 3x^5 + 3x^3 - 8$
D)    $4x^8 - 2x^7 - 3x^5 + 3x^3 - 8$

10. For what real value of x is the following function undefined?

$$f(x) = \frac{1+p^2}{x^2 - 2px + 1 + p^2}$$

A)    $x = -p$

B)    $x = p$

C)    $x = p^2$

D)    The function is defined for all real values of x.


11. Which of the following polynomials could produce a graph that looks like the one below?

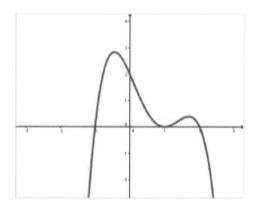

A)    $y = -(x+1)(x+2)(x-1)^2$

B)    $y = (x+1)(x+2)(x-1)^2$

C)    $y = -(x+1)(x+2)(x-1)$

D)    $y = (x+1)(x+2)(x-1)$


12. If the graph of $\dfrac{2x^2 + 2x}{x^3 - x}$ has $a$ holes, $b$ vertical asymptotes and $c$ horizontal asymptotes, what is the sum of $a, b,$ and $c$?

A)    1

B)    2

C)    3

D)    4


13. Which of the diagrams below could be the graph of $\dfrac{3(x-1)^2}{2x(x+2)}$?

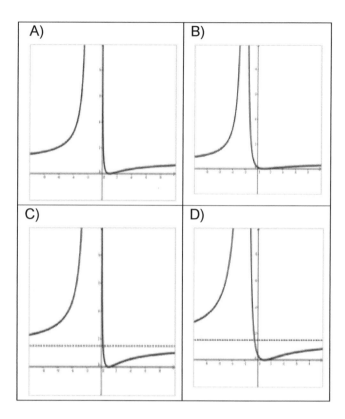

A)    B)    C)    D)


14. Which of the following statements are true about the graph of $y = \dfrac{1}{x^2}$?

   I.   The graph is tangent to the x-axis.

   II.   The graph has horizontal and vertical asymptotes

   III   The graph never crosses the x-axis or the y-axis

A)    I only

B)    I and II only

C)    II and III only

D)    I, III and III

# 3.9 Solutions to practice problems on higher order polynomials

**1. (D)**

$x^3 + 2x^2 - 3x = x(x^2 + 2x - 3) = x(x+3)(x-1)$

Zeros are at x=0, x=-3 and x=1

**2. (D)**

$$5 \begin{array}{|rrrr} 1 & -5 & -1 & 5 \\ & 5 & 0 & -5 \\ \hline 1 & 0 & -1 & 0 \end{array}$$

The reduced polynomial is $x^2 - 1 = (x+1)(x-1)$

Zeros are at x=-1 and x=1.

**3. (A)**

by the remainder theorem, $p(-1) = 3$
$p(-1) = -1 + 1 + b + 2 = 3,\ b + 2 = 3,\ b = -1$

**4. (A)**

$$\begin{array}{r} x+2 \\ x^2 - x - 1\overline{)x^3 + x^2 - x + 2} \\ \underline{|x^3 - x^2 - x} \\ 2x^2 \qquad + 2 \\ \underline{|2x^2 - 2x - 2} \\ 2x + 4 \end{array}$$

**5 (B)**

$$-2 \begin{array}{|rrrr} 1 & 1 & -1 & 2 \\ & -2 & 2 & -2 \\ \hline 1 & -1 & 1 & 0 \end{array}$$

Use quadratic formula to solve the reduced

polynomial $x^2 - x + 1 = 0$.

$x = \dfrac{1 \pm \sqrt{1-4}}{2} = \dfrac{1 \pm 3i}{2}$

There is only one real zero to the polynomial.

**6. (B)**

Do synthetic division using 2 as a root  Make sure
to use zero placeholders for the $x^3$ and $x$ terms.

$$2 \begin{array}{|rrrrr} 1 & 0 & 5 & 0 & -36 \\ & 2 & 4 & 18 & 36 \\ \hline 1 & 2 & 9 & 18 & 0 \end{array}$$

Further reduce the polynomial using -2 as a root by
doing another synthetic division.

$$-2 \begin{array}{|rrrr} 1 & 2 & 9 & 18 \\ & -2 & 0 & -18 \\ \hline 1 & 0 & 9 & 0 \end{array}$$

You are left with $x^2 + 9$ which gives $\pm 3i$ as the
remaining two roots.

**7. (A)**

If $2x - 1$ is a factor then 1/2 is a zero and

$p\left(\dfrac{1}{2}\right) = 8\left(\dfrac{1}{2}\right)^5 - b\left(\dfrac{1}{2}\right)^2 + 6\left(\dfrac{1}{2}\right) - 10 = 0$

$\dfrac{1}{4} - \dfrac{b}{4} + 3 - 10 = 0,\ -\dfrac{b}{4} - \dfrac{-27}{4} = 0,\ b = -27$

**8. (D)**

$$\begin{array}{r} 3x^2 - 5x + 5 \\ x^2 + 2x + 1\overline{)3x^4 + x^3 - 2x^2 + x + 8} \\ \underline{|3x^4 + 6x^3 + 3x^2} \\ -5x^3 - 5x^2 + x + 8 \\ \underline{|-5x^3 - 10x^2 - 5x} \\ 5x^2 + 6x + 8 \\ \underline{|5x^2 + 10x + 5} \\ -4x + 3 \end{array}$$

**9. (C)**

$x^8 - 3x^5 + 6x^3 - 8 - (-3x^8 - 2x^7 + 3x^3) =$
$x^8 + 3x^8 + 2x^7 - 3x^5 + 6x^3 - 3x^3 - 8 =$
$4x^8 + 2x^7 - 3x^5 + 3x^3 - 8$

**10. (D)**

A ratio of polynomials is undefined where a vertical
asymptote (or hole) exists.  A vertical asymptote
exists when the denominator is zero.

$$\dfrac{1 + p^2}{x^2 - 2px + 1 + p^2} = \dfrac{1 + p^2}{(x-p)^2 + 1}$$

But the denominator can never be zero because it
is the sum of a square and positive 1.

**11. (A)**

A tangent at x=1 means that the factor x-1 is raised
to an even power.  The degree must be even and
the leading coefficient must be negative because
the graph starts and ends negative.

**12. (D)**

$\dfrac{2x^2 + 2x}{x^3 - x} = \dfrac{2x(x+1)}{x(x+1)(x-1)}$

Holes at x=0 and x=-1, VA at x=1 and HA at y=0.
2+1+1=4

**13. (C)**

The graph must have a horizontal asymptote at
y=3/2 because the degrees are the same.  That
eliminates A and B.  There must be two vertical
asymptotes are at x=0 and x=-2 .  That eliminates D
which has only one vertical asymptote at x=-2.

**14. (C)**

I is false.  The y-value can never be zero because
when y is zero x is undefined.

II is true.  The graph has a horizontal asymptote at
y=0 and a vertical asymptote at x=0.

III is true.  The x-value cannot be zero because the
graph is not defined at x=0

## 3.10  Absolute value

Absolute value problems can be tricky, especially inequalities.  But there are techniques that will help you solve them easily.  First, we begin with a definition of absolute value:

$$\text{When } x \geq 0, \ |x| = x. \quad \text{When } x < 0, \ |x| = -x.$$

Note that the absolute value of a number is always positive.  If x is positive in the first place, leave the sign alone.  If x is negative, change the sign to positive.

Absolute value has a physical meaning as well as a mathematical one.  The absolute value of the difference of two numbers is the distance between them.  For example $|5--3|$ is the distance between 5 and -3, which is 8.  We could also find this distance using $|-3-5|$, which is also 8.  It does not matter which endpoint we use as the starting number, as long as we remember to subtract.

In general, the expression $|x-c|$ can be used to represent the distance between $x$ and $c$.

### Absolute value equalities always produce two points

The simplest absolute value problems to solve are equalities, where the absolute value of some expression is set equal to a non-negative constant.  (If the constant is negative, there are no solutions.)  The figure below illustrates how two equations are created from the absolute value and where the solutions fall on a number line.

When the absolute value of an expression (represented by the happy face above) is set equal to a non-negative constant, the expression is either equal to the constant or equal to the negative of the constant.  Note that the solution is always two points.

Suppose we wanted to know the points on a number line that are five units away from -3.  To solve this we would set up the equation $|x--3| = 5$, in words this would be asking what values of x are exactly five units away from -3.  The happy face in this example is the expression x--3 which simplifies to x+3.  To solve this absolute value equality we set up two equations, x+3=5 or x+3=-5.  Solving these gives the solutions x=2 or x=-8.  In other words the values of 2 and -8 are exactly five units away from 3.

### Absolute value less than (or less than or equal to) inequalities always produce barbells

Absolute values can also appear in inequalities where the absolute value of some expression is set to be less than (or less than or equal to) a non-negative constant.  (If the constant is negative there are no solutions.)  The figure below shows how a compound inequality is created to find the solutions to the absolute value inequality.

When the absolute value of an expression (represented by the happy face above) is less than a constant, the expression is placed into the middle of a compound inequality.  Note that the solution is always a closed interval. If the inequality is strictly less than, the endpoints are open. If the inequality is less than or equal to, the endpoints are closed (filled).

$$|\text{☺}| < c$$

$$-c < \text{☺} < c$$

Suppose we wanted to manufacture a ball bearing, which is a steel sphere, and the ball bearing had to have a radius of 5 cm. If the radius of the ball bearing was beyond 0.1 cm, then the ball bearing would have to be discarded and a new one manufactured. To find the acceptable sizes of the ball bearing we could write the inequality $|x-5| \le 0.1$. That would be solved by creating the compound inequality $-0.1 \le x-5 \le 0.1$. Adding 5 to each part of the inequality gives us $4.9 \le x \le 5.1$. In other words the radius of the ball bearing must be at least 4.9 cm but not more than 5.1 cm in order to satisfy the manufacturer's specification.

**Absolute value greater than (or greater than or equal to) inequalities always produce two intervals**

Absolute values can also appear in inequalities where the absolute value of some expression is set to be greater than (or greater than or equal to) a non-negative constant. (If the constant is negative then the solution is the set of all real numbers.) The figure below shows how two inequalities are created to find the solutions to the absolute value inequality.

$$|\text{☺}| > c$$

$$\text{☺} < -c \quad \text{or} \quad \text{☺} > c$$

When the absolute value of an expression (represented by the happy face above) is greater than a constant, two inequalities must be created. Note that the solution is always two intervals. If the inequality is strictly greater than, the endpoints are open. If the inequality is greater than or equal to, the endpoints are closed (filled).

Suppose that the point -2 on the number line represents the location of a toxic waste dump. In order to be safe, people need to live at least 20 units away from the dump. What locations on the number line are safe? To find the solution we start with the inequality $|x--2| \ge 20,$ which simplifies to $|x+2| \ge 20$. This inequality is split into two inequalities: $x+2 \le -20$ or $x+2 \ge 20$. Solving each of these inequalities gives us the intervals $x \le -22$ or $x \ge 18$. It is safe to live west of -22 or east of 18 because each of these points is twenty miles away from -2.

**Graphs of absolute value equality and inequalities**

The graph of an absolute value equality will always have a V shape. The graph can be translated (location change), or it can be reflected across the x-axis to give it an inverted V shape, etc. The various ways to move and flip graphs are covered in unit 3.14. The graphs of the parent equation, $y = |x|$, and its inequalities look like those below (solution regions for the inequalities are shaded):

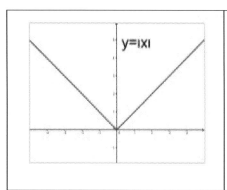

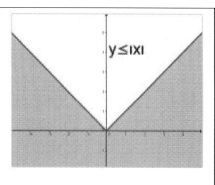

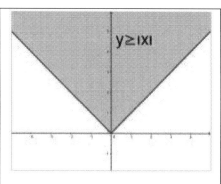

|  **Calculator Tip:** | Suppose you have an absolute value equality or inequality to solve. For this example we will used $\|x-1\|$ for the absolute value expression and 2 for the constant. |
|---|---|
| | Enter the absolute value expression into the first line of the *Y=* equation editor. The absolute value function can be found at *math-num-abs*. Then enter 2 into the second line of the Y= equation editor. The equations are shown in the first screen shot on the left. |
| | If you want a graph that matches the one on the right below, press the *window* key to adjust the window to the settings shown below. |
| | Next press *graph*. You should have a graph that matches the one below. If you want to solve $\|x-1\|=2$ then find the intersections of the two graphs. You can do this by pressing the *trace* button and moving the cursor to an intersection. The coordinates will be displayed at the bottom of the screen. Or you can use *2nd-calc-intersect* and follow the dialog to find each intersection. If you want to solve $\|x-1\|<2$ the solution is the interval of the x-axis that lies in-between the intersections. If you want to solve $\|x-1\|>2$ the solutions are the intervals of the x-axis that lie on either side of the intersections. |

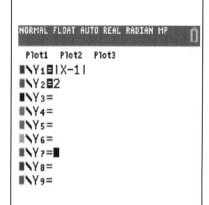

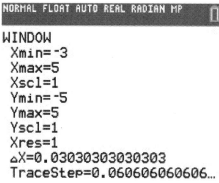

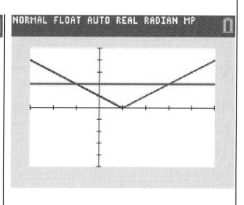

106

## 3.10 Practice problems on absolute value
### Solve these problems by hand first and then verify on the calculator

1. The solutions to the equation $5|x-2|=20$ are:

A)    x=-2 and x=2

B)    x=-2 and x=6

C)    x=-4 and x=2

D)    x=-4 and x=4

2. The solution to the inequality $2|x+5|<8$ is:

A)    $-9<x<-1$

B)    $-9<x<1$

C)    $-1<x<9$

D)    $1<x<9$

3. The solution to the inequality $5|x-3|-5\leq0$ is:

A)    $-4\leq x\leq-2$

B)    $-4\leq x\leq2$

C)    $-2\leq x\leq4$

D)    $2\leq x\leq4$

4. The solution to the inequality $3|x+8|\geq6$ is:

A)    $-10\geq x \ or \ x\geq-6$

B)    $-10\geq x \ or \ x\geq6$

C)    $-6\geq x \ or \ x\geq10$

D)    $6\geq x \ or \ x\geq10$

5. The solution to the inequality $|2x-5|\geq9$ is:

A)    $-7\geq x \ or \ x\geq-2$

B)    $-7\geq x \ or \ x\geq2$

C)    $-2\geq x \ or \ x\geq7$

D)    $-2\geq x \ or \ x\geq-7$

6. The solution to the inequality $5|3x|>-15$ is:

A)    $-1\geq x \ or \ x\geq1$

B)    $1\geq x \ or \ x\geq-1$

C)    All real values of $x$

D)    No real solution

7. The solution to the inequality $|2x|<-2$ is:

A)    $-2<x<1$

B)    $-1<x<1$

C)    All real values of $x$

D)    No real solution

8. In order to be admitted to a ride in an amusement park, children must be older than three and younger than seven. Which of the inequalities below represents the admission requirement?

I.    $3<x<7$

II.    $|x-3|<7$

III.    $|x-5|<2$

A)    I only

B)    II only

C)    I and II only

D)    I and III only

9. A certain automobile part must be 2 inches thick, with a tolerance of one-tenth of one inch. Which of the inequalities below represents acceptable thicknesses?

A)    $|x|\leq0.1$

B)    $|x|\leq2$

C)    $|x-2|\leq0.1$

D)    $|x-0.1|\leq2$

10. Suppose the safe level of lead in water is 15 parts per billion (ppb), but the equipment used to measure lead is only accurate to within 3 ppb. Which inequality below best represents the range of readings on the measurement equipment that could be considered acceptable?

A) $x \leq 18$

B) $12 \leq x$

C) $12 \leq x \leq 18$

D) $x \leq 15$

11. To minimize electrical resistance, the cable connecting electrical generators to homes must be no greater than 100 feet long. If a home is located at coordinate -30 on a number line, which of the inequalities below could be solved to determine the coordinates where must the generator be located?

A) $|x - 30| \leq 100$

B) $|x + 30| \leq 100$

C) $|x - 100| \leq 30$

D) $|x + 100| \leq 30$

12. Radio station WMATH broadcasts important math facts and its broadcast signal can travel up to 150 km from the tower. If the broadcast tower is located at coordinate 5 on a number line, what are the furthest coordinates you could travel and still listen to important math facts?

A) $-155 \leq x \leq 145$

B) $-155 \leq x \leq 155$

C) $-155 \leq x \leq 145$

D) $-145 \leq x \leq 155$

13. Due to the risk of explosion, Town regulations require that underground propane tanks be at least 30 units away from the nearest structure. If a tank is buried at coordinate 10 on a number line, at what coordinates could the closest structures exist?

A) $x \leq -20$ or $x \geq 40$

B) $x \leq -40$ or $x \geq 20$

C) $x \geq -20$ or $x \leq 40$

D) $x \geq -40$ or $x \leq 20$

14. The shaded region of which of the graphs below could illustrate the solution to the inequality $|x + 2| \geq 3$ ?

A)

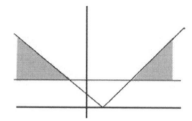

B)

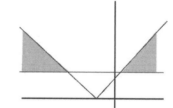

C)

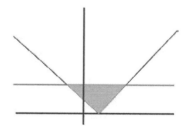

D)

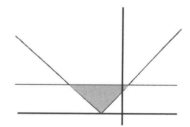

# 3.10 Solutions to practice problems on absolute value

**1. (B)**

Isolate the absolute value:

$$|x-2| = \frac{20}{5} = 4$$

First equation: $x-2 = -4, \quad x = -2$

Second equation: $x-2 = 4, \quad x = 6$

**2. (A)**

Isolate the absolute value: $|x+5| < \frac{8}{2} = 4$

$-4 < x+5 < 4$

$-9 < x < -1$

**3. (D)**

Isolate the absolute value:

$5|x-3| \leq 5, \quad |x-3| \leq 1$

$-1 \leq x-3 \leq 1$

$2 \leq x \leq 4$

**4. (A)**

Isolate the absolute value:

$3|x+8| \geq 6, \quad |x+8| \geq 2$

First inequality: $-2 \geq x+8, \quad -10 \geq x$

Second inequality: $x+8 \geq 2, \quad x \geq -6$

**5. (C)**

First inequality:

$-9 \geq 2x-5, \quad -4 \geq 2x, \quad -2 \geq x$

Second inequality: $2x-5 \geq 9, \quad 2x \geq 14, \quad x \geq 7$

**6. (C)**

Isolate the absolute value: $5|3x| > -15, \quad |3x| > -3$

This inequality is true for all real values of x. The absolute value of any quantity is always non-negative.

**7. (D)**

This inequality is never true for any real value of x. The absolute value of any quantity is always non-negative.

**8. (D)**

I. obviously is correct.

II is incorrect:

$$|x-3| < 7$$

$$-7 < x-3 < 7, \quad -4 < x < 10$$

III is correct

$$|x-5| < 2$$

$$-2 < x-5 < 2, \quad 3 < x < 7$$

**9. (C)**

$|x-2| \leq 0.1$

$-0.1 \leq x-2 \leq 0.1$

$1.9 \leq x \leq 2.1$

**10. (A)**

If you chose (B) or (C) you got immersed in the math but lost track of the context. There is no reason to think that a measurement of less than 12 is unacceptable, in fact it is excellent.

**11. (B)**

$|x+30| \leq 100, \quad -100 \leq x+30 \leq 100, \quad -130 \leq x \leq 70$

**12. (D)**

$|x-5| \leq 150, \quad -150 \leq x-5 \leq 150, \quad -145 \leq x \leq 155$

**13. (A)**

$|x-10| \geq 30$

First inequality: $x-10 \geq 30, x \geq 40$

Second inequality: $x-10 \leq -30, x \leq -20$

**14. (B)**

The bottom two graphs are illustrating a less than inequality (x values are constrained to be between a lower bound and an upper bound, or "bar bells"). So the these graphs are wrong.

The upper two graphs illustrate a greater than inequality because there are two open intervals for the x-values. When you solve the inequality you get

$|x+2| \geq 3, x+2 \geq 3$ or $x+2 \leq -3$

$x \geq 1$ or $x \leq -5$

The end points of 1 and -5 match graph B

## 3.11   Exponents and radicals

Previous units contain examples of a variable raised to a power, such as $x^3$. In words we would say "x to the third power." In this example the **base** is the variable x and the **power** is 3. This unit covers how to perform operations on variables raised to powers and how to perform operations on radicals.

### Laws of exponents

Laws governing the operations on exponents are as follows:

Multiplication (same base)

$$x^a \cdot x^b = x^{a+b}$$

Division (same base)

$$\frac{x^a}{x^b} = x^{a-b}, \; x \neq 0$$

Exponentiation (non-zero exponent )

$$\left(x^a\right)^b = x^{ab}$$

Exponentiation (exponent is zero)

$$x^0 = 1, \; x \neq 0$$

Negative exponents

$$x^{-a} = \frac{1}{x^a}, \; x \neq 0 \quad \text{and} \quad \frac{1}{x^{-a}} = x^a$$

Laws of exponents are often used to simplify expressions, such as

$$x^{a+2} \cdot x^{-2} = x^a$$

$$\frac{x^5}{x^{-3}} = x^5 \cdot x^3 = x^8$$

### Equations involving exponents

Sometimes you will see equations involving exponents. The technique to use here is to convert both sides of the equation to the same base. Once the bases are the same, you can equate the exponents. For example:

$4^x = 128$          original equation

$\left(2^2\right)^x = 2^7$          convert both sides to use base 2

$2^{2x} = 2^7$          simplify the left-hand side using a law of exponents

$2x = 7, \; x = 3.5$          equate exponents; solve for x.

### Important facts about the square root

Please remember that the square root symbol $\sqrt{\phantom{x}}$ means the positive square root. There is an invisible + sign in front of the radical. Although it is invisible, it is very important. For example, $\sqrt{9}$ is positive 3, not negative 3. In words, this would be "the positive square root of nine is positive three, not negative three."

When we mean to indicate the negative square root, we write $-\sqrt{9} = -3$. In words, this would be "the negative square root of nine is negative three." When we mean to indicate the positive **and** negative square roots, we write $\pm\sqrt{9} = \pm 3$. In words, this would be "the positive and negative square roots of nine are positive and negative three."

Positive and negative square roots are used mostly for solving equations, such as

$$x^2 = 64$$
$$x = \pm\sqrt{64} = \pm 8$$

In words, this would be "the solutions to the equation $x^2 = 64$ are $x = 8$ and $x = -8$". Remember that the $\pm$ symbol means positive AND negative. So the symbol $\pm\sqrt{\phantom{x}}$ means the positive and negative square root, while the symbol $\pm 8$ means positive 8 AND negative 8.

Check these:

$$\sqrt{25} = 5 \text{ only}, \quad \text{and} \quad -\sqrt{25} = -5 \text{ only}$$
$$\pm\sqrt{25} = 5 \text{ and -5 (you could also write } \pm 5)$$

Remember:

$\pm$ means positive AND negative

$\sqrt{\phantom{x}}$ means positive square root

## The relationship between exponents and radicals

When using square roots, written as $\sqrt{x}$, sometimes students lose sight of the fact that there is an invisible 2 that is part of the square root radical. In fact the square root could be written as $\sqrt[2]{x}$. For the sake of convenience we omit the number 2 from the radical, but that little 2 is incredibly important because

$$\sqrt{x} = \sqrt[2]{x} = x^{\frac{1}{2}} \text{ and in general } \sqrt[n]{x} = x^{\frac{1}{n}}.$$

Once you understand this relationship between radicals and exponents you can apply the laws of operations to either exponents or radicals, because they are the same thing.

## Operations on exponents and radicals

| Operation | Exponent Version | Radical Version |
|---|---|---|
| Multiplication (different bases, same power) | $(xy)^a = x^a \cdot y^a$ | $\sqrt[n]{xy} = \sqrt[n]{x} \cdot \sqrt[n]{y}$ |
| Division (different bases, same power) | $\left(\dfrac{x}{y}\right)^a = \dfrac{x^a}{y^a}$ | $\sqrt[n]{\dfrac{x}{y}} = \dfrac{\sqrt[n]{x}}{\sqrt[n]{y}}$ |
| Exponentiation (non-zero exponents) | $\left(x^{\frac{1}{a}}\right)^b = x^{\frac{b}{a}} = \left(x^b\right)^{\frac{1}{a}}$ | $\left(\sqrt[a]{x}\right)^b = x^{\frac{b}{a}} = \sqrt[a]{x^b}$ |

Operations on radicals are typically used to simplify a radical, such as

$$\sqrt{50} = \sqrt{50 \cdot 2} = \sqrt{25} \cdot \sqrt{2} = 5\sqrt{2}$$
$$\sqrt[3]{192} = \sqrt[3]{64 \cdot 3} = \sqrt[3]{64} \cdot \sqrt[3]{3} = 4\sqrt[3]{3}$$

$$\sqrt{\frac{18}{64}} = \frac{\sqrt{18}}{\sqrt{64}} = \frac{\sqrt{9 \cdot 2}}{8} = \frac{3\sqrt{2}}{8}$$

but they also can be used to deal with tricky powers and roots such as

$$\sqrt[7]{x^3} = \left(x^3\right)^{\frac{1}{7}} = x^{\frac{3}{7}} \quad \text{and} \quad \left(\sqrt[7]{x}\right)^3 = \left(x^{\frac{1}{7}}\right)^3 = x^{\frac{3}{7}}.$$

|  **Calculator Tip:** | Dealing with exponents and radicals is easy to do on the calculator. |
|---|---|
| | For exponents, make use of the caret key ^. To raise 2 to the eighth power, press 2-^-8 and then press *enter*. You will see the result shown on the left below. |
| | For radicals, use fractions as exponents. To find the 5$^{\text{th}}$ root of 7776, simply enter *7776- ^- (- 1- ÷- 5- )* into your calculator and then press *enter*. Your display should look like the one shown on the right below. |
| | Note that the dashes in the calculator instructions above are used to separate keystrokes, they are not negatives to be entered into the calculator. |

| NORMAL FLOAT AUTO REAL RADIAN MP | NORMAL FLOAT AUTO REAL RADIAN MP |
|---|---|
| $2^8$ | $7776^{(1/5)}$ |
| 256 | 6 |

## Radicals in the denominator

An expression is not considered to be simplified if there are radicals in the denominator. Clearing a square root out of the denominator is easy, just multiply top and bottom by the square root, as in

$$\frac{\sqrt{5}}{2\sqrt{3}} = \left(\frac{\sqrt{5}}{2\sqrt{3}}\right)\left(\frac{\sqrt{3}}{\sqrt{3}}\right) = \frac{\sqrt{15}}{2 \cdot 3} = \frac{\sqrt{15}}{6}$$

To clear a more complicated radial, multiply top and bottom by the radical raised to the power that will clear the denominator, as in:

$$\frac{5}{2\sqrt[5]{3}} = \left(\frac{5}{2\sqrt[5]{3}}\right)\left(\frac{\left(\sqrt[5]{3}\right)^4}{\left(\sqrt[5]{3}\right)^4}\right) = \frac{5\left(\sqrt[5]{3}\right)^4}{2\left(\sqrt[5]{3}\right)^5} = \frac{5\left(\sqrt[5]{3}\right)^4}{2 \cdot 3} = \frac{5\left(\sqrt[5]{3}\right)^4}{6}$$

Another example is where the denominator contains a square root that is being added or subtracted. In that case we use the **conjugate** to clear the square root. For example

$$\frac{6}{2-\sqrt{5}} = \left(\frac{6}{2-\sqrt{5}}\right)\left(\frac{2+\sqrt{5}}{2+\sqrt{5}}\right) = \frac{12+6\sqrt{5}}{4-2\sqrt{5}+2\sqrt{5}-5} = \frac{12+6\sqrt{5}}{-1} = -12-6\sqrt{5}$$

We multiply the top and bottom by the conjugate of the denominator. The conjugate of $a+b\sqrt{x}$ is $a-b\sqrt{x}$. When the denominator is FOILed out, the square root disappears.

# 3.11 Practice problems on exponents and radicals
## Solve these problems by hand first and then verify on the calculator

1. $\sqrt{49}$ is equivalent to:

A)   7 only

B)   -7 only

C)   -7 or 7

D)   -7 and 7

2. $\sqrt[3]{-27}$ is equivalent to:

A)   3 only

B)   -3 only

C)   -3 or 3

D)   -3 and 3

3. Which of the following is the solution to the equation $x^2 - 5 = 20$?

A)   5 only

B)   -5 only

C)   -5 and 5

D)   $\pm\sqrt{15}$

4. $\sqrt{72}$ is equivalent to:

   I.   $6\sqrt{2}$

   II.  $3\sqrt{8}$

   III. $2\sqrt{18}$

A)   I only

B)   II only

C)   I and III only

D)   I, II and III

5. $\sqrt[3]{-384}$ is equivalent to:

A)   $8\sqrt{6}$

B)   $-8\sqrt{6}$

C)   $4\sqrt[3]{6}$

D)   $-4\sqrt[3]{6}$

6. $16^{\frac{2}{3}}$ is not equivalent to:

A)   $\sqrt[3]{16^2}$

B)   $\left(\sqrt{16}\right)^3$

C)   $\sqrt[3]{4^4}$

D)   $2^{\frac{8}{3}}$

7. The solution to the equation
   $1 - \sqrt{x} = \dfrac{-7}{2}$ is:

A)   $x = 1.5$

B)   $x = 2$

C)   $x = 4$

D)   $x = 20.25$

8. 497 is ten less than three times the square of a number. The value of that number is:

   I.   $-13$

   II.  13

   III. 12.74

A)   I only

B)   II only

C)   III only

D)   I and II only

9. If $\sqrt[4]{x} + \sqrt[3]{-125} = \sqrt{81}$ then $x$ is equal to:

A)   16

B)   196

C)   256

D)   32,416

10. The expression $\left(3 + \sqrt{x}\right)^2$ is equal to:

A)   $9 + x$

B)   $9 + 3\sqrt{x} + x^2$

C)   $9 + 6\sqrt{x} + x$

D)   $9 + 6x + x^2$

113

11. The quantity $\dfrac{\sqrt{15}}{\sqrt{20}}$ simplifies to:

A) $\quad \dfrac{\sqrt{3}}{4}$

B) $\quad \dfrac{\sqrt{3}}{2}$

C) $\quad \sqrt{3}$

D) $\quad 2\sqrt{3}$

12. The expression $\dfrac{\sqrt{x}+\sqrt{x}}{\sqrt{2x}}$ simplifies to:

A) $\quad 1$

B) $\quad \sqrt{2}$

C) $\quad 2$

D) $\quad \dfrac{\sqrt{2}}{2}$

13. If $x^2 = -(x-10)(x+10)$ then the value of $x$ could be:

A) $\quad 2\sqrt{5}$

B) $\quad 5\sqrt{2}$

C) $\quad 5$

D) $\quad 10$

14. The expression $x^3 \cdot x^{\frac{a}{3}}$ simplifies to

(A) $\quad x^3$

(B) $\quad x^a$

(C) $\quad x^{\frac{1+a}{3}}$

(D) $\quad x^{\frac{9+a}{3}}$

15. The expression $\dfrac{x^{a+2}}{x^{a+3}}$ simplifies to

A) $\quad x^{2a+5}$

B) $\quad \dfrac{1}{x}$

C) $\quad x$

D) $\quad x^{a^2+5a+6}$

16. The expression $\sqrt{3^{30}x^4}$ simplifies to:

A) $\quad (3x)^{34}$

B) $\quad (3x)^{17}$

C) $\quad 3^{15}x^2$

D) $\quad 3^{60}x^8$

17. The expression $\sqrt[3]{x^3 y^{10}}$ simplifies to:

A) $\quad x^9 y^{30}$

B) $\quad xy\sqrt[3]{y}$

C) $\quad xy^2\sqrt[3]{y}$

D) $\quad xy^3\sqrt[3]{y}$

18. Simplify $\dfrac{x^2 y}{z} \div \dfrac{x}{zy}$

A) $\quad xy^2$

B) $\quad x^2 y^2$

C) $\quad x^3 y^2$

D) $\quad \dfrac{x^3}{z^2}$

19. Simplify $\dfrac{\sqrt[3]{x^{15}}\, y^{-2}}{x^{-3} y^3}$

A) $\quad x^{48} y^{-5}$

B) $\quad x^{4.5} y$

C) $\quad x^5 y^5$

D) $\quad \dfrac{x^8}{y^5}$

114

20. Solve $\sqrt{x+a} = \sqrt[3]{125}$ for $x$:

A) $\qquad 5-a$

B) $\qquad 5+a$

C) $\qquad 25-a$

D) $\qquad 25+a$

21. If $x^{-1} = \dfrac{\sqrt{2}}{2}$, then $x^2$ must be:

A) $\qquad \dfrac{1}{4}$

B) $\qquad \dfrac{1}{2}$

C) $\qquad 2$

D) $\qquad 4$

22. Which of the equations below is <u>not</u> equivalent to the other three equations?

A) $\qquad 128 = 4^x$

B) $\qquad 2^x = 32$

C) $\qquad 2x = 7$

D) $\qquad 2^7 = 4^x$

23.. Solve $9^{x+1} = \sqrt{3^{x+2}}$ for $x$:

A) $\qquad x = -\dfrac{2}{3}$

B) $\qquad x = 0$

C) $\qquad x = \dfrac{2}{3}$

D) $\qquad x = 1$

24. Solve $81^x = \sqrt[3]{27^2}$ for $x$:

A) $\qquad x = \dfrac{1}{2}$

B) $\qquad x = \dfrac{3}{4}$

C) $\qquad x = \dfrac{4}{3}$

D) $\qquad x = 2$

25. The fully simplified form of the expression $\sqrt{\dfrac{5}{12}}$ is:

A) $\qquad \dfrac{5}{12}$

B) $\qquad \dfrac{\sqrt{5}}{\sqrt{12}}$

C) $\qquad \dfrac{5}{2\sqrt{3}}$

D) $\qquad \dfrac{\sqrt{15}}{6}$

26. The fully simplified form of the expression $\dfrac{1+\sqrt{3}}{1-\sqrt{3}}$ is:

A) $\qquad 0$

B) $\qquad 2$

C) $\qquad -2-\sqrt{3}$

D) $\qquad 2+\sqrt{3}$

27. <u>You may use a calculator</u>: The fully simplified form of the expression $\dfrac{6\sqrt{2}}{\sqrt[5]{486}}$ is:

A) $\qquad 2^{13/10}$

B) $\qquad 2^{17/10}$

C) $\qquad 2^{4/5}$

D) $\qquad 2^{-4/5}$

115

# 3.11 Solutions to practice problems on exponents and radicals

**1. (A)**

$\sqrt{49} = +7$ only

**2. (B)**

$\sqrt[3]{-27} = -3$ because $(-3)(-3)(-3) = -27$

**3. (C)**

$x^2 - 5 = 20$, $x^2 = 25$, $x = \pm5$

**4. (D)**

Start by dividing perfect squares into 72

$\sqrt{72} = \sqrt{36 \cdot 2} = \sqrt{36} \cdot \sqrt{2} = 6\sqrt{2}$

$\sqrt{72} = \sqrt{9 \cdot 8} = \sqrt{9} \cdot \sqrt{8} = 3\sqrt{8}$

$\sqrt{72} = \sqrt{4 \cdot 18} = \sqrt{4} \cdot \sqrt{18} = 2\sqrt{18}$

**5. (D)**

Start by dividing perfect cubes into 384

$\sqrt[3]{-384} = \sqrt[3]{-64 \cdot 6} = \sqrt[3]{-64} \cdot \sqrt[3]{6} = -4\sqrt[3]{6}$

**6. (B)**

$16^{\frac{2}{3}} = \sqrt[3]{16^2} = \sqrt[3]{\left(4^2\right)^2} = \sqrt[3]{\left(\left(2^2\right)^2\right)^2} = 2^{\frac{8}{3}}$

**7. (D)**

$1 - \sqrt{x} = \dfrac{-7}{2}$, $\sqrt{x} = \dfrac{9}{2}$, $x = \dfrac{81}{4} = 20.25$

**8. (D)**

$3x^2 - 10 = 497$, $3x^2 = 507$

$x^2 = 169$, $x = \pm13$

**9. (D)**

$\sqrt[4]{x} + \sqrt[3]{-125} = \sqrt{81}$, $\sqrt[4]{x} - 5 = 9$, $\sqrt[4]{x} = 14$, $x = 14^4$

**10. (C)**

$\left(3 + \sqrt{x}\right)^2 = \left(3 + \sqrt{x}\right)\left(3 + \sqrt{x}\right)$

$\qquad = 9 + 3\sqrt{x} + 3\sqrt{x} + x$

**11. (B)**

$\dfrac{\sqrt{15}}{\sqrt{20}} = \dfrac{\sqrt{15}}{2\sqrt{5}} = \left(\dfrac{1}{2}\right)\left(\sqrt{\dfrac{15}{5}}\right) = \dfrac{\sqrt{3}}{2}$

**12. (B)**

$\dfrac{\sqrt{x} + \sqrt{x}}{\sqrt{2x}} = \dfrac{2\sqrt{x}}{\left(\sqrt{2}\right)\left(\sqrt{x}\right)} = \dfrac{2}{\sqrt{2}} = \sqrt{2}$

**13. (B)**

$x^2 = -(x-10)(x+10) = -(x^2 - 100)$

$2x^2 = 100$, $x^2 = 50$, $x = \pm\sqrt{50} = \pm5\sqrt{2}$

**14. (D)**

$x^3 \cdot x^{\frac{a}{3}} = x^{3 + \frac{a}{3}} = x^{\frac{9}{3} + \frac{a}{3}} = x^{\frac{9+a}{3}}$

**15. (B)**

$\dfrac{x^{a+2}}{x^{a+3}} = x^{(a+2)-(a+3)} = x^{-1} = \dfrac{1}{x}$

**16. (C)**

$\sqrt{3^{30} x^4} = \left(3^{30}\right)^{\frac{1}{2}} \left(x^4\right)^{\frac{1}{2}} = 3^{15} x^2$

**17. (D)**

$\sqrt[3]{x^3 y^{10}} = \sqrt[3]{x^3 y^9}\sqrt[3]{y} = xy^3\sqrt[3]{y}$

**18. (A)**

$\dfrac{x^2 y}{z} \div \dfrac{x}{zy} = \left(\dfrac{x^2 y}{z}\right)\left(\dfrac{zy}{x}\right) = xy^2$

**19. (D)**

$\dfrac{\sqrt[3]{x^{15}} y^{-2}}{x^{-3} y^3} = \dfrac{x^5 y^{-2}}{x^{-3} y^3} = x^{(5--3)} y^{(-2-3)} = x^8 y^{-5} = \dfrac{x^8}{y^5}$

**20. (C)**

$\sqrt{x+a} = \sqrt[3]{125}$, $\sqrt{x+a} = 5$, $x + a = 25$, $x = 25 - a$

**21. (C)**

$x^2 = \left(\dfrac{1}{x^{-1}}\right)^2 = \left(\dfrac{2}{\sqrt{2}}\right)^2 = \dfrac{4}{2} = 2$

**22. (B)**

$128 = 4^x$, $2^7 = \left(2^2\right)^x$, $2^7 = 2^{2x}$, $7 = 2x$, $3.5 = x$

**23. (A)**

$9^{x+1} = \sqrt{3^{x+2}}$, $\left(3^2\right)^{x+1} = \left(3^{x+2}\right)^{\frac{1}{2}}$,

$2(x+1) = \dfrac{1}{2}(x+2)$, $\dfrac{3x}{2} = -1$, $x = \dfrac{-2}{3}$

**24. (A)**

$81^x = \sqrt[3]{27^2}$, $\left(3^4\right)^x = \left(\left(3^3\right)^2\right)^{\frac{1}{3}}$, $3^{4x} = 3^2$, $x = 0.5$

**25. (D)**

$\sqrt{\dfrac{5}{12}} = \dfrac{\sqrt{5}}{\sqrt{12}} = \dfrac{\sqrt{5}}{2\sqrt{3}} = \left(\dfrac{\sqrt{5}}{2\sqrt{3}}\right)\left(\dfrac{\sqrt{3}}{\sqrt{3}}\right) = \dfrac{\sqrt{15}}{6}$

**26. (C)**

$\dfrac{1+\sqrt{3}}{1-\sqrt{3}} = \left(\dfrac{1+\sqrt{3}}{1-\sqrt{3}}\right)\left(\dfrac{1+\sqrt{3}}{1+\sqrt{3}}\right) = \dfrac{1+2\sqrt{3}+3}{1-3} = \dfrac{4+2\sqrt{3}}{-2} = -2 - \sqrt{3}$

**27. (A)**

$\dfrac{6\sqrt{2}}{\sqrt[5]{486}} = \dfrac{6\sqrt{2}}{\sqrt[5]{243}\sqrt[5]{2}} = \dfrac{2\sqrt{2}}{\sqrt[5]{2}} = \dfrac{2^{3/2}}{2^{1/5}} = 2^{13/10}$

## 3.12   Exponential growth and decay

Exponential growth and decay occur in nature. For example, populations might grow exponentially, or radioactive material might decay exponentially. In the world of finance, the value of an investment can grow exponentially and the value of an asset, like a house or a car, could decrease exponentially. It is important for you to understand exponential growth and decay models, and to be able to distinguish them from linear models.

### Exponential models

The equation

$$y = ab^x$$

describes the exponential model, where $a$ is usually referred to as the **starting amount** and $b$ is referred to as the **base**. The variable $x$ usually represents time. When time is zero (the starting time), $y = ab^0 = a(1) = a$ (the starting amount). Exponential growth occurs when $b > 1$ and exponential decay occurs when $0 < b < 1$. The graphs of exponential growth and decay are show below.

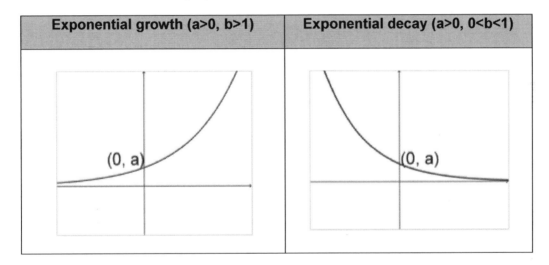

| Exponential growth (a>0, b>1) | Exponential decay (a>0, 0<b<1) |

### Determining the base ($b$) and the power ($x$)

It is fairly easy to determine the base, keeping in mind that $0 < b < 1$ produces decay and $b > 1$ produces growth. SAT® problems may use the idea of a rate. For example an investment grows at a rate of 5%, or population of an endangered species is decreasing at a rate of 3%. To find the proper base, just use the formulas:

For growth: $b = 1 + r$     For decay: $b = 1 - r$

For the base in the investment example we would use $b = 1 + .05 = 1.05$. Notice that the base is larger than 1. For the base in the endangered species example we would use $b = 1 - r = 1 - .03 = 0.97$. Notice that the base is smaller than 1.

<u>Power and base must agree</u>

Finding the power is simple if the units of time in the growth or decay rate and the units of time in the power already agree. In the investment example, let's say that the investment grows at a rate of 5% per month and that we want to know what the investment would be worth 20 months after an initial investment of $500. We would use the formula $500(1.05)^{20}$ to find the value of the investment after 20 months. In the endangered species example, suppose that the animal population decreases at 3% per year and that we want to know how many animals will remain 10 years from now if there are 5,000 animals today. We would use the formula $5000(.97)^{10}$ to find the animal population in 10 years.

But what if the units of time do not agree? Then you should adjust the power so that its units of time match the units of time in the base. Suppose the investment grows at a rate of 5% per month and we want to know what the investment would be worth 20 years after an initial investment of $500. In that case we would use the formula $100(1.05)^{(20)(12)}$. Note that the time units of the power (240 months) match the time units of the base (5% per month). Suppose the endangered species population decreases at 3% per year and we want to know how many animals will be remaining after 30 months if there are 5,000 animals today. In that case we would use the formula $5000(0.97)^{\frac{30}{12}}$. Note that the time units of the power (30/12 years) match the time units of the base (3% per year).

**Exponential versus linear models**
Suppose you buy two cars, each costs $15,000 and after four years of ownership they are both worth $6,144. The values of the cars for each year of ownership are shown in the table below. Which car decreased in value exponentially and which are decreased in value linearly?

| Years of ownership | Car A | Car B |
|---|---|---|
| 0 | 15,000 | 15,000 |
| 1 | 12,000 | 12,786 |
| 2 | 9,600 | 10,572 |
| 3 | 7,680 | 8,358 |
| 4 | 6,144 | 6,144 |

The way to distinguish between exponential versus linear decay is to look at how the values are changing. Notice that for Car A the annual values are decreasing every year by the <u>same rate</u>: 12000/150000 is 80%, 9600/12000 is also 80%, 7680/9600 is also 80%, etc. For Car B notice that the annual values are decreasing by the <u>same amount</u> every year: 12786-15000 is -2214, 10572-12786 is also -2214, 8358-10572 is also -2214, etc. This enables us to conclude that Car A is decreasing exponentially whereas Car B is decreasing linearly.

The distinction between exponential decay and linear decay is very important. Suppose you wanted to know what these cars would be worth in 6 years? Although they are worth the same in the fourth year that does not mean they will continue to be worth the same. The exponential decay in Car A can be modeled by $15000(1-0.2)^x$ because we know the starting value was 15,000 and the rate of decay is 20% per year. The linear decay in Car B can be modeled by $15000-2214x$ because the initial value (y-intercept) is 15,000 and the annual change in value (slope) is -2214 every year. If we plug 6 into each of these expressions we find that Car A will be worth $3,932 in six years, whereas Car B will be worth $1,716 in six years. The graph of these car values are shown below: In the longer run, Car A will hold its value far better than Car B.

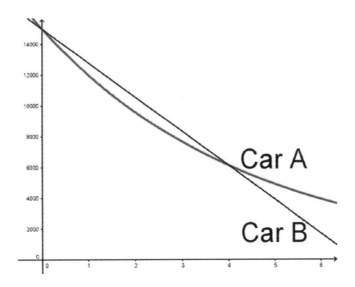

| | |
|---|---|
|  **Calculator Tip:** | An exponential growth or decay function can easily be entered into the graphing calculator.  But the only way to solve a certain type of exponential problem (without using logarithms) is to use the calculator.

Suppose you deposit $2 in a bank account that pays 3% interest every year.  How many years will it take for your money to double?  The equation to be solved is $4 = 2(1.03)^x$ and it can be solved easily with logarithms, which are not required knowledge for the SAT®.  You could try testing values of x on your calculator, but a more elegant way is to enter the equations as shown in left screen below.  Next adjust the window to match the settings shown below.  When you press the *graph* key your screen  should look like the one on the right below.  If you are working on a multiple choice problem you can toggle the cursor onto the intersection to get a solution that is close enough, but if you want an exact answer you can follow the *2nd-calc-intersect* dialog.  The solution is 23.5 years. |
| 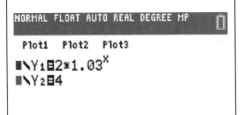 | 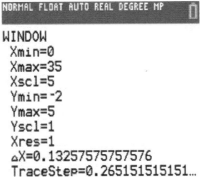 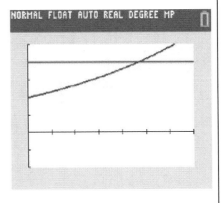 |

## 3.12 Practice problems on exponential growth and decay
## calculator is permitted

1. Suppose you deposit $500 in a bank account that pays 4% interest per year. What would your account balance be if you leave your money in the bank for 10 years?

A)    $.04(10)+500$

B)    $10(.04)(500)$

C)    $500(.04)^{10}$

D)    $500(1.04)^{10}$

2. Suppose a certain endangered species declines 20% every 10 years. If there are $x$ animals of that species alive today how many will be alive in 50 years?

A)    $50(.8)x$

B)    $x(.8)^{5}$

C)    $x(.2)^{5}$

D)    $x(.8)^{50}$

3. See the calculator tip: Suppose E. coli bacteria double in quantity every 30 minutes. If an animal is currently infected with 500 E. coli cells, how long will it take the number of cells to reach 128,000?

A)    2 hours

B)    3 hours

C)    4 hours

D)    5 hours

4. Suppose the half life of a radioactive isotope is 20 minutes, that is every 20 minutes the amount of isotope remaining is half the previous amount. If you have a sample of 50 grams, what will be the weight of the sample at the same time tomorrow?

A)    25

B)    $50^{\frac{1}{2}}$

C)    $50(.5)^{24}$

D)    $50(.5)^{3(24)}$

5. Alexandra is trying to choose a bank in which she will deposit $1,000 and leave it there for 5 years. If Bank A pays 3% interest and Bank B pays 4% interest, at the end of 5 years how much more money will she have at Bank B than Bank A?

A)    $10.00

B)    $57.37

C)    $91.14

D)    $186.35

---

**Questions 6-7 refer to the following information.**

The data below describe the size of a sink hole (a mysterious hole that forms in the ground) over a period of three weeks.

| Week | Diameter (in feet) |
|------|--------------------|
| 0 | 38.0 |
| 1 | 41.8 |
| 2 | 46.0 |
| 3 | 50.6 |

6. Which of the following best describes the change in size over time?

A)    increasing linear

B)    decreasing linear

C)    increasing exponential

D)    decreasing exponential

7. Which of the equations below best relates the diameter of the sink hole (in feet) to time (in weeks)?

A)    $d=4w+38$

B)    $d=38-4w$

C)    $d=38(1.1)^{w}$

D)    $d=38(0.9)^{w}$

## 3.12 Solutions to practice problems on exponential growth and decay

### 1. (D)

The starting amount is 500, the rate is .04, and this is growth: $500(1+.04)^{10} = 500(1.04)^{10}$

### 2. (B)

The starting amount is $x$, the rate is .20 and this is decay: But the rate is per 10-year period so the power must be adjusted.

$x(1-.2)^{\frac{50}{10}} = x(.8)^5$

### 3. (C)

Plug the answer choices into $500(2)^{2x}$. Or put $Y1 = 500(2)^{2x}$ and $Y2 = 128000$ into the equation editor of the graphing calculator and find the intersection.

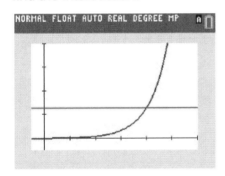

NORMAL FLOAT AUTO REAL DEGREE MP

### 4. (D)

The starting amount is 50, the rate is .5 and this is decay. But the rate is per 20 minutes and there are 3(24) 20 minute periods in 24 hours. $50(1-.5)^{3(24)}$

### 5. (B)

$1000(1.04)^5 - 1000(1.03)^5$
$= 1216.65 - 1159.28 = 57.37$

### 6. (C)

This is growth, but is it linear or exponential? Notice that diameter increases by <u>different</u> <u>amounts</u> each week (3.8, 4.2, and 4.6) but size always increases by the <u>same rate</u>, namely 10%, each week:

$(41.8 = 1.1(38), \ 46 = 1.1(41.8),$ etc.$)$.

So the growth is exponential, not linear.

### 7. (C)

In question 6, it was established that the relationship is exponential growth with a growth rate of 10% and a starting diameter of 38.

$d = 38(1+.1)^w = 38(1.1)^w$

## 3.13  Functions

A function defines a relationship between every possible value that can be accepted by the function (this set is called the domain) to every possible value that can be produced by the function (this set is called the range). For example the function $f(x) = x + 3$ establishes a relationship between every domain value and its corresponding range value. The relationship is simple: take the domain value and add three in order to obtain the range value. A useful graphic representation of a function is shown below.

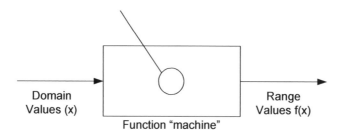

Function "machine"

Imagine that you feed a value from the domain (the x-value) into the function machine. Next, turn the crank on the machine. Then out comes the corresponding value from the range (the y-value or the $f(x)$ value). For a particular domain value that is placed into it, a function can only crank out one range value (otherwise it is not a function). When functions are graphed, they pass the "vertical line test," meaning that if a vertical line is drawn anywhere on the graph, it passes through the graph of the function at one and only one point.

## Notation

On the SAT® many of the problems involve interpreting function notation. Doing this means replacing the y with the function name and argument (usually functions are named $f$ or some other lower case letter and the argument is named $x$ or some other lower case letter). For example, instead of writing an equation as $y = mx + b$ we write $f(x) = mx + b$. They are both equations but the second one uses function notation.

Changing the argument: To confuse matters, sometimes the SAT® will change the argument from a simple $x$ to something else. Do not let this throw you off your game; just remember that the function is a kind of machine. Whatever goes into the function (the argument, or domain) gets treated the same way every time.

For example suppose we are given the function $f(x) = 2x + 1$. If the argument is changed from $x$ to $a$, just replace the letter $x$ with the letter $a$ and find that $f(a) = 2a + 1$. No matter what is placed into this function, it is multiplied by 2 and then it is added to 1. Similarly $f(x^2 - 1) = 2(x^2 - 1) + 1 = 2x^2 - 1$.

We could even go so far as to replace $x$ with something really weird, like $f(\Omega) = 2\Omega + 1$. That makes no sense mathematically speaking but it follows the rules of how this particular function works.

Solving equations: Consider the equation $y = a(x - 1)^2 - 2$. If you are told that the graph of the equation travels through the point (3, -14) and asked to find the value of $a$, you would set up the equation $-14 = a(3 - 1)^2 - 2$ and solve that equation for $a$. Re-writing that equation in function notation we could say $h(x) = a(x - 1)^2 - 2$. Nothing has changed except we chose $h$ instead of $f$ for the name of the function and we replaced $y$ with $h(x)$. Because we are in function notation you would be told that $h(3) = -14$ and be asked to find the value of $a$. The process is identical even though the notation is different: you would solve the equation $-14 = a(3-1)^2 - 2$ for $a$.

## Graphs

It is important to be able to navigate graphs of functions. A general graph of a function is

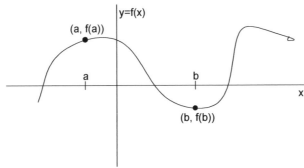

Notice that the domain is the horizontal axis (x-axis) and the range is the vertical axis (y-axis). The function maps each value in the domain to a single value in the range (passes the vertical line test). Any point that lies on the graph must satisfy the function rule. For example if the function were $f(x) = x^2 + 1$ then any arbitrary point on the graph of that function would have the coordinates of $(a, a^2 + 1)$.

Consider the function $f$ graphed below, which is defined on the interval [-3, 6]. We can say that the following things about this function are true:

- The maximum value of the function is 5.
- The minimum value of the function is -1
- $f(-2) = -1$
- On the interval [0, 2] the minimum value of the function is zero.
- On the interval [0,2] the maximum value of the function is one.
- Throughout the domain [-3,6], $f(x) = 1$ twice, once when x=1 and again when x=4

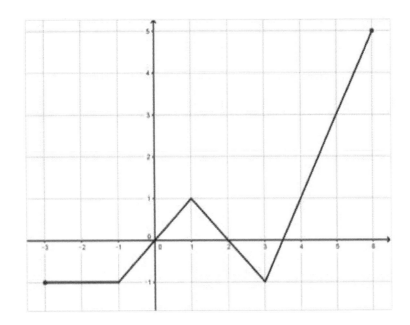

## Tables

Functions may also appear in tabular form. Consider the table below for two functions, named $g$ and $h$:

| $x$ | $g(x)$ | $h(x)$ |
|---|---|---|
| -10 | 70 | 6 |
| 2 | 10 | 15 |
| 6 | -10 | 20 |
| 8 | -20 | 45 |
| 20 | -80 | 65 |
| 30 | -130 | 74 |

You may be asked to estimate $g(25)$, assuming that $g$ is a linear function (see Unit 3.3 for more on linear relations, an extremely popular topic on the test). Start by finding the slope over the interval [20,30] as $\dfrac{-130-(-80)}{30-20} = \dfrac{-50}{10} = -5$. That same slope must also apply to the interval [20, 25] therefore $-5 = \dfrac{g(25)-g(20)}{25-20}$, $-5 = \dfrac{g(25)+80}{5}$, $-25 = g(25)+80$, $-105 = g(25)$.

## Combinations of functions

Sometimes functions are combined together, using addition subtraction, multiplication or division. Using the table above, for example: $g(8)-h(2) = -20-15 = -35$, $g(20)\cdot h(6) = -80(20) = -1600$, and $\dfrac{h(6)}{g(2)} = \dfrac{20}{10} = 2$.

Sometimes functions are combined in a special way to form **composite functions**. Suppose we want to find the value of $h(g(6))$. The first step is to find $g(6) = -10$. Then just replace $g(6)$ with -10 as follows: $h(g(6)) = h(-10) = 6$. Another example is $g(h(6)) = g(20) = -80$.

Less often you might be asked to combine functions that have variables. The process is exactly the same. For example suppose $f(x) = x+2$ and $g(x) = x^2$. For addition/subtraction we can write $f(x) - g(x) = x+2-x^2$. Whereas for composites we can write $f(g(x)) = f(x^2) = x^2 + 2$.
Note above that the first step for the composite is just substituting $x^2$ for $g(x)$. Then the $f$ function is applied to the argument $x^2$, yielding $x^2 + 2$. We could go the other way around, namely $g(f(x)) = g(x+2) = (x+2)^2$. The expression $x+2$ replaces $f(x)$ and then the $g$-function is applied to the argument $x+2$, yielding $(x+2)^2$.

1. If $g(x) = \dfrac{x+c}{x^2}$ and $x \neq 0$ and $g(-1) = -4$

then which equation below could be used to find the value of $c$?

A) $\dfrac{x-1}{x^2} = -4$

B) $\dfrac{x-4}{x^2} = -1$

C) $c - 1 = -4$

D) $c - 1 = -1$

2. If $f(x) = ax^2 + x + c$ and $f(0) = 5$ and $f(2) = 15$, what is the value of $a - c$?

A) -3
B) 2
C) 3
D) 5

3. If $f(x + a) = x$ then $f(x)$ could be which of the following expressions?

A) $x + a$

B) $x - a$

C) $x^2$

D) $\dfrac{x}{a}$

4. If $f(x) = 2x + 3$ which of the following is an expression for $f(x + c) - f(x)$?

A) $2c + 3$
B) $c$
C) $2c$
D) $2c + 6$

5. If $f(x) = 2x^2 + x + a$ and the graph of $f(x - a)$ passes through the point (2, 20), what is the value of $a$?

A) -1
B) 0
C) 1
D) 2

**Questions 6 and 7 refer to the following information:**

The data below describe the average height of tomato plants over time (in days). Some plants were given organic fertilizer and others were given non-organic fertilizer.

| Elapsed Time, $t$ (in days) | Average Height ( in cm) | |
| --- | --- | --- |
| | Organic Fertilizer $f(t)$ | Inorganic Fertilizer $g(t)$ |
| 6 | 4 | 6 |
| 8 | 6 | 10 |
| 9 | 7 | 12 |
| 10 | 8 | 14 |
| 14 | 12 | 16 |

6. Which of the following statements are <u>false</u>?

I. $g(8) - f(8) = f(6)$
II. $g(f(10)) = f(14) - 2$
III. $f(g(6)) = \dfrac{g(14)}{g(6)}$

A) I only
B) II only
C) III only
D) None are false

7. Which of the following statements are <u>false</u>?

I. $f(t + 4) = g(9)$ when $t = 10$
II $g(t) - f(t) = f(t - 4)$ when $t = 8$
III $\dfrac{g(t)}{t} = \dfrac{f(6)}{3}$ when $t = 9$

A) I only
B) II only
C) III only
D) None are false

8. If $g(a) = a^2$ and $h(a) = \dfrac{a}{2}$ then what is the expression for $g(h(2a-2))$?

A)    $a^2 + 1$

B)    $2a^2 + 2$

C)    $a^2 - 2a + 1$

D)    $2a^2 - 4a + 2$

---

**Questions 9-15 refer to the following information:**

The function $g(x)$ is defined over the interval [-1, 4] as shown in the graph below.

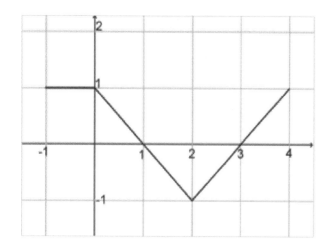

9. For what value of $x$ is $g(x)$ at its maximum?

A)        -1

B)        1

C)        2

D)        4

10. For what value of $x$ is $g(x)$ at its minimum?

A)        -1

B)        1

C)        2

D)        4

11. At how many points is $g(x) = \dfrac{1}{2}$?

A)        0

B)        1

C)        2

D)        More than two

12. If $g(a) = g(b) = 0$ then what is the value of $a - b$?

A)        -2

B)        -1

C)        0

D)        1

13. What is the value of $\dfrac{g(0)}{g(2)}$?

A)        -1

B)        0

C)        1

D)        2

14. Which of the following are equal to 1?

I.            $g(-1)$

II.           $g(1)$

III.          $g(2)$

A)    I only

B)    II only

C)    III only

D)    None are equal to 1

15. What is the value of $g(g(2))$?

A)        -1

B)        0

C)        1

D)        2

# 3.13 Solutions to practice problems on functions

**1. (C)**

$$g(x) = \frac{x+c}{x^2}, \quad -4 = \frac{-1+c}{(-1)^2}, \quad -4 = c-1$$

**2. (A)**

(0,5) means c=5.

(2,15) means

$$15 = a(2)^2 + 2 + 5, \quad 8 = 4a, \quad 2 = a$$

$$a - c = 2 - 5 = -3$$

**3. (B)**

Backsolve this one.

If $f(x) = x - a$ then $f(x+a) = (x+a) - a = x$

**4. (C)**

$$f(x+c) - f(x) = [2(x+c)+3] - (2x+3) = 2c$$

**5. (A)**

$$f(x) = 2x^2 + x + a$$

$$f(x-a) = 2(x-a)^2 + (x-a) + a = 2x^2 - 4ax + 2a^2 + x$$

at $(2,20)$  $20 = 2(4) - 4a(2) + 2a^2 + 2$

$$0 = 2a^2 - 8a - 10 = 2(a-5)(a+1)$$

$$a = 5 \text{ or } a = -1$$

**5. (B)**

$$1000(1.04)^5 - 1000(1.03)^5$$

$$= 1216.65 - 1159.28 = 57.37$$

**6. (C)**

I.  true because $g(8) - f(8) = 10 - 6 = 4 = f(6)$

II  true because
$$g(f(10)) = g(8) = 10 = f(14) - 2 = 12 - 2$$

III false because $f(g(6)) = f(6) = 4$, whereas
$$\frac{g(14)}{g(6)} = \frac{16}{6}$$

**7. (B)**

I. is true because
$$g(8) - f(8) = 10 - 6 = 4 = f(6)$$

II is true because
$$g(f(10)) = g(8) = 10 = f(14) - 2 = 12 - 2$$

III is false because $f(g(6)) = f(6) = 4$,

whereas $\dfrac{g(14)}{g(6)} = \dfrac{16}{6}$

**8. (C)**

$$g(h(2a-2)) = g\left(\frac{2a-2}{2}\right) = g(a-1)$$
$$= (a-1)^2 = a^2 - 2a + 1$$

**9. (B)**

Remember that $g(x)$ is the height of the graph.

**10. (A)**

Remember that $g(x)$ is the height of the graph.

**11. (C)**

Remember that $g(x)$ is the height of the graph.

**12. (A)**

$a$ and $b$ are equal to 1 and 3. So $a - b$ could be -2 or it could be 2.

**13. (A)**

$$\frac{g(0)}{g(2)} = \frac{1}{-1} = -1$$

**14. (A)**

I is true because $g(-1) = 1$

II is false because $g(1) = 0$

III is false because $g(2) = -1$

**15. (C)**

$$g(g(2)) = g(-1) = 1$$

127

## 3.14   Transformations of functions

There are three categories of ways that functions can be transformed:  translations (moving the graph up, down, left and right), reflections (flipping the graph over the x-axis or y-axis) and scale changes (altering the shape of the graph by multiplying the function by a constant).  But before we cover these transformations it is important to become familiar with the popular parent functions.

### Parent functions

Students are expected to be able to sketch the more popular parent functions by hand.  Most transformation problems appear in the no calculator section.  Even if a transformation problem appears in the calculator section it could be easier and faster to solve the problem by hand.

The more popular parent functions and their graphs are shown below:

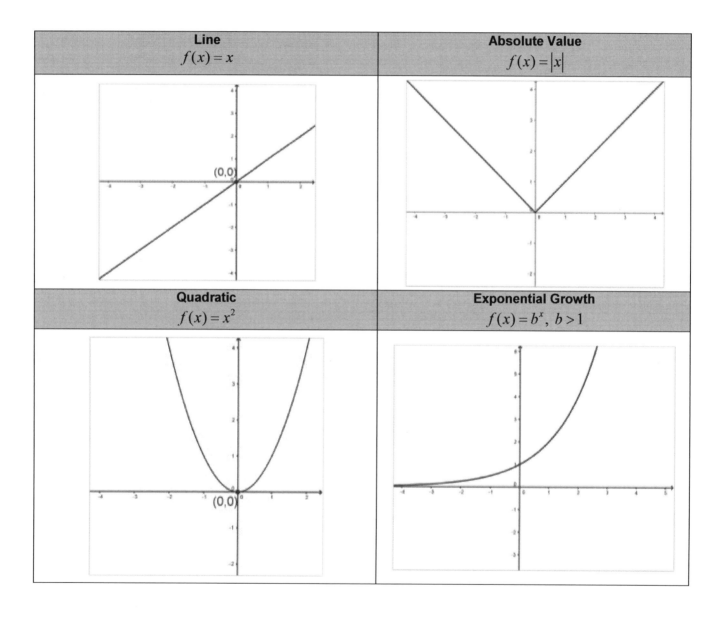

| Line $f(x) = x$ | Absolute Value $f(x) = |x|$ |
| Quadratic $f(x) = x^2$ | Exponential Growth $f(x) = b^x,\ b > 1$ |

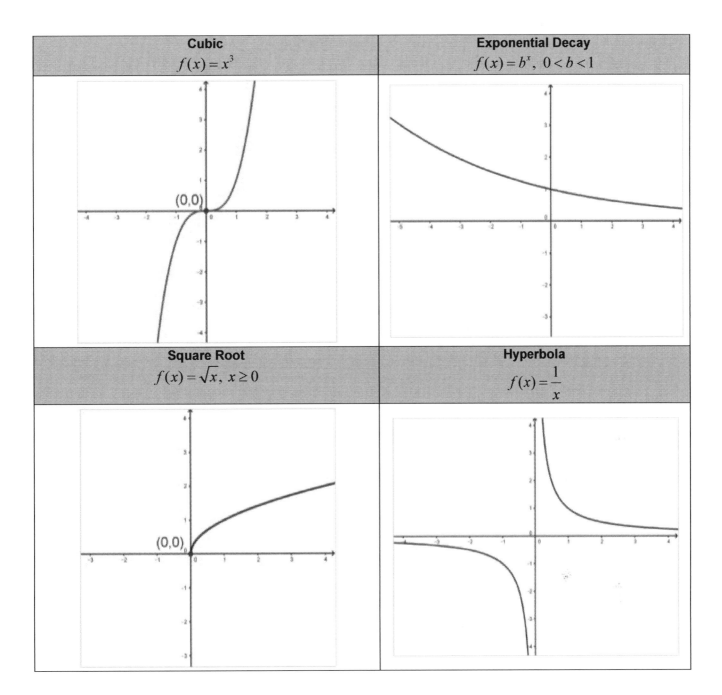

## Translations

A translation involves sliding the graph of the function left or right, or up or down. The popular parent functions all have a critical point, which is labeled in the graphs above. A translation moves that critical point along with the rest of the curve, but does not change the shape of the curve.

If you want to translate the curve left or right, just replace $f(x)$ with $f(x-h)$, where $h$ is the number of horizontal units to be moved. If $h$ itself is positive then the curve moves right, whereas if $h$ itself is negative the curve moves left. If you want to translate the curve up or down, just replace $f(x)$ with $f(x)+k$, where $k$ is the number of vertical units to be moved. If $k$ is positive then the curve moves up, whereas if $k$ is negative the curve moves down.

Notice that the critical point moves from its original location to its translated location of $(h,k)$.

The table below shows the parent functions before and after they are translated left 1 unit $(h=-1)$ and down 2 units $(k=-2)$.

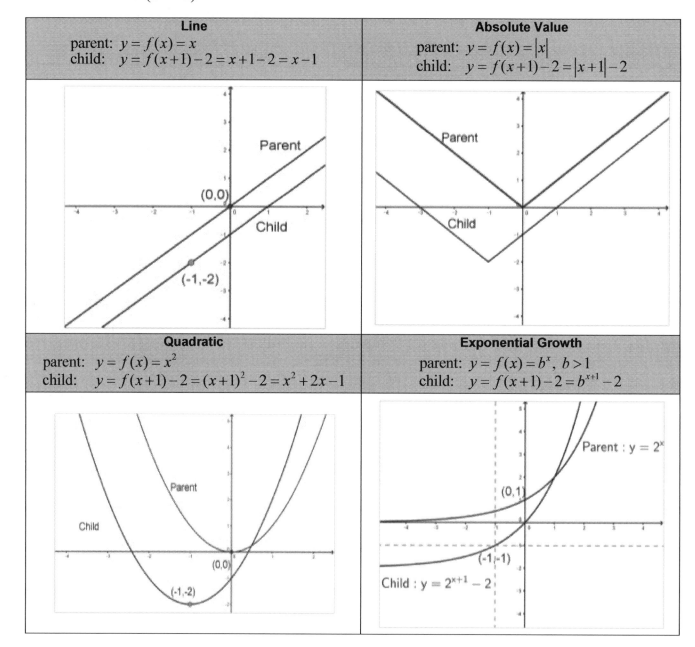

| Line | Absolute Value |
|---|---|
| parent: $y=f(x)=x$ <br> child: $y=f(x+1)-2=x+1-2=x-1$ | parent: $y=f(x)=\lvert x\rvert$ <br> child: $y=f(x+1)-2=\lvert x+1\rvert-2$ |
| Quadratic | Exponential Growth |
| parent: $y=f(x)=x^2$ <br> child: $y=f(x+1)-2=(x+1)^2-2=x^2+2x-1$ | parent: $y=f(x)=b^x,\ b>1$ <br> child: $y=f(x+1)-2=b^{x+1}-2$ |

| Cubic | Exponential Decay |
|---|---|
| parent: $y = f(x) = x^3$ | parent: $y = f(x) = b^x$, $0 < b < 1$ |
| child: $y = f(x+1) - 2 = (x+1)^3 - 2$ | child: $y = f(x+1) - 2 = b^{x+1} - 2$ |

(0,0)
(−1,−2)
Parent
Child

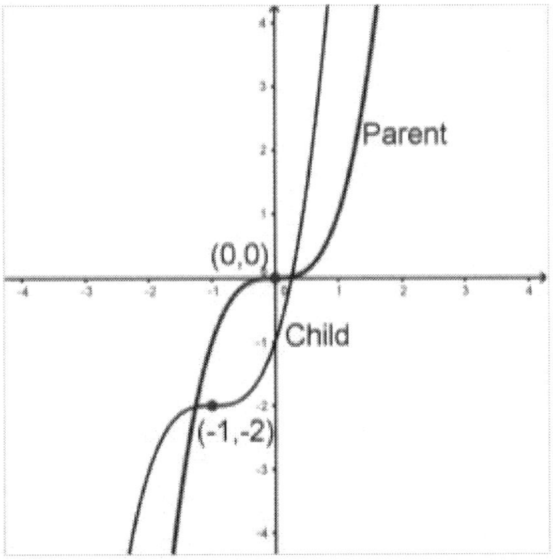

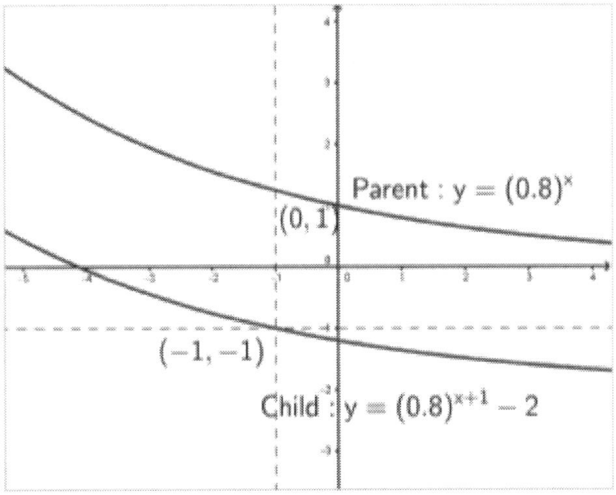

Parent : $y = (0.8)^x$
(0, 1)
(−1, −1)
Child : $y = (0.8)^{x+1} - 2$

| Square Root | Hyperbola |
|---|---|
| parent: $y = f(x) = \sqrt{x}$, $x \geq 0$ | parent: $y = f(x) = \dfrac{1}{x}$   child: $y = f(x+1) - 2 = \dfrac{1}{x+1} - 2$ |
| 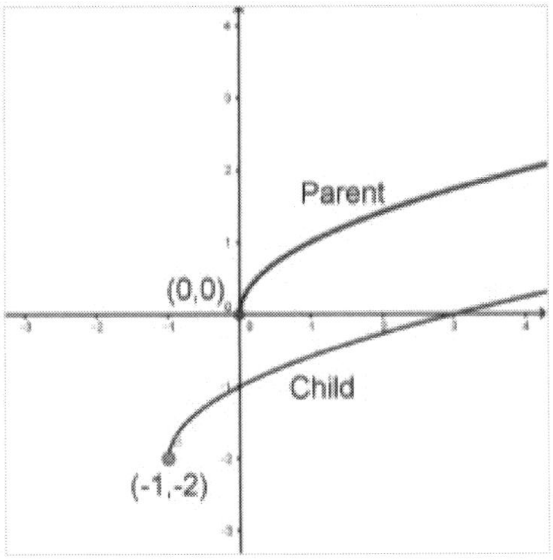 child: $y = f(x+1) - 2 = \sqrt{x+1} - 2$, $x \geq -1$ | 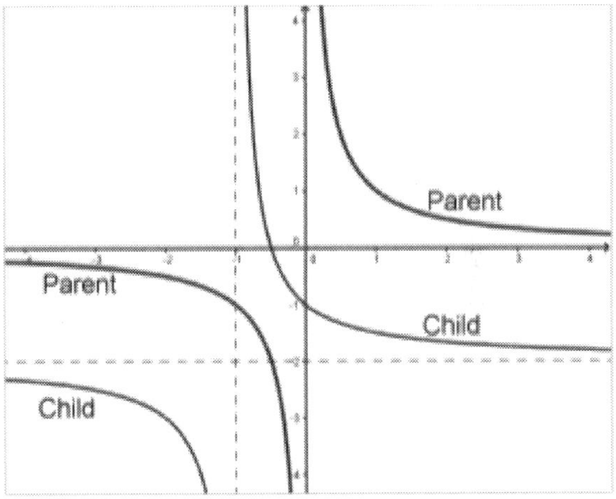 |

(0,0)
Parent
Child
(−1,−2)

Parent
Parent
Child
Child

**Reflections**

A reflection is achieved by flipping the graph over the x-axis or over the y-axis. Reflections do not change the shape of the curve, just its orientation. To reflect over the x-axis, $y = f(x)$ is replaced by $y = -f(x)$. To reflect over the y-axis, $y = f(x)$ is replaced by $y = f(-x)$. The table below shows examples of reflecting the parent functions.

131

| **Line** | **Absolute Value** |
|---|---|
| parent: $y = f(x) = x$ <br> reflected over the x-axis: $y = -f(x) = -x$ | parent: $y = f(x) = |x|$ <br> reflected over the x-axis: $y = -f(x) = -|x|$ |

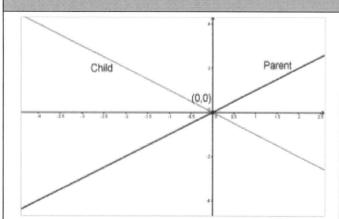
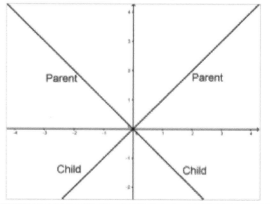

| **Quadratic** | **Exponential Growth** |
|---|---|
| parent: $y = f(x) = x^2$ <br> reflected over the x-axis: $y = -f(x) = -x^2$ | parent: $y = f(x) = b^x$, $b > 1$ <br> reflected over the x-axis: $y = -f(x) = -b^x$ |

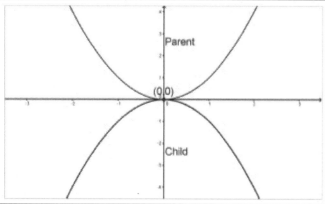
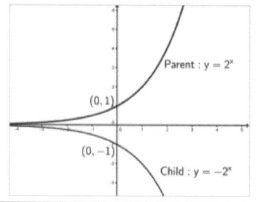

| **Cubic** | **Exponential Decay** |
|---|---|
| parent: $y = f(x) = x^3$ <br> reflected over the y-axis: $y = f(-x) = (-x)^3$ | parent: $y = f(x) = b^x$, $0 < b < 1$ <br> reflected over the y-axis: $y = f(-x) = b^{-x}$ |

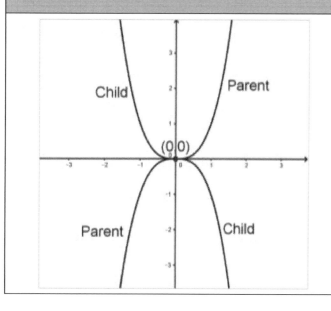
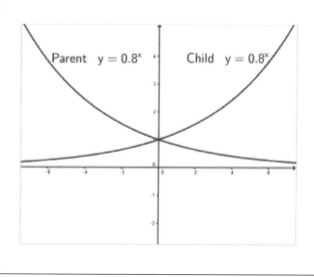

132

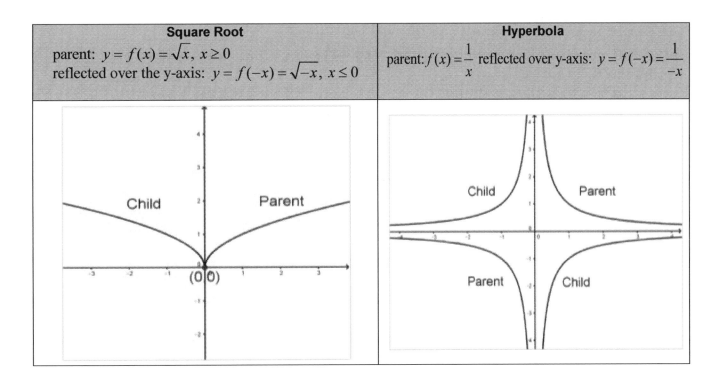

| Square Root | Hyperbola |
|---|---|
| parent: $y = f(x) = \sqrt{x}, \; x \geq 0$ <br> reflected over the y-axis: $y = f(-x) = \sqrt{-x}, \; x \leq 0$ | parent: $f(x) = \dfrac{1}{x}$ reflected over y-axis: $y = f(-x) = \dfrac{1}{-x}$ |

**Scale changes**

In this book we will cover what are called vertical scale changes (scale change questions are rare and are more likely to be vertical scale changes). A vertical stretch is caused when $y = f(x)$ is replaced by $y = cf(x)$ and $c > 1$. A vertical shrink is caused when $y = f(x)$ is replaced by $y = cf(x)$ and $0 < c < 1$. Vertical shrinks and stretches are illustrated below for two of the parent functions. In a vertical stretch, for any given value of x, the y-value increases. This causes the parabola to get narrower and it causes the absolute value slopes to increase. The vertical shrink does the opposite: for any given value of x, the y-value decreases. This causes the parabola to get wider and it causes the absolute value slope to decrease.

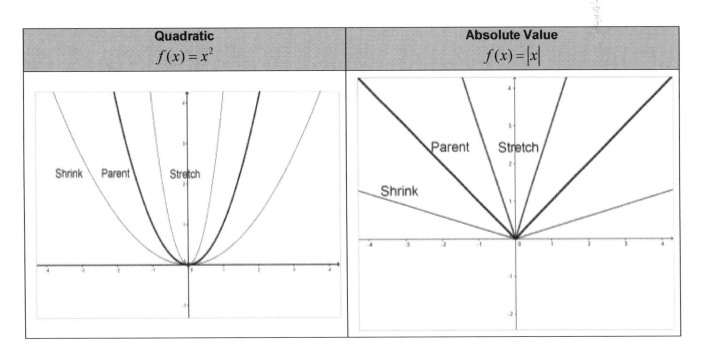

| Quadratic <br> $f(x) = x^2$ | Absolute Value <br> $f(x) = |x|$ |
|---|---|

## Combinations of transformations

It is possible that you will encounter a transformation that is a combination of translations, reflections and sometimes scale changes. Two combinations are illustrated below.

| Square Root | Exponential Growth |
|---|---|
| parent: $y = f(x) = \sqrt{x}$, $x \geq 0$ <br> reflect over y-axis, then move right 1 and down 2 <br> $y = \sqrt{-x}$ then $y = \sqrt{-x+1} - 2$, $x \leq 1$ | $y = f(x) = b^x$, $b > 1$ <br> reflect over x-axis, then move left 1 and down 1 <br> $y = -b^x$ then $y = -b^{x+1} - 1$ |
| 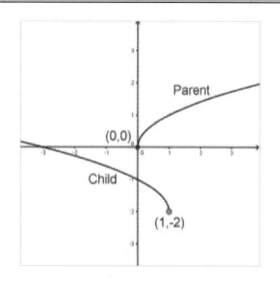 | 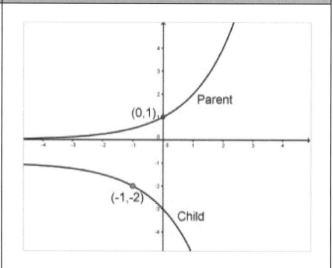 |
| | Note that the critical point moves from (0,1) to (0,-1) because of the reflection. Then it moves from (0,-1) to (-1,-2) because of the translation. |

## 3.14 Practice problems on transformations of functions
## Solve these problems by hand first and then check them on the graphing calculator.

1. Which of the functions below has a graph that goes through the origin (0,0)?

A) $f(x) = \dfrac{1}{x}$

B) $f(x) = \sqrt{x}$

C) $f(x) = 1.5^x$

D) $f(x) = 0.5^x$

2. Which of the functions below has been translated left 2 and down 2?

A) $f(x) = (x-2)^2 - 2$

B) $f(x) = 3^{x-2} - 2$

C) $f(x) = 1.5^{x+2} - 2$

D) $f(x) = -2|x| - 2$

3. Which of the following functions has been reflected over the x-axis only?

A) $f(x) = -\sqrt{-x}$

B) $f(x) = |-x|$

C) $f(x) = 2^{-x}$

D) $f(x) = -|x|$

4. A parent function f(x) and a child function g(x) are graphed below. Which of the following could be an expression for g(x)?

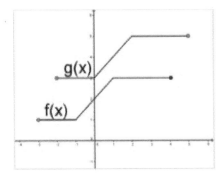

A) $g(x) = f(x+1) + 2$

B) $g(x) = f(x+1) - 2$

C) $g(x) = f(x-1) + 2$

D) $g(x) = f(x-1) - 2$

5. Which of the graphs of the following functions never goes below the x-axis?

A) $f(x) = (x-2)^2$

B) $f(x) = 5^x - 2$

C) $f(x) = -2|-x|$

D) $f(x) = \sqrt{x} - 2$

6. If $f(x) = \dfrac{1}{x}$ which of the following is the graph of $-f(x+2)$?

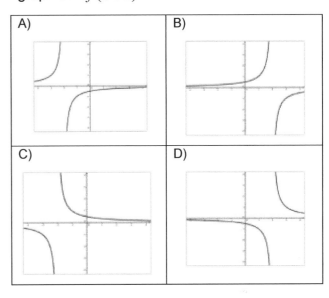

7. The graph below shows $f(x)$ and $g(x) = cf(x)$. What can be concluded about the value of $c$?

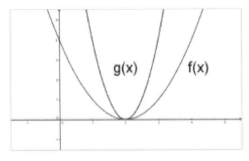

A) $c \le 0$

B) $0 < c < 1$

C) $c = 1$

D) $c > 1$

# 3.14 Solutions to practice problems on transformations of functions

**1. (B)**

$f(0) = \sqrt{0} = 0$

**2. (C)**

In the parent function, replace $x$ with $x+2$ and then subtract 2.

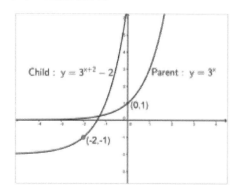

**3. (D)**

Parent: $y = f(x) = |x|$

Child: $y = -f(x) = -|x|$

If $f(x) = x - a$ then $f(x+a) = (x+a) - a = x$

**4. (C)**

f(x) has been translated right 1 and up 2.
Replace $x$ with $x-1$ and add 2.

**5. (A)**

$f(x) = (x-2)^2$ is a parabola shifted right two units. It is tangent to the x-axis but does not go below it.

**6. (A)**

A) shifted left 2 units and reflected over x-axis.

B) shifted right 2 units and reflected over x-axis.

C) shifted left 2 units but not reflected

D) shifted right 2 units but not reflected.

**7. (D)**

This is a vertical stretch so $c > 1$. If $c < 0$ the graph would be reflected over the x-axis. If $c = 1$ the graph does not change. If $0 < c < 1$ there would be a vertical shrink.

# 4. Geometry and trigonometry

Although the SAT® does not place as much weight on geometry as it does on algebra, geometry can play an important role in your score. For most students it will necessary to be able to solve the easier geometry problems in order to achieve a mid-range target, say 550-650. For those students with higher targets the more difficult geometry problems might prove to be the key to success. Geometry uses different circuitry in your brain from that used by algebra. If you have not done geometry in a while you will probably need to get those wheels turning again.

Similar comments about score targets apply to trigonometry. Some trigonometry will typically be required in order to achieve a mid-range target score. Basic right triangle trigonometry is something you probably learned in geometry or algebra 2, but there can also be more advanced trigonometry on the test that you might not see until you take pre-calculus (this varies from school to school).

## 4.1 Graphs and equations of lines

This unit continues our conversation about linear models. Earlier units, Unit 3.3 equations and Unit 3.2 ratios, covered the ideas of slope and intercept from the algebraic point of view of equations and average rate of change, respectively. This unit has a focus on the graphs of linear models in the x-y coordinate plane.

### Given two points, find the equation

Remember how to find the equation of a line? The most useful form of a linear equation is called the slope-intercept form, which is

$$y = mx + b,$$

where $m$ is the slope of the line and $b$ is where the line crosses the y-axis (the y-intercept).

The equation of a line can be determined if you know two of the points through which it travels (two points determine a line). We denote the points as $(x_1, y_1)$ and $(x_2, y_2)$. The first step is to find the slope

$$m = \frac{y_2 - y_1}{x_2 - x_1}.$$

Once we have the slope, we can use one of the points to find the equation of the line. For example, suppose we want the equation of the line that passes through (1,2) and (5, 14). We determine the slope to be

$$m = \frac{14 - 2}{5 - 1} = \frac{12}{4} = 3.$$

Next write the partial equation

$$y = 3x + b.$$

Substitute the values (1,2) in the partial equation and solve for b:

$$2 = 3 \cdot 1 + b, \quad -1 = b.$$

So we know that the equation is: $y = 3x - 1$.

**Given one point and a slope, find the equation**

Instead of providing two points, some problems will provide the slope of the line and a single point (the slope and a point determine a line). If a problem gives the slope and a point, simply write the partial equation, plug in the point and solve for b. For example, given a slope of -3 and the point (2,3) we write the partial equation

$$y = -3x + b$$

then plug in (2,3) to solve for b

$$3 = -3(2) + b, \ 9 = b \ .$$

The equation of the line is $y = -3x + 9$.

**Parallel and perpendicular lines**

Rather than provide the slope directly, sometimes the slope is provided indirectly through information about another line. In order to do this type of problem you must remember that:

- The slopes of parallel lines are the same
- The slopes of perpendicular lines are negative reciprocals of each other.

For example, if a line has a slope of 3 then all lines parallel to it must also have a slope of 3; whereas all lines perpendicular to it must have a slope of $-\dfrac{1}{3}$.

**Special cases of slope**

There are two special cases of slope to keep in mind:

- The slope of a horizontal line is zero. For example, the line $y = 3$ has a slope of zero.
- The slope of a vertical line is undefined. For example, the slope of the line $x = 3$ is undefined.

**Given an equation, graph the line**

Suppose you are given the equation of a line in slope-intercept format, say $y = 2x - 4$. The first step is to graph the y-intercept, which is the point where the graph crosses the y-axis. In this case the point is (0, -4). Next, place your pencil on the y-intercept and use the idea that slope is just rise over run, in this case the rise is 2 and the run is 1 because the slope is 2/1. Move your pencil up to units and then to the right two units and mark another point at (1, -2). You can repeat the process using the slope to find other points if desired. The last step is to connect the points.

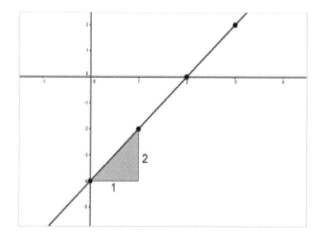

**Distance formula**

The distance formula is something that you should memorize, or if memorizing does not suit you, remember that it is a simple application of the Pythagorean Theorem. You are given two points and need to find the distance between them.

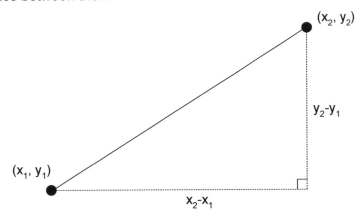

Notice that the vertical distance is just $y_2 - y_1$ and the horizontal distance is just $x_2 - x_1$. Applying the Pythagorean Theorem gives

$$d^2 = (y_2 - y_1)^2 + (x_2 - x_1)^2$$
$$d = \sqrt{(y_2 - y_1)^2 + (x_2 - x_1)^2}$$

**Midpoint formula**

The midpoint of the line segment with endpoints $(x_1, y_1)$ and $(x_2, y_2)$ has the coordinates:

$$\text{midpoint} = \left( \frac{x_1 + x_2}{2}, \ \frac{y_1 + y_2}{2} \right)$$

**Quadrants**

In the x-y coordinate plane, the four quadrants are numbered. Sometimes students are not taught this until they take pre-calculus, but it is a topic that can come up on the SAT®. The numbering scheme is simple, running counter-clockwise as show below, and Roman numerals are used.

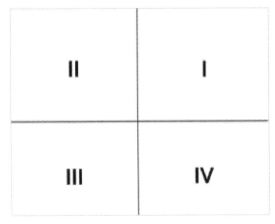

# 4.1 Problems on graphs and equations of lines
## Solve these problems by hand first and then verify on the calculator.

1. The equation of the line passing through points (5,7) and (-15, 23) is:

A)      $y = -0.8x + 11$

B)      $y = -0.8x + 3$

C)      $y = 0.8x + 12.6$

D)      $y = -1.25x + 13.25$

2. What is the length of the line segment whose endpoints are (5,7) and (-15, 23)?

A)      4.0

B)      25.6

C)      31.6

D)      36.0

3. Find the equation of the line that passes through (1,3) and is perpendicular to the line with the equation $3x - 2y = 5$.

A)      $2y = 3x + 3$

B)      $2y = -3x + 9$

C)      $3y = 2x + 4$

D)      $3y = -2x + 11$

4. What is the slope of the line that passes through the points (3, -2) and (3, 2)?

A)      0.0

B)      0.4

C)      0.6

D)      Cannot be determined

5. The diameter of a circle has as its endpoints (-1,2) and (9, 24). What are the coordinates of the center?

A)      (4, 11)

B)      (4, 13)

C)      (5, 11)

D)      (5, 13)

6. If two vertices of rectangle ABCD are at A=(1,2) and B=(5,8), what is the slope of $\overline{BC}$?

A)      $-2/3$

B)      $-3/2$

C)      $2/3$

D)      $3/2$

7. What is the equation of the perpendicular bisector of the line segment whose endpoints are (5,7) and (-5,11)?

A)      $y = -0.4x + 9$

B)      $y = -0.4x - 9$

C)      $y = 2.5x + 9$

D)      $y = 2.5x - 5.5$

8. The line $y = 3$ does <u>not</u> pass through

     I.    (1,3)

     II.    (3,1)

     III.    (3,3)

A)      I only

B)      II only

C)      III only

D)      II and III only

9. Which quadrant does the graph of $y = -x - 3$ <u>not</u> travel through?

A)      Quadrant I

B)      Quadrant II

C)      Quadrant III

D)      Quadrant IV

10. If a line passes through points (1,5), (3,8) and (x,-10) then x must be equal to:

A)      -11

B)      -9

C)      9

D)      11

11. If a line passes through points (1,5) and (3,8) then it must also pass through which points?

    I.   (-1, 2)

    II.  (3, 2)

    III.  (2,3)

A)          I only

B)          II only

C)          III only

D)          I and II only

---

The diagram below is used in problems 12-14.

$\overline{AB}$ is a diameter of the circle and it is 12 units long. Point $M$ is the midpoint of $\overline{AC}$.

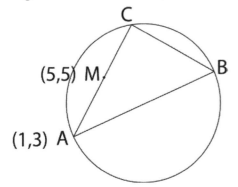

12. What are the coordinates of point C?

A)          (-3,1)

B)          (7,9)

C)          (9,7)

D)          (11,13)

13. What is the slope of $\overline{BC}$?

A)          -2.0

B)          --1.0

C)          1.0

D)          2.0

14. What is the length of $\overline{BC}$?

A)          4

B)          8

C)          $2\sqrt{31}$

D)          $2\sqrt{41}$

---

15.

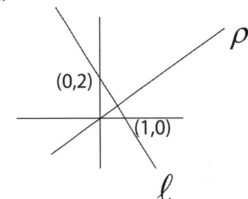

In the diagram above, line $\ell$ passes through points (0,2) and (1,0). If line $\rho$ is perpendicular to line $\ell$, then the two lines intersect at the point:

(A)          (.4, .2)

(B)          (.4, .8)

(C)          (.5, 1)

(D)          (.8, .4)

16. The graph below shows the progress of a swimming pool being drained of water. The initial height of the water was 4 feet and it took 3 hours to drain the pool. During what period of time was the pool draining at the fastest rate?

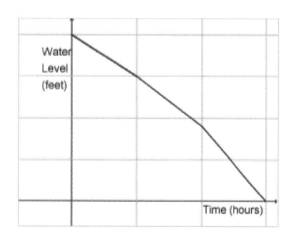

A)     0-1 hours (the first hour)

B)     1-2 hours (the second hour)

C)     2-3 hours (the last hour)

D)     The pool drained at about the same rate throughout the 3 hour time period.

17. Which of the graphs below could be the graph of the equation $y = -x - 2$?

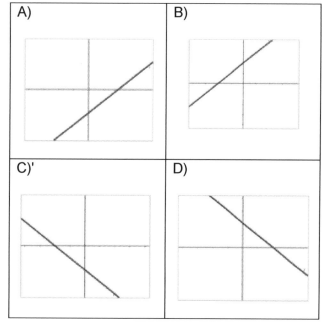

18. Line $\ell$ (shown below) and line $v$ (not shown below) intersect at the point (1.2, 3.4). If the lines are perpendicular, line $v$ must travel through which of the following points?

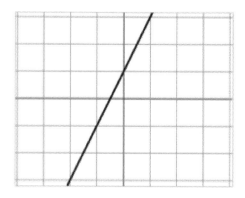

A)          (-7, 4.9)

B)          (0, 0)

C)          (7,2)

D)          (10,-1)

19. If the graph of a line passes through the points (1,2) and (2, $a$) what is the equation of the line?

A)          $y = (a-2)x + (4-a)$

B)          $y = (a-2)x + (5-2a)$

C)          $y = (a-2)x + (a-4)$

D)          $y = (a-2)x + (2a-5)$

142

# 4.1 Solutions to problems on graphs and equations of lines

**1. (A)**

$$m = \frac{23-7}{-15-5} = \frac{-4}{5}, \quad y = \frac{-4}{5}x + b$$

at $(5,7)$ $\quad 7 = \frac{-4}{5}(5) + b, \quad 11 = b$

$y = (-4/5)x + 11$

**2. (B)**

$$d = \sqrt{(23-7)^2 + (-15-5)^2} = \sqrt{656}$$

**3. (D)**

$$3x - 2y = 5, \quad -2y = -3x + 5, \quad y = \frac{3}{2}x - 2.5$$

$y = \frac{-2}{3}x + b \quad$ at $(1,3) \quad 3 = \frac{-2}{3}(1) + b, \quad \frac{11}{3} = b$

$y = \frac{-2}{3}x + \frac{11}{3} \quad$ or $\quad 3y = -2x + 11$

**4. (D)**

This a vertical line with the equation is $x = 3$. Its slope is undefined.

**5. (B)**

$$\text{center=midpoint} = \left(\frac{-1+9}{2}, \frac{2+24}{2}\right) = (4,13)$$

**6. (A)**

slope of AB $= \frac{8-2}{5-1} = \frac{3}{2}$

slope BC=(-2/3)

**7. (C)**

original slope $= \frac{11-7}{-5-5} = \frac{4}{-10}$

desired slope = 10/4 = 2.5

midpoint $= \left(\frac{5-5}{2}, \frac{11+7}{2}\right) = (0,9)$

at (0, 9), equation is $y = 2.5x + 9$

**8. (B)**

I. is false because the line passes through (1,3)

II is true because the line does not pass through (3,1)

III is false because the line passes through (3,3)

**9. (A)**

The graph looks like this

**10. (B)**

$$m = \frac{y_2 - y_1}{x_2 - x_1} = \frac{8-5}{3-1} = \frac{3}{2}$$

$\frac{3}{2} = \frac{-10-5}{x-1}, \quad 3x - 3 = -30, \quad x = -9$

**11. (A)**

A line has constant slope. The slope must be:

$$m = \frac{y_2 - y_1}{x_2 - x_1} = \frac{8-5}{3-1} = \frac{3}{2}. \quad \text{Test the other points:}$$

$\frac{2-5}{-1-1} = \frac{3}{2}, \quad \frac{2-5}{3-1} = \frac{-3}{2}, \quad \frac{3-5}{2-1} = -2$

**12. (C)**

$5 = \frac{1+x}{2}, \ x = 9 \quad 5 = \frac{y+3}{2}, \ y = 7$

**13. (A)**

$slope \ \overline{AC} = \frac{5-3}{5-1} = \frac{1}{2}, \quad slope \ \overline{BC} = neg \ reciprocal = -2$

**14. (B)**

$$AC = 2 \cdot AM = 2\sqrt{(5-3)^2 + (5-1)^2} = 2\sqrt{20} = \sqrt{80}$$

$$CB = \sqrt{12^2 - AC^2} = \sqrt{144 - 80} = \sqrt{64} = 8$$

**15. (D)**

Equation of line $\ell$: $y = -2x + 2$

Equation of line $\rho$: $y = (1/2)x$

At the point of intersection:

$-2x + 2 = \frac{1}{2}x, \quad -4x + 4 = x,$

$-5x = -4, \quad x = \frac{4}{5} \quad$ and $\quad y = \frac{1}{2}x = \frac{4}{10} = \frac{2}{5}$

**16. (C)**

Slope is the rate at which the pool was draining.
Slope was steepest during the last hour, 2-3.

**17 (C)**

Must have negative slope and negative y-intercept.

**18. (D)**

Looking at the graph we see that the slope is 2 and that the y-intercept is 1. So the equation of line $\ell$ must be $y = 2x + 1$. The slope of line $v$ must be -1/2. At the point (1.2, 3.4) the equation of line $v$ is

$y = -.5x + b, \ 3.4 = -.5(1.2) + b, \ 3.4 = -.6 + b, \ 4 = b$

Test answer choices to satisfy $y = -.5x + 4$.

**19. (A)**

The slope is $(a-2)/(2-1) = a - 2$ giving the partial equation $y = (a-2)x + b$. At (1,2) we get

$2 = (a-2)(1) + b, \ 2 = a - 2 + b, \ 4 - a = b$

## 4.2    Angles and parallel lines

There are three types of angles to know:

$$0° < \text{acute angle} < 90°$$

$$\text{right angle} = 90°$$

$$90 < \text{obtuse angle} < 180°$$

Supplementary angles comprise a straight angle (they sum to 180 degrees); whereas complementary angles comprise a right angle (they sum to 90 degrees).

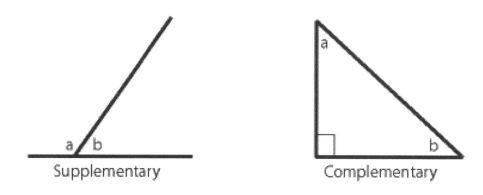

Supplementary                        Complementary

Remember that vertical angles are congruent (they have the same measure).

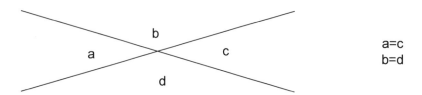

a=c
b=d

The bulk of what you need to remember about angles and lines has to do with parallel lines with a transversal line.  The picture looks like this:

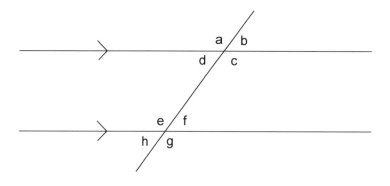

There is a bit of terminology to be mastered with this. The interior angles are those angles that lie inside the parallel lines, namely c, d, e and f. The exterior angles are those that lie outside the parallel lines, namely a, b, h and g.

There are several sets of congruent pairs to remember, as you can see in the table below.

| Vertical angles | a=c |
| | b=d |
| | e=g |
| | f=h |
| Alternate interior angles | c=e |
| | d=f |
| Corresponding angles | a=e |
| | d=h |
| | b=f |
| | c=g |
| Alternate exterior angles | a=g |
| | b=h |

# 4.2 Problems on angles and parallel lines
## calculator permitted

**Questions 1 and 2 refer to the diagram below.**

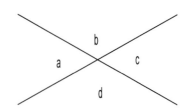

1. Which of the following must be true?

    I.   a=c

    II.  a=d

    III. a+b=c+d

A)         I only

B)         II only

C)         III only

D)         I and III only

2. Which of the following may not be supplementary?

A)         a and b

B)         a and c

C)         a and d

D)         b and c

**Questions 3, 4 and 5 refer to the diagram below.**

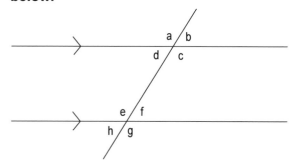

3. Which of the following must be true?

    I.   a=c

    II.  a=h

    III. a+c=e+g

A)         I only

B)         II only

C)         I and II only

D)         I and III only

4. Which of the following must be true?

    I.   a=g

    II.  b+e=180

    III. d=h

A)         I only

B)         II only

C)         III only

D)         All must be true

5. What is the measure of $2c+f+h$?

A)         90 degrees

B)         180 degrees

C)         270 degrees

D)         360 degrees

---

6. If A and B are complementary angles and the measure of A is 20 degrees, what is the measure of B?

A)         70 degrees

B)         90 degrees

C)         160 degrees

D)         180 degrees

7 If a and b are supplementary angles, and a and c are complementary angles, then which of the following must be true?:

A)         a+b+c = 270 degrees

B)         b - a = 90 degrees

C)         b −c = 90 degrees

D)         a+b-c = 90 degrees

# 4.2 Solutions to problems on angles and parallel lines

## 1 (D)

I is true (a and c are vertical angles). II is not necessarily true. III is true (a+b=180=c+d).

## 2. (B)

A and C are congruent because they are vertical angles; however they are not necessarily supplementary. The only way they could be supplementary would be if the lines were perpendicular.

## 3. (D)

I is true because a and c are vertical. II is false because a and h are not alternate exterior. III is true because a=c and e=g (vertical) and c=e (alternate interior). Therefore a=c=e=g and a+c=e+g.

## 4. (D)

I is true because a and g are alternate exterior angles.

II is true because b=d, d=h and h+e=180.may not be true.

III is always true because d and h are corresponding angles.

## 5. (D)

e+f+g+h=360
c=g (corresponding angles)
c=e (alternate interior angles)
So e+f+g+h=c+f+c+h=2c+f+h=360.

## 6. (A)

$$A + B = 90, \quad B = 90 - 20 = 70$$

## 7. (C)

This is a pair of equations:

$$a + b = 180$$
$$a + c = 90$$
$$b - c = 180 - 90 = 90$$

## 4.3    Triangles

Triangles are a big part of standardized tests, especially right triangles.  But first we begin with information about triangles in general.  There are three types of triangles:

|  | Sides | Angles |
|---|---|---|
| **Equilateral** | All congruent | All 60 degrees |
| **Isosceles** | Two congruent | Two congruent |
| **Scalene** | None congruent | None congruent |

The formulas for the area of a triangle are:

| Any triangle | $A = \dfrac{1}{2}bh$ |
|---|---|
| Right triangle | $A = \dfrac{1}{2}leg_1 \cdot leg_2$ |
| Equilateral triangle | $A = \dfrac{s^2\sqrt{3}}{4}$ |

### Triangle Inequality

For reasons that are unclear, standardized tests are fond of the triangle inequality, though so far this has not been a favorite of the SAT®.  The triangle inequality simply states that any leg of any triangle is strictly less than the sum of the other two legs.  Graphically, it looks like this:

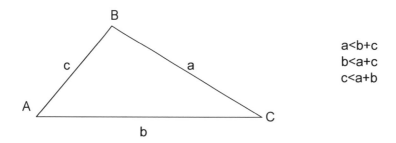

a<b+c
b<a+c
c<a+b

Note that it is only necessary to test whether the longest leg is strictly less than the sum of the other two legs.  In the diagram above, it is only necessary to test whether $b$ is less than $a + c$.  Using a variety of means, a question may ask whether a particular triplet can form a triangle, for example 1,2,3.  That cannot be a triangle because 3=1+2.  However 1,2,2 can be a triangle because 2<1+2.

## Largest and Smallest Angles and Sides

Along with the triangle inequality, remember that the longest side (b in the diagram above) is opposite the largest angle (B in the diagram); whereas the shortest side (c in the diagram) is opposite the smallest angle (C in the diagram). A special case is the right triangle. The hypotenuse of a right triangle is the longest side (and it is opposite the largest angle, the right angle).

## Congruent triangles

In school, a lot of time is spent proving that triangles are congruent. Although the syllabus for the SAT® includes congruence, this topic has not been popular so far, and the test does not require proofs. Nonetheless please remember that there are four ways to prove congruence for any triangles, SSS, SAS, ASA, and AAS. If you are trying to establish congruence for right triangles, HL can be used. Note that HL is just a variation of SSS because if the hypotenuse and one of the legs are congruent the other leg must be congruent because of Pythagorean Theorem.

## Similar Triangles

Although congruence has not proved to be popular so far, similarity has. Two triangles are similar if their corresponding angles are congruent and their corresponding sides are proportional. Similar triangles are illustrated below: In the diagram below, $\triangle ABC \sim \triangle DEF$. Take careful note of the corresponding angles and sides. Also note that angles are labeled with capital letters; sides are labeled with lower case letters.

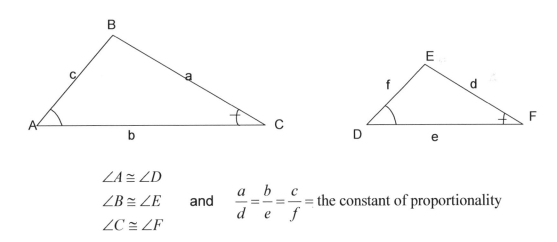

$$\angle A \cong \angle D$$
$$\angle B \cong \angle E \quad \text{and} \quad \frac{a}{d} = \frac{b}{e} = \frac{c}{f} = \text{the constant of proportionality}$$
$$\angle C \cong \angle F$$

A special case of similar triangles is where a line has been drawn through a triangle so that the line is parallel to one of the sides of the triangle, as shown below. The result is two similar triangles, where the larger triangle is similar to the smaller triangle.

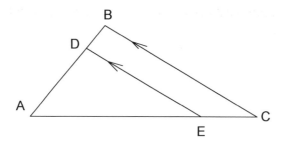

Note that $\angle ADE$ and $\angle ABC$ are congruent because they are corresponding angles of parallel lines. The same is true for $\angle AED$ and $\angle ACB$. Having proved angles to be congruent we can conclude that the triangles are similar (remember AA?). When writing out the similar statement, make sure you get the corresponding sides lined up correctly, $\triangle ABC \sim \triangle ADE$. Do you see how the corresponding sides line up? The proportionality relationships are

$$\frac{AD}{AB} = \frac{AE}{AC} = \frac{DE}{BC}$$

## Right Triangles

The most famous theorem in all of math, the Pythagorean Theorem, applies to right triangles. The theorem states

$$a^2 + b^2 = c^2$$

where $c$ is the length of the hypotenuse, and $a$ and $b$ are the lengths of the legs.

It is absolutely necessary to memorize the relationships of the sides of the two special triangles shown below, even though these are supplied on the SAT®. You should recognize these relationships when they show up on the test, without flipping pages back and forth when a formula is needed.

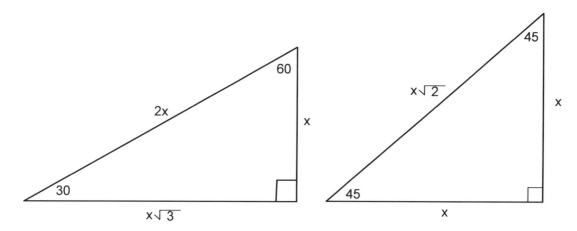

Be on the lookout for these special right triangles because they are very popular on standardized tests. The table below gives some tips on how to spot them.

| When you see: | Look out for: |
|---|---|
| $\sqrt{3}$ | 30-60-90 |
| A side that is $\dfrac{1}{2}$ the hypotenuse | 30-60-90 |
| A hypotenuse that is twice the length of a side | 30-60-90 |
| An equilateral triangle | 30-60-90 |
| $\sqrt{2}$ | 45-45-90 |
| The diagonal of a square | 45-45-90 |

A useful exercise is to use the Pythagorean Theorem to prove the relationships of the sides of each of the special right triangles. The proof for the 45-45-90 triangle is shown below as an example, and the 30-60-90 triangle is left as an exercise.

$$x^2 + x^2 = \left(x\sqrt{2}\right)^2$$
$$2x^2 = \sqrt{2}\cdot\sqrt{2}\cdot x\cdot x = 2x^2$$

# 4.3 Practice problems on triangles
## calculator permitted, diagrams are not drawn to scale

**This diagram pertains to problems 1-3.**

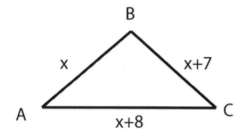

1. What is the perimeter of $\triangle ABC$?

A)        $3x+15$

B)        $x+15$

C)        $x(x+7)(x+8)$

D)        $x^2+(x+7)^2+(x+8)^2$

2. If B is a right angle, what is the area of $\triangle ABC$?

A)        $3x+15$

B)        $\dfrac{1}{2}x(x+7)$

C)        $\dfrac{1}{2}x(x+8)$

D)        $\dfrac{1}{2}(x+7)(x+8)$

3. If B is a right angle, what is the value of $x$?

A)        3

B)        4

C)        5

D)        12

---

4. What is the perimeter of an equilateral triangle whose area is $4\sqrt{3}$?

A)        4

B)        8

C)        12

D)        16

5. What is the side of an equilateral triangle whose altitude is 3?

A)        $\sqrt{3}$

B)        $2\sqrt{3}$

C)        3

D)        6

6. What is the area of a square whose diagonal is 2?

A)        1

B)        2

C)        $\sqrt{2}$

D)        4

7. One leg of a right triangle is 5 and its hypotenuse is 10. What is the size of its smallest angle?

A)        15 degrees

B)        30 degrees

C)        45 degrees

D)        60 degrees

8. One leg of a right triangle is 7 and the hypotenuse is 10. What is the length of the other leg?

A)        6

B)        $\sqrt{51}$

C)        36

D)        $\sqrt{149}$

9. One side of a triangle is 7 and another side is 10. Which of the values below could be the third side of the triangle?

     I.    2          IV   16

     II.    3          V.   17

     III.    4         VI.   18

A)        I and IV only

B)        II and V only

C)        III and IV only

D)        I, II and III only

10. In the diagram below, $\triangle ABC \sim \triangle DEF$.
What is the value of y-x?

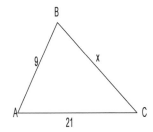

A)          -8

B)          5/3

C)          7

D)          -63

11. Which of the following statements would
be sufficient to conclude that $\triangle ABC \cong \triangle DEF$ ?

    I.  AB=DE, AC=DF, $\angle A \cong \angle D$

    II.  BC=EF, AC=DF, $\angle A \cong \angle D$

    III.  BC=EF, $\angle A \cong \angle D$, $\angle C \cong \angle F$

A)          I only

B)          II only

C)          I and III only

D)          II and III only

12. In the diagram below, if $\overline{AB} \parallel \overline{ED}$, then
what is the value of $x$ ?

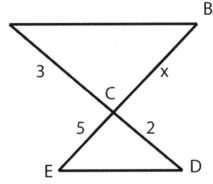

A)          2.0

B)          3.5

C)          5.0

D)          7.5

13. In $\triangle ABC$, side c=3 and side a=7.  If $\angle B$ is
the largest angle, then side b could be:

A)          3

B)          4

C)          9

D)          10

14. If $\triangle ABC$ and $\triangle EDB$ are right triangles and
CB=35, what is the value of CD ?

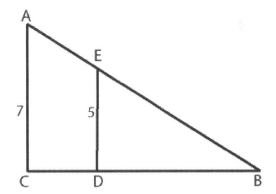

A)          10

B)          14

C)          25

D)          49

# 4.3 Solutions to practice problems on triangles

1. (A)

$x + (x+7) + (x+8) = 3x + 15$

2. (B)

$A = \dfrac{1}{2}bh = \dfrac{1}{2}(x)(x+7)$

3. (C)

$x^2 + (x+7)^2 = (x+8)^2$

$x^2 + (x^2 + 14x + 49) = x^2 + 16x + 64$

$x^2 - 2x - 15 = 0, \ (x-5)(x+3) = 0, \ x = 5$

4. (C)

$A = s^2 \dfrac{\sqrt{3}}{4}$

$4\sqrt{3} = \dfrac{s^2\sqrt{3}}{4}, \ s^2 = 16, \ s = 4, \ P = 12$

5. (B)

The altitude of an equilateral triangle forms two 30-60-90 triangles. The altitude is opposite the 60 degree angle, and the side opposite the 30 degree angle is s/2. So if the altitude is 3 then

$3 = \dfrac{s}{2}\sqrt{3}, \quad \dfrac{6}{\sqrt{3}} = s, \quad 2\sqrt{3} = s$.

6. (B)

The diagonal of a square forms two 45-45-90 triangles, with the diagonal being the hypotenuse of each right triangle. So if the diagonal is 2 then

$s^2 + s^2 = 2^2, \ 2s^2 = 4, \ s = \sqrt{2}, \ A = s^2 = 2$.

7. (B)

This must be a 30-60-90 triangle because the hypotenuse is twice as long as of one of the sides. Therefore the smallest angle is 30 degrees.

8. (B)

$x^2 + 7^2 = 10^2, \ x^2 = 100 - 49 = 51, \ x = \sqrt{51}$

9. (C)

I. False $10 \ not < \ 2+7$

II False $10 \ not < \ 3+7$

III. True $10 < 4+7$

IV True $16 < 7+10$

V. False $17 \ not < \ 7+10$

VI. False $18 \ not < \ 7+10$

10. (A)

$\dfrac{3}{9} = \dfrac{y}{21}, \qquad 9y = 63, \qquad y = 7$

$\dfrac{3}{9} = \dfrac{5}{x}, \quad 3x = 45, \ x = 15$

$y - x = 7 - 15 = -8$

11. (C)

I. True by SAS

II. False, SSA is not a condition for congruence

III. True by AAS

12. (D)

$\triangle ABC \sim \triangle DEC$ because of alternate interior angles, $\angle E \cong \angle B$ and $\angle A \cong \angle D$.

$\dfrac{2}{3} = \dfrac{5}{x}, \ 2x = 15, \ x = 7.5$

13. (C)

Side b is the longest side because angle B is the largest angle. Therefore b must be greater than 3 or 7. On the other hand, the triangle inequality requires b to be less than 3+7=10.

14. (A)

$\dfrac{35}{35 - CD} = \dfrac{7}{5}, \ 175 = 245 - 7CD, \ 10 = CD$

## 4.4    Circles

There are just a few things to remember about circles, and most of them are things you probably know already.  Everyone remembers that the central angle of an entire circle measures 360 degrees and that the measure of the entire arc of a circle is 360 degrees.  But you must also remember the relationship between arcs, central angles, and inscribed angles, as shown below.

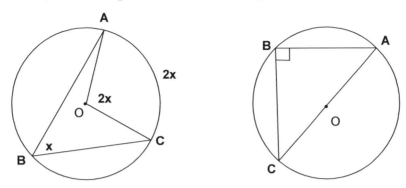

Take a look at circle O on the left.  It has a central angle $\angle AOC$ ($\angle AOC$ is a central angle because its vertex is the center of the circle).  Note that the measure of central angle $\angle AOC$ is the same as the measure of its inscribed arc, $\overset{\frown}{AC}$.  On the other hand, $\angle ABC$ is an inscribed angle, not a central angle (its vertex is not at the center of the circle).  Its measure is one-half the measure of its inscribed arc, $\overset{\frown}{AC}$.

Circle O on the right above illustrates a special case of an inscribed angle.  $\angle ABC$ is inscribed in a semi-circle, where chord $\overline{AC}$ is a diagonal of the circle.  Therefore $\overset{\frown}{AC}$ is a semi-circle and must be 180 degrees (half of a 360 degree circle).  Because $\angle ABC$ is inscribed in a semi-circle, its measure must be 90 degrees (half of the 180 degree arc in which it is inscribed).  For some reason, questions about inscribed right angles are popular.

### Sectors

Another favorite topic has to do with sectors of circles.  Think of these as slices from a pizza pie.  You need to memorize formulas for the area of the pizza slice (area of the sector) and the length of the crust of the pizza slice (arc length).  These are shown below.

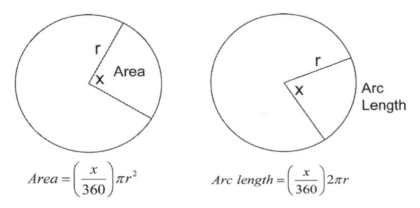

$$Area = \left(\frac{x}{360}\right)\pi r^2 \qquad\qquad Arc\ length = \left(\frac{x}{360}\right)2\pi r$$

In the figures above, notice that the central angle, which is x degrees, is the key to understanding how these formulas work. As x increases, the size of the slice increases. If the slice were half of the pizza, x would be 180 degrees. The formulas simply take the fraction of the whole that the central angle represents and then multiply that fraction by the area of the whole pie ($\pi r^2$) or by the circumference of the whole pie ($2\pi r$).

To learn how to solve a problem where the central angle is measured in radians, see Unit 4.7.

### Equation of a circle and completing the square

Another favorite topic is the equation of a circle. If you know the coordinates of the center of the circle $(h, k)$ and you know that the radius is $r$, then the equation of the circle is:

$$(x-h)^2 + (y-k)^2 = r^2$$

Unfortunately test problems may not be quite so straightforward. More advanced problems may ask you to find the equation of a circle by completing the square, a technique that was covered in Unit 3.7 concerning equations of parabolas. If you are not comfortable with completing the square please review that earlier unit. In this unit we complete the square in two variables. For example, suppose you are asked to find the center and radius of a circle with the equation $x^2 - 2x + y^2 + 4y = -4$.

Group the terms involving x and y separately $\qquad (x^2 - 2x) + (y^2 + 4y) = -4$

Add $(b/2)^2$ to the x terms and y terms $\qquad (x^2 - 2x + 1) + (y^2 + 4y + 4) = -4 + 1 + 4$

Factor the x terms and y terms $\qquad (x-1)(x-1) + (y+2)(y+2) = 1$

Simplify $\qquad (x-1)^2 + (y+2)^2 = 1^2$

The circle in question has a center at (1, -2) and a radius of 1.

### Tangents

Lastly, it is necessary to remember that the tangent to a circle forms a right angle with the radius of a circle at the point where the tangent and radius meet. This is illustrated below.

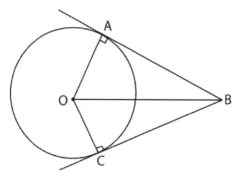

In addition to the right angles that are formed at the points of tangency, notice that we have two congruent right triangles, $\triangle AOB \cong \triangle COB$. Of particular interest is that the external point B is equidistant from the points of tangency, or $\overline{AB} \cong \overline{CB}$.

## Circle graphs (pie charts)

Most people rely on computers to construct a circle graph (also known as a pie chart). But sometimes you will see a question that asks you to construct it by hand.. To see how, consider a sock drawer with 10 red socks, 40 white socks and 30 blue socks. To construct a circle graph, just calculate the size of the central angle for each color:

$$red = \left(\frac{10}{80}\right)360 = 45°, \ white = \left(\frac{40}{80}\right)360 = 180°, \ blue = \left(\frac{30}{80}\right)360 = 135°$$

Once the central angles are calculated, it is easy to draw the circle graph. In this case it would look like:

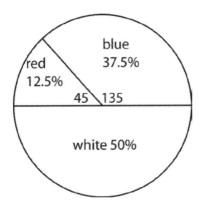

# 4.4 Practice problems on circles
## calculator permitted

1. If circle A has a radius that is twice the length of the radius of circle B, then the following must be true:

    I. The area of circle A is two times the area of circle B.

    II. The circumference of circle A is two times the circumference of circle B.

    III. The area of circle A is four times the area of circle B.

A)        I only

B)        II only

C)        III only

D)        II and III only

2. In the figure below, which of the following must be true?

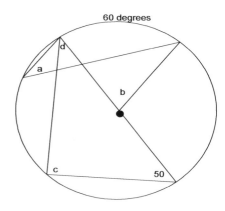

    I. a=60

    II. c-d=50

    III. b=120

A)        I only

B)        II only

C)        III only

D)        I and II only

3. If a circle is divided into eight congruent sectors and each sector has an area of $8\pi$, what is the radius of the circle?

A)        4

B)        8

C)        12

D)        18

4. If a sector has an arc length of $\pi$ and a radius of 10, what is the size of its central angle (in degrees)?

A)        4

B)        8

C)        12

D)        18

5. Billy ordered a pizza with a crust that is $10\pi$ inches long. What is the area of the pizza?

A)        $5\pi$

B)        $10\pi$

C)        $20\pi$

D)        $25\pi$

6. A tangent is drawn to a circle from an external point that is 20 inches from the center of the circle. If the external point is 10 inches from the point of tangency, what is the radius of the circle?

A)        10

B)        $10\sqrt{3}$

C)        $10\sqrt{5}$

D)        20

7. About 20% of the clothes that Rachel has are from Italy. If she were to construct a circle graph of her clothes, what would be the size (in degrees) of the central angle representing Italy?

A)        20

B)        36

C)        72

D)        80

8. If the area of a circle is $25\pi$ and the area of a sector of that circle is $7\pi$ then what is the measure of the central angle of that sector?

A)        4 degrees

B)        8 degrees

C)        55 degrees

D)        101 degrees

9. About 20% of the clothes that Rachel has are from Italy. If she were to construct a circle graph of her clothes using a circle with a radius of 1 inch, what would be length of the arc of the portion of the circle representing Italy?

A)        $0.2\pi$

B)        $0.4\pi$

C)        $2\pi$

D)        $4\pi$

10. If a sector of a circle has an area of $\pi$ units squared and the measure of its central angle (in degrees) is an integer, then the radius of the circle must be:

A)        $\pi$

B)        6

C)        10

D)        36

11. In the diagram below, find the value of $x$ (in degrees).

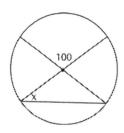

A)        20

B)        30

C)        40

D)        50

12. A circle graph is to be constructed from the data below. What is the size (in degrees) of the angle representing math majors?

| Major | Number of Students |
|---|---|
| Math | 50 |
| Science | 150 |
| Business | 300 |
| Other | 400 |

A)        .05

B)        5

C)        10

D)        20

13. If a circle is tangent to the x-axis at x=5 and is tangent to the y-axis at y=-5, what is the equation of the circle?

A)        $(x+5)^2+(y+5)^2=25$

B)        $(x+5)^2+(y-5)^2=25$

C)        $(x-5)^2+(y+5)^2=25$

D)        $(x-5)^2+(y-5)^2=25$

14. What are the coordinates of the center of a circle whose equation is $x^2+6x+y^2-2y=6$.

A)        (6, -2)

B)        (-6, 2)

C)        (3, -1)

D)        (-3, 1)

## 4.4 Solutions to practice problems on circles

**1 (D)**

I is false and III is true:

$$\frac{A_A}{A_B} = \frac{\pi r_A^2}{\pi r_B^2} = \frac{(2r_B)^2}{r_B^2} = 4$$

II is true:

$$\frac{C_A}{C_B} = \frac{2\pi r_A}{2\pi r_B} = \frac{r_A}{r_B} = \frac{2r_B}{r_B} = 2$$

**2. (B)**

I is false; a=30, inscribed angle

II is true because c=90 and therefore d=40

III is false because b=60, central angle.

**3. (B)**

$$8\pi = \left(\frac{45}{360}\right)\pi r^2,\ 8 = \frac{1}{8}r^2,\ 64 = r^2,\ 8 = r$$

**4. (D)**

$$\pi = \left(\frac{x}{360}\right)2\pi \cdot 10,\ 1 = 20\left(\frac{x}{360}\right)$$

$$\frac{1}{20} = \frac{x}{360},\quad x = 18$$

**5. (D)**

$2\pi r = 10\pi,\ r = 5$

$A = \pi r^2 = 25\pi$

**6. (B)**

$r^2 + 10^2 = 20^2$

$r^2 = 400 - 100 = 300$

$r = \sqrt{300} = 10\sqrt{3}$

**7. (C)**

$.20(360) = 72$

**8. (D)**

$$\frac{7\pi}{25\pi} = \frac{x}{360},\ x = 100.8$$

**9. (B)**

$$l = \left(\frac{72}{360}\right)2\pi \cdot 1 = 0.4\pi$$

**10. (B)**

$$\pi = \left(\frac{n}{360}\right)\pi r^2$$

$$1 = \frac{n}{360}r^2$$

$360 = nr^2,\ n = 10\ \text{and}\ r^2 = 36,\ r = 6$

**11. (C)**

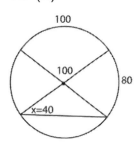

**12. (D)**

$$\left(\frac{50}{900}\right)360 = 20$$

**13. (C)**

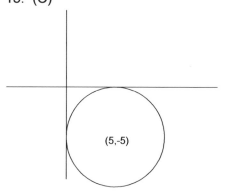

center$=(5,-5)$, radius=5

$(x\text{-}5)^2 + (y+5)^2 = 5^2$

**14. (D)**

Complete the square

$(x^2 + 6x) + (y^2 - 2y) = 6$

$(x^2 + 6x + 9) + (y^2 - 2y + 1) = 6 + 9 + 1$

$(x+3)^2 + (y-1)^2 = 16$

## 4.5    Polygons

A polygon is a closed shape with n straight sides.  If n=3 the polygon is a triangle.  If n=4 the polygon is a quadrilateral, etc. There are two formulas to be memorized for polygons:

$$\text{sum of interior angles} = (n-2)180$$
$$\text{sum of exterior angles} = 360$$

A **regular polygon** has all sides congruent and all interior angles congruent.  A three sided regular polygon is an equilateral triangle, whereas a four sided regular polygon is a square.  To find the measure of an angle of a regular polygon, take the sum of the angles and divide by the number of sides.

### Quadrilaterals

The most popular polygon is the four-sided polygon or quadrilateral.  There are quite a few properties to remember about quadrilaterals, and the easiest way to remember them is to use a "quadrilateral tree," as shown below.

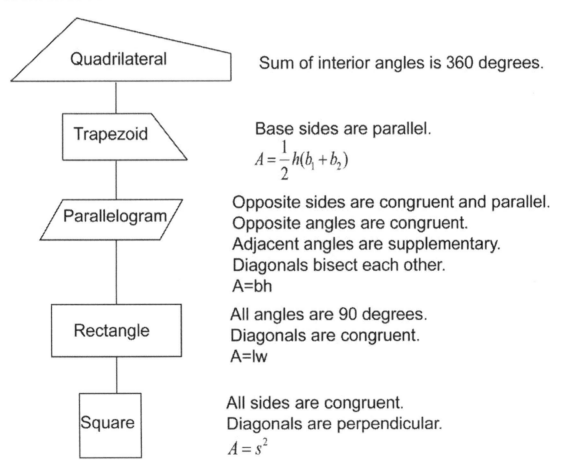

Quadrilateral — Sum of interior angles is 360 degrees.

Trapezoid — Base sides are parallel.
$$A = \frac{1}{2}h(b_1 + b_2)$$

Parallelogram — Opposite sides are congruent and parallel.
Opposite angles are congruent.
Adjacent angles are supplementary.
Diagonals bisect each other.
A=bh

Rectangle — All angles are 90 degrees.
Diagonals are congruent.
A=lw

Square — All sides are congruent.
Diagonals are perpendicular.
$$A = s^2$$

The key to understanding the tree is that properties are inherited by the "children" from the "parents."  The parallelogram is a special type of quadrilateral, the rectangle is a special type of parallelogram, and the square is a special type of rectangle.  For example, the diagonals of a rectangle bisect each other because that property is inherited from the parallelogram.

# 4.5 Practice problems on polygons
## calculator permitted

1.  How large (in degrees) is the interior angle of a regular pentadecagon (all 15 sides are congruent)?

A)     40

B)     110

C)     125

D)     156

2.  How large (in degrees) is the exterior angle of a regular dodecagon (all 12 sides are congruent)?

A)     15

B)     30

C)     60

D)     90

3.  If sum of the interior angles of a regular polygon is 1800 degrees, how many sides does it have?

A)     6

B)     8

C)     12

D)     14

4.  In the parallelogram below, what is the measure of z (in degrees)?

A)     15

B)     30

C)     45

D)     60

5.  If a rectangle has an area of 60 units and a width of 5 units, what is the length of its diagonal?

A)     $\sqrt{61}$

B)     12

C)     13

D)     $\sqrt{119}$

6.  In the parallelogram below, what is the measure (in degrees) of z?

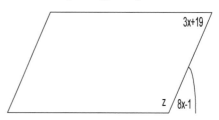

A)     14.7

B)     63.2

C)     116.8

D)     149

7.  If the base of a parallelogram is doubled and its height is tripled, the ratio of the area of the new parallelogram to the area of the old parallelogram is:

A)     2

B)     3

C)     6

D)     36

8.  If the area of a square is 10 square units, what is the sum of its diagonals?

A)     $2\sqrt{5}$

B)     $4\sqrt{5}$

C)     $2\sqrt{10}$

D)     $4\sqrt{10}$

9.  If the area of the trapezoid below is 140 square units, what is the height?

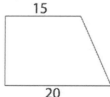

A)          4
B)          6
C)          8
D)          28

---

**Questions 10-11 refer to the following information.**

Point E is the center of square ABCD.

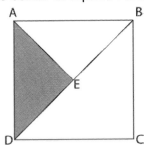

10. If the area of $\triangle ADE$ is 4/3, then the area of square ABCD would be:

A)          9/4
B)          3/1
C)          4/1
D)          16/3

11. If DE is 5 units long, then the area of square ABCD would be:

(A)          $5\sqrt{2}$
(B)          10
(C)          25
(D)          50

---

**Questions 12-13 refer to the following information.**

Quadrilateral ABCD is a parallelogram and $\triangle ABE$ is equilateral.

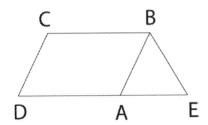

12. If AE is 10 units long, then how long is CD?

A)          5
B)          10
C)          15
D)          20

13. What is the measure (in degrees) of $\angle C$ ?

A)          30
B)          45
C)          60
D)          120

---

14. A circle is inscribed in a square, as shown below. If the diagonal of the square is 36 units, what is the diameter of the circle?

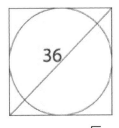

A)          $3\sqrt{2}$
B)          $9\sqrt{2}$
C)          $18\sqrt{2}$
D)          $36\sqrt{2}$

15. If the area of the regular hexagon below is 18 and its perimeter is 12, what is the height (h) of the triangle shown?

A)          1
B)          2
C)          3
D)          4/3

163

# 4.5 Solutions to practice problems on polygons

**1. (D)**

Interior angles sum to $(15-2)180 = 2340$.

Each interior angle must be 2340/15 = 156 degrees.

**2. (B)**

Each exterior angle must be 360/12 = 30 degrees.

**3. (C)**

$$1800 = (n-2)180$$
$$10 = n-2, \quad n = 12 \text{ sides}$$

**4. (B)**

Because they are supplementary,
$$2x + (5x+75) = 180, \quad x = 15$$
$$z = 2x = 2 \cdot 15 = 30$$

**5. (C)**

$$5l = 60, \quad l = 12$$
$$5^2 + 12^2 = d^2, \quad 169 = d^2, \quad 13 = d$$

**6. (D)**

Because of alternate interior angles of parallel lines,
$$3x + 19 = 8x - 1, \; 5x = 20, \; x = 4$$

Angle z and 8x-1 are supplementary, so
$$z + (8x-1) = 180, \quad z + 31 = 180, \quad z = 149$$

**7. (C)**

$$old = bh$$
$$new = (2b)(3h) = 6bh$$
$$new/old = 6/1$$

**8. (B)**

$$\left(\sqrt{10}\right)^2 + \left(\sqrt{10}\right)^2 = d^2$$
$$10 + 10 = d^2$$
$$d = \sqrt{20} = 2\sqrt{5}$$
$$d + d = 4\sqrt{5}$$

**9. (C)**

$$140 = \frac{1}{2}h(20+15), \; 280 = 35h, \; 8 = h$$

**10. (D)**

The shaded region comprises 1/4 of the square. So the area of the square is four times the area of the shaded region, $A = 4\left(\frac{4}{3}\right) = \frac{16}{3}$

**11. (D)**

If DE=5 then AE=5. By Pythagorean Theorem:

$$Area = AD^2 = 5^2 + 5^2 = 50$$

**12. (B)**

If AE is 10 units long then AB is also 10 units long because triangle ABE is equilateral. If AB is 10 units long then CD is 10 units long because opposite sides of a parallelogram are congruent.

**13. (D)**

If triangle ABE is equilateral then $\angle BAE$ is 60 degrees. Then $\angle BAD$ is 120 degrees because it is supplemental. Therefore $\angle C$ must also be 120 degrees because opposite angles of a parallelogram are congruent.

**14. (C)**

The diameter of the circle is equal to the side of the square. By Pythagorean Theorem:

$$s^2 + s^2 = 36^2, \; s^2 = 648, \; s = \sqrt{648} = 18\sqrt{2}$$

**15. (C)**

If the perimeter is 12 then the base is 2. If the area is 18 and there are six congruent triangles that could be drawn in the hexagon, then each triangle has an area of 3.

$$A = \frac{1}{2}bh, \; 3 = \frac{1}{2}(2)h, \; 3 = h$$

## 4.6 Solids

Although the volume formulas for the six solid shapes are provided on the SAT® it is very helpful if you become familiar with them (or memorize them) rather than scramble to look them up under test conditions.

### Rectangular solids

Take a look below at a diagram of a rectangular solid. Think of a sandbox filled with sand. It has a certain width and a certain length, which define the base of the sandbox, and it has a certain height. The box has six faces. Each face is a rectangle with a surface area (SA) equal to the area of its respective rectangle. The total surface area of the rectangular solid is the sum of the surface areas of the faces.

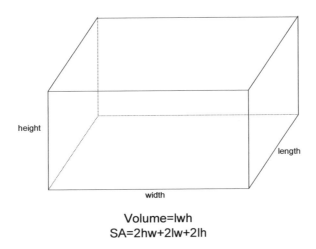

height

length

width

Volume=lwh
SA=2hw+2lw+2lh

### Diagonals of rectangular solids

An important type of question that you might see on a standardized test involves the diagonal of a rectangular solid. When you see a question of this sort, use the Pythagorean Theorem twice. First find the legs of the right triangle formed by the diagonal, then find the diagonal itself.

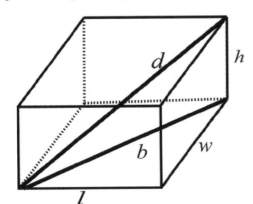

$$First: \quad b^2 = l^2 + w^2$$
$$Second: \quad d^2 = b^2 + h^2$$

### Cubes

An important special case of the rectangular solid is the cube. The width, length and height of a cube are all the same, represented by the letter $s$ which stands for side. The volume and surface area of the cube are:

$$Volume = lwh = s \cdot s \cdot s = s^3$$
$$SA = 2hw + 2lw + 2lh = 2s^2 + 2s^2 + 2s^2 = 6s^2$$

## Cylinders

The cylinder is the most popular solid on the test. When you think of a cylinder, think of a can of soup (or soda or beer, whichever you prefer). The volume of a cylinder is the area of the circular base times the height of the cylinder.

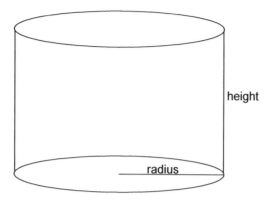

$$Volume = \pi r^2 h$$

## Spheres

In many ways the sphere is the easiest solid because the only variable to be concerned with is the radius (r). Any plane that slices through the center of a sphere will produce a circle with that radius.

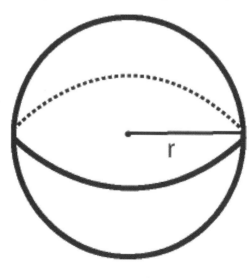

$$Volume = \frac{4}{3}\pi r^3$$

## Cones

The cone has a circular base with a radius (r). The height of the cone is measured by dropping a perpendicular line from the vertex at the top of the cone to the center of the circular base. An easy way to remember the volume of the cone is that it is one-third the volume of the cylinder.

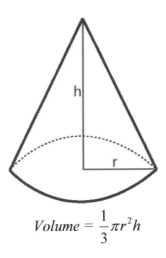

$$Volume = \frac{1}{3}\pi r^2 h$$

## Pyramids

The four sided pyramid has a rectangular (or square) base. The height of the pyramid is measured by dropping a perpendicular line from the vertex at the top down to the center of the rectangular base. An easy way to remember the volume of the pyramid is that it is one-third the volume of the rectangular solid.

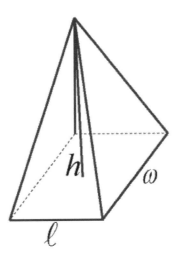

$$Volume = \frac{1}{3}\ell\omega h$$

## How many small things fit in a big thing?

Another important type of problem involving solids is the question of how many small solids can fit in a large solid. To find the answer, calculate the volume of the large solid and then divide by the volume of the small solid. For a fun example, find the number of glasses of beer that can be served from a keg (assuming all glasses are the same and all participants are over 21) by dividing the volume of the keg by the volume of the glass. **IMPORTANT NOTE:** This same reasoning can be applied to area. How many tiles are needed to cover a floor? Calculate the area of the floor and divide by the area of each tile.

## 4.6 Practice problems on solids
### calculator permitted

1. What is the width of a rectangular solid that has a volume of 375, a length of 5 and a height of 5?

A)     5

B)     15

C)     25

D)     75

2. How many cubes of length 2 would it take to fill a rectangular solid with a volume of 120?

A)     15

B)     30

C)     45

D)     60

3. What is the height of a cylinder whose volume is $18\pi$ and whose radius is 3?

A)     2

B)     4

C)     6

D)     8

4. How long is the edge of a cube whose surface area is $150a^2$ square units?

A)     $2a$

B)     $5a$

C)     $2.5a\sqrt{6}$

D)     $5a\sqrt{6}$

5. Amy is building a new silo to store grain. If the dimensions of the silo are as shown below, how much grain could the silo hold (assuming it is filled to the top)?

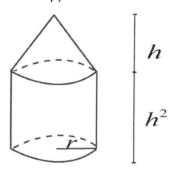

A)     $2\pi r^2 h$

B)     $\pi r^2 h^2$

C)     $(4/3)\pi r^3 h$

D)     $\pi r^2 h(h+(1/3))$

6. What is the length of the diagonal of a cube whose side is 3 units?

A)     $2\sqrt{2}$

B)     $2\sqrt{3}$

C)     $3\sqrt{2}$

D)     $3\sqrt{3}$

7. A roll of wallpaper is 3 feet wide and 25 feet long. How many rolls will be needed to cover a cube whose edge is 15 feet?

A)     3

B)     12

C)     16

D)     18

8. What is the length of the diagonal of a rectangular solid with a length of 4 and a width of 3 and a height of 6?

A)     6

B)     7.8

C)     8.5

D)     9

9. If 50 guests are expected at a party, and each guest is expected to drink 3 cylindrical glasses of punch, and each glass has a radius of 5 cm and a height of 10 cm, what must be the minimum capacity of the punch bowl (in cubic centimeters)?

A)     $7500\pi$

B)     $12500\pi$

C)     $25000\pi$

D)     $37500\pi$

# 4.6 Solutions to practice problems on solids

**1. (B)**

$375 = 5 \cdot 5 \cdot h, \quad 15 = h$.

**2. (A)**

$\dfrac{120}{2^3} = 15$

**3. (A)**

$18\pi = \pi 3^2 h, \quad 2 = h$

**4. (B)**

$SA = 150a^2 = 6s^2$

$25a^2 = s^2, \ 5a = s$

**5. (D)**

The volume of the base cylinder is $\pi r^2 h^2$ and the volume of the cone is $\dfrac{1}{3}\pi r^2 h$.

$\pi r^2 h^2 + \dfrac{1}{3}\pi r^2 h = \pi r^2 h(h + (1/3))$

**6. (D)**

Find the diagonal of the base:

$3^2 + 3^2 = d^2, \quad 3\sqrt{2} = d$

Find the diagonal of the cube:

$3^2 + \left(3\sqrt{2}\right)^2 = d^2, \quad 9 + 18 = d^2, \quad 3\sqrt{3} = d$

**7. (D)**

Each roll has $3 \cdot 25 = 75$ square feet.

Cube has $15 \cdot 15 \cdot 6 = 1350$ square feet.

1350/75 = 18 rolls

**8. (B)**

Find the diagonal of the base:

$3^2 + 4^2 = d^2, \quad 5 = d$

Find the diagonal of the cube:

$6^2 + 5^2 = d^2, \quad 36 + 25 = d^2, \quad \sqrt{61} = d$

**9. (D)**

Glasses are $50 \cdot 3 = 150$

Each glass holds $\pi \cdot 5^2 \cdot 10 = 250\pi$

Capacity must be $150 \cdot 250\pi = 37500\pi$

## 4.7    Trigonometric ratios

Most of the time the SAT® contains some trigonometry problems.  But many of them are easy if you know the basic information that is reviewed here.  It is not necessary to be a trigonometry wizard to do well on the test.

This unit contains the trigonometry derived from the properties of right triangles.  The main idea is captured in the infamous mnemonic, SOHCAHTOA.  Take a look at this diagram:

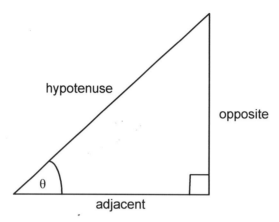

Notice that we have a right triangle, and we want to find the trigonometric ratios for one of its angles, labeled $\theta$ in the diagram.  The three basic ratios, sine, cosine and tangent are remembered through SOHCAHTOA:

S =    $\sin\theta$ is equal to

O=    opposite over

H=    hypotenuse.

C=    $\cos\theta$ is equal to

A=    adjacent over

H=    hypotenuse.

T=    $\tan\theta$ is equal to

O=    opposite over

A=    adjacent.

The other three trigonometric ratios are the reciprocal functions:  secant, cosecant and cotangent.  These are defined below:

$$\sec\theta = \frac{1}{\cos\theta} \qquad \csc\theta = \frac{1}{\sin\theta} \qquad \cot\theta = \frac{1}{\tan\theta}$$

### Complementary angles

You may remember from geometry that if two angles are complementary their measures add up to 90 degrees.  It turns out that trigonometric ratios behave in an interesting way when two angles are complementary, and this is illustrated below.

170

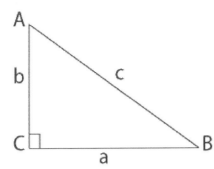

$$\sin A = \frac{a}{c} \qquad \sin B = \frac{b}{c}$$

$$\cos A = \frac{b}{c} \qquad \cos B = \frac{a}{c}$$

$$\tan A = \frac{a}{b} \qquad \tan B = \frac{b}{a}$$

Notice that angles A and B are complementary. Also notice that $\sin A = \cos B$, $\cos A = \sin B$, and $\tan A = \cot B$. This gives rise to the following relationships between complementary angles:

$$\sin(90-\theta) = \cos\theta, \quad \cos(90-\theta) = \sin\theta, \quad \tan(90-\theta) = \cot\theta$$

## Special right triangles (reference angles)

There are certain angles, called reference angles, and for these angles you are expected to know the exact values of their trigonometric ratios. Fortunately these can be derived easily from the special right triangles that were covered earlier in Unit 4.3, Triangles. The 30-60-90 and 45-45-90 triangles are shown below, along with a table of their trigonometric ratios.

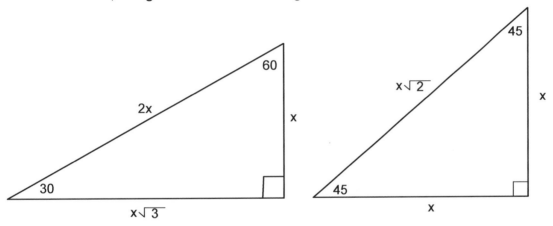

| Reference Angle | $\sin\theta$ | $\cos\theta$ | $\tan\theta$ |
|---|---|---|---|
| 0 | 0 | 1 | 0 |
| 30 | $\dfrac{x}{2x} = \dfrac{1}{2}$ | $\dfrac{x\sqrt{3}}{2x} = \dfrac{\sqrt{3}}{2}$ | $\dfrac{x}{x\sqrt{3}} = \dfrac{1}{\sqrt{3}} = \dfrac{\sqrt{3}}{3}$ |
| 45 | $\dfrac{x}{x\sqrt{2}} = \dfrac{1}{\sqrt{2}} = \dfrac{\sqrt{2}}{2}$ | $\dfrac{x}{x\sqrt{2}} = \dfrac{1}{\sqrt{2}} = \dfrac{\sqrt{2}}{2}$ | $\dfrac{x}{x} = 1$ |
| 60 | $\dfrac{x\sqrt{3}}{2x} = \dfrac{\sqrt{3}}{2}$ | $\dfrac{x}{2x} = \dfrac{1}{2}$ | $\dfrac{x\sqrt{3}}{x} = \sqrt{3}$ |
| 90 | 1 | 0 | Undefined |

**Similar triangles**

This may sound obvious, but the sine of a 30 degree angle is always one-half, no matter how large or how small the right triangle happens to be. This is true because the trigonometric functions are ratios, and the ratio of the opposite side to the hypotenuse is always one-half, provided the angle is 30 degrees. From the triangles Unit 4.3 you may recall that if two triangles have congruent angles and proportional sides, they are similar. If you know the measure of the angles and the sides in one triangle these can be used to find the angles and sides in the similar triangle.

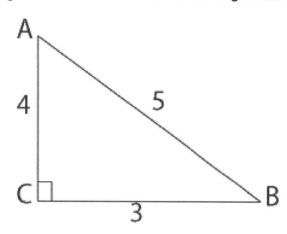 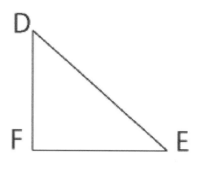

In the diagram above, suppose triangle ABC is similar to triangle DEF, $\triangle ABC \sim \triangle DEF$. Because

angles A and D are congruent, $\sin A = \sin D = \dfrac{3}{5}$. If you were given that DE=3 then you could find the

EF by using the fact that $\sin D = \dfrac{3}{5} = \dfrac{EF}{DE} = \dfrac{EF}{3}$.

**Identities**

There are two identities from trigonometry that might be useful on a test. They are:

$$\frac{\sin \theta}{\cos \theta} = \frac{\dfrac{opp}{hyp}}{\dfrac{adj}{hyp}} = \frac{opp}{adj} = \tan \theta \text{ and}$$

$$\sin^2 \theta + \cos^2 \theta = 1$$

The first can be proved using SOHCAHTOA and the second can be proved using the Pythagorean Theorem.

# 4.7 Practice problems on trigonometric ratios
## calculator permitted

**Use the figure below to solve problems 1-3.**

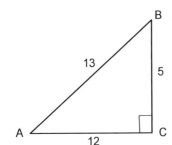

1. For the right triangle above, the $\sec A$ is:

A)        12/5

B)        13/5

C)        12/13

D)        13/12

2. For the triangle above, $\sin A + \cos B$ equals

A)        10/13

B)        17/13

C)        24/13

D)        30/13

3. The following are equal to $5/12$ EXCEPT:

A)        $\tan A$

B)        $\cos B$

C)        $\cot(90 - A)$

D)        $1/\cot A$

4. If the $\sin \theta = 5/7$ then the $\cot \theta$ equals:

A)        $5/12$

B)        $7/12$

C)        $13/12$

D)        $2\sqrt{6}/5$

5. The expression $\dfrac{\sin^2 \theta - \sin^4 \theta}{\cos^4 \theta}$ simplifies to:

A)        $\sin^2 \theta$

B)        $\cos^2 \theta$

C)        $\tan^2 \theta$

D)        $\tan^4 \theta$

6. The $(\cos 30°)(\sin 45°)$ is equal to:

A)        $\dfrac{\sqrt{5}}{2}$

B)        $\dfrac{\sqrt{5}}{4}$

C)        $\dfrac{\sqrt{6}}{2}$

D)        $\dfrac{\sqrt{6}}{4}$

7. If the ratio of the angles in a triangle is 3:2:1 then the sine of the smallest angle is:

A)        $1/2$

B)        $\sqrt{2}/4$

C)        $\dfrac{\sqrt{3}}{2}$

D)        $\dfrac{\sqrt{3}}{3}$

8. If $\sin x = \cos y$ then which of the following is <u>false</u>?

    I.   $\cos x = \sin y$

    II.  $\tan x = \tan y$

    III.  $x + y = 90^{O}$

A)        I only

B)        II only

C)        III only

D)        None are false

9. If $\sin \theta = .75$ what is the secant of $\theta$?

A)          $\sqrt{5}/3$

B)          $\sqrt{7}/4$

C)          $4/\sqrt{7}$

D)          $\sqrt{5}/4$

10. In the diagram below, if $\sin y = \dfrac{a}{b}$ then $\sin x$ would be:

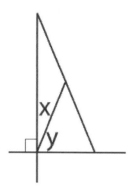

A)          $\dfrac{a}{b}$

B)          $\dfrac{b}{a}$

C)          $\dfrac{b-a}{b}$

D)          $\dfrac{\sqrt{b^2-a^2}}{b}$

11. If $\sin x = \dfrac{d^2 - e^2}{e}$ and $\cos x = \dfrac{d-e}{e^2}$ then $\tan x$ would be:

A)          $\dfrac{e}{d+e}$

B)          $\dfrac{e}{d-e}$

C)          $\dfrac{d^3 - e^3}{e^3}$

D)          $\dfrac{e^3 - d^3}{e^3}$

12. If $\sin x = \cos y$ and $x - y = a$ then $y$ can be expressed as

A)          $90 - a$

B)          $a - 90$

C)          $45 - \dfrac{a}{2}$

D)          $\dfrac{a}{2} - 45$

13. In the diagram below, $\overline{AB}$ is parallel to $\overline{DE}$. If $\sin E = a$, then the $\cos A$ would be equal to:

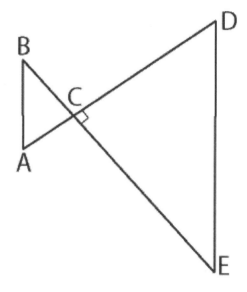

A)          $\dfrac{a}{2}$

B)          $a$

C)          $\dfrac{a}{\sqrt{1-a^2}}$

D)          $\sqrt{1-a^2}$

# 4.7 Solutions to practice problems on trigonometric ratios

**1 (D)**

$$\cos A = \frac{12}{13}$$

$$\sec A = \frac{1}{\cos A} = \frac{13}{12}$$

**2. (A)**

$$\sin A + \cos B = \frac{5}{13} + \frac{5}{13} = \frac{10}{13}$$

**3. (B)**

$$\cos B = \frac{5}{13}$$

**4. (D)**

If a right triangle has a hypotenuse of 7 and one of its legs is 5, then the length of the other leg is:

$$\sqrt{7^2 - 5^2} = \sqrt{49 - 25} = \sqrt{24} = 2\sqrt{6}$$

$$\cot \theta = \frac{2\sqrt{6}}{5}$$

**5. (C)**

$$\frac{\sin^2 \theta - \sin^4 \theta}{\cos^4 \theta} = \left(\frac{\sin^2 \theta}{\cos^2 \theta}\right)\frac{(1 - \sin^2 \theta)}{\cos^2 \theta}$$

$$= \tan^2 \theta \left(\frac{\cos^2 \theta}{\cos^2 \theta}\right) = \tan^2 \theta$$

**6. (D)**

$$(\cos 30°)(\sin 45°) = \frac{\sqrt{3}}{2} \cdot \frac{\sqrt{2}}{2} = \frac{\sqrt{6}}{4}$$

**7. (A)**

This is a 30-60-90 triangle. It can be found using the approach to mixture problems from Unit 3.6:

$$3x + 2x + x = 180, \; 6x = 180, \; x = 30$$

$$\sin 30 = \frac{1}{2}$$

**8. (B)**

If $\sin x = \cos y$ then $x$ and $y$ are complementary angles.

**9. (C)**

**10. (D)**

Because x and y are complementary

$$\sin y = \cos x = \frac{a}{b}.$$

$$\sin^2 x = 1 - \cos^2 x = 1 - \frac{a^2}{b^2} = \frac{b^2 - a^2}{b^2}$$

**11. (A)**

$$\tan x = \frac{\sin x}{\cos x} = \frac{\dfrac{d^2 - e^2}{e}}{\dfrac{d - e}{e^2}} = \left(\frac{(d-e)(d+e)}{e}\right)\left(\frac{e^2}{d-e}\right) = \frac{e}{d+e}$$

**12. (C)**

Because x and y are complementary we have a system of equations $\begin{matrix} x + y = 90 \\ x - y = a \end{matrix}$. Subtracting these gives $2y = 90 - a$.

**13. (B)**

Because D and E are complementary, $a = \sin E = \cos D$. $\angle D \cong \angle A$ because they are alternate interior angles of parallel lines. Therefore $a = \cos D = \cos A$.

## 4.8    Radians and circles

This unit covers more advanced topics in trigonometry that do not appear frequently on the test.  But if your target score is 750+ these topics could make the difference.

### Radians

A radian is just another way to measure the size of an angle.  It can be more convenient to measure an angle using radians rather than degrees.  The best example of how this can be convenient comes from sectors of circles, a topic covered in Unit 4.4 using degrees.    It turns out that the arc length of a sector is just the measure of the central angle times the radius.

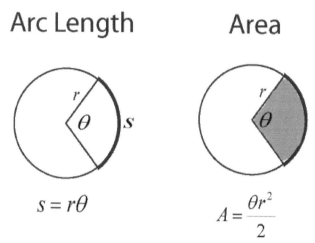

Arc Length                     Area

$$s = r\theta$$

$$A = \frac{\theta r^2}{2}$$

As you can see in the diagram above, the formulas for arc length and area are simpler when the central angle ($\theta$) is measured in radians.  If the circle happens to be a **unit circle** where the radius of the circle is equal to one, the formulas become even simpler.  In particular, the arc length is equal to the radian measure of the central angle when you have a unit circle.

### Converting between degrees and radians

Converting the measure of an angle in degrees to radians or from radians to degrees is easy.  If you consider the unit circle where the radius is one, the circumference of the circle would be $2\pi$.  So an arc that represents one full rotation of the circle (360 degrees) would be $2\pi$ radians.  Similarly a half rotation of the circle (180 degrees) would be $\pi$ radians.  To convert, just use ratios.  Suppose you want to convert 30 degrees to radians, use the ratios:

$$\frac{180}{\pi} = \frac{30}{r}, \; r = \frac{30\pi}{180} = \frac{\pi}{6}$$

To convert $\pi/3$ radians to degrees, start with the same ratio equation:

$$\frac{180}{\pi} = \frac{d}{\pi/3}, \; \frac{180\pi}{3} = \pi d, \; 60 = d$$

It can be extremely useful to memorize the degree and radian measures for the reference angles (see Unit 4.7) as given in the table below.

| Degrees | 0 | 30 | 45 | 60 | 90 |
|---------|---|----|----|----|----|
| Radians | 0 | $\pi/6$ | $\pi/4$ | $\pi/3$ | $\pi/2$ |

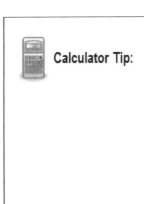

| Calculator Tip: | To convert 30 degrees to radians, press the *mode* key to make sure that the calculator is set to radians (the first screen below). | To convert $\pi/4$ radians to degrees, press the *mode* key to make sure that the calculator is set to degrees (the first screen below). |
|---|---|---|
| | 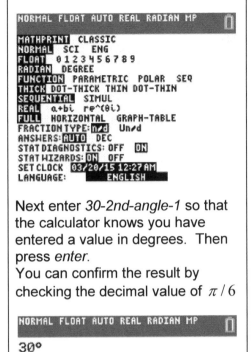 | 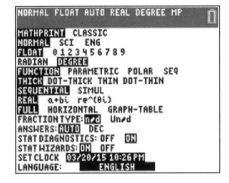 |
| | Next enter *30-2nd-angle-1* so that the calculator knows you have entered a value in degrees. Then press *enter*.<br>You can confirm the result by checking the decimal value of $\pi/6$ | Next enter *(-2nd-$\pi$-÷4-)-2nd-angle-3* so that the calculator knows you have entered a value in radians. Then press enter. |
| | |  |
| | NORMAL FLOAT AUTO REAL RADIAN MP<br>30°<br>$\phantom{xxxxxxxxx}$ 0.5235987756<br>$\pi/6$<br>$\phantom{xxxxxxxxx}$ 0.5235987756 | |

## Working with angles in the first quadrant and beyond

Finding the values of the trigonometric ratios is easy when the angle in question lies in the first quadrant, that is when the angle is between 0 and 90 degrees, or 0 and $\pi/2$ radians. In the top right portion of the figure below, you can see the angle of interest, $\theta$, drawn in a counter-clockwise direction starting from zero. Then draw a vertical line to form a right triangle, and use SOHCAHTOA and the special right triangles to find the desired ratio.

But what if you want the cosine of 120 degrees or $2\pi/3$ radians. When you start moving counter-clockwise from zero you end up in the second quadrant. In this example, $\theta = 2\pi/3$ but in order to find the $\cos(2\pi/3)$ you need to work with the reference angle, x. In the second quadrant $x = \pi - \theta = \pi - 2\pi/3 = \pi/3$ radians or 60 degrees. From the special right triangles you know that $\cos(\pi/3) = 1/2$. But the x coordinate of the reference angle is negative which means the cosine is negative, which yields $\cos(2\pi/3) = -\cos(\pi/3) = -1/2$. You can practice these on your own and check them on your calculator (when you do this on the calculator make sure it is in radian mode).

If you want $\tan(7\pi/6)$ you find the angle to be in the third quadrant where the reference angle is $x = \theta - \pi = (7\pi/6) = \pi = \pi/6$ radians or 30 degrees. From the special right triangles you know that $\tan(\pi/6) = \sqrt{3}/3$. In the third quadrant the x coordinate and the y coordinate are negative, so the tangent would be positive, which yields $\tan(7\pi / 6) = \tan(\pi / 6) = \sqrt{3} / 3$.

If you want $\cos(7\pi / 4)$ you find the angle to be in the fourth quadrant where the reference angle is $x = 2\pi - \theta = 2\pi - 7\pi / 4 = \pi / 4$ radians or 45 degrees. From the special right triangles you know that $\cos(\pi / 4) = \sqrt{2} / 2$. In the fourth quadrant the x coordinate is positive, so the cosine would be positive, which yields $\cos(7\pi / 6) = \cos(\pi / 4) = \sqrt{2} / 2$.

| | |
|---|---|
| **Second Quadrant**<br>reference angle $= x = \pi - \theta$<br>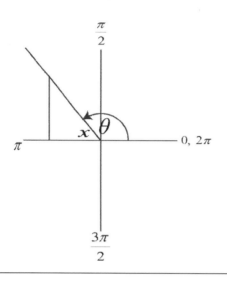 | **First Quadrant**<br>reference angle $= \theta$<br>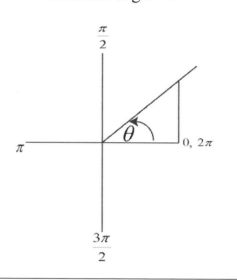 |
| **Third Quadrant**<br>reference angle $= x = \theta - \pi$<br>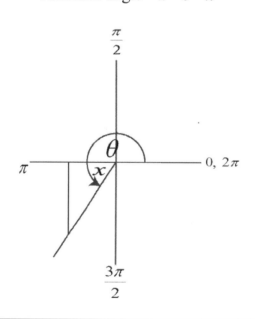 | **Fourth Quadrant**<br>reference angle $= x = 2\pi - \theta$<br>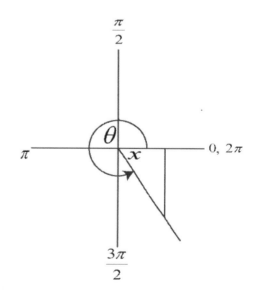 |

# 4.8 Practice problems on radians and circles
## Solve these problems by hand first and then confirm on a calculator

1. An angle that measures $4\pi/9$ radians is equivalent to:

A)     60 degrees

B)     70 degrees

C)     80 degrees

D)     90 degrees

2. An angle that measures 42 degrees is equivalent to:

A)     7/30 radians

B)     30/7 radians

C)     $7\pi/30$ radians

D)     $30\pi/7$ radians

---

**The diagram below pertains to problems 3 and 4.**

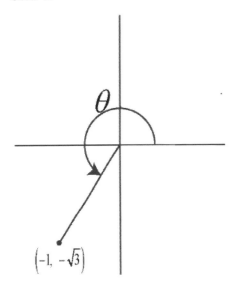

3. Given the coordinates of the endpoint shown, what is the radian measure of the obtuse angle $\theta$?

A)        $\pi/3$

B)        $\pi/6$

C)        $4\pi/3$

D)        $7\pi/6$

4. What is the secant of angle $\theta$?

A)        -1/2

B)        -2

C)        $-\sqrt{3}/2$

D)        $-2/\sqrt{3}$

---

5. What is the length of an arc of a circle with a radius of 5 cm, intercepted by a central angle of 36 degrees?

A)        $\pi/2$ cm

B)        3 cm

C)        $\pi$ cm

D)        4 cm

6. If $\sin\theta < 0$ and $\cos\theta > 0$ then $\theta$ must be in which quadrant?

A)        I

B)        II

C)        III

D)        IV

7. What is the measure of $\theta$ if its reference angle is $\pi/4$ and $\theta$ lies in quadrant IV?

A)        $7\pi/4$

B)        $5\pi/4$

C)        $3\pi/4$

D)        $\pi/4$

8. Which two angles have the same sine?

A)        $\pi/2$ and $3\pi/2$

B)        $\pi/4$ and $3\pi/4$

C)        $\pi/3$ and $4\pi/3$

D)        $2\pi/3$ and $5\pi/3$

# 4.8 Solutions to practice problems on radians and circles

### 1. (C)

$$\frac{180}{\pi} = \frac{d}{4\pi/9}, \quad d = \frac{180 \cdot 4}{9} = 80$$

### 2. (C)

$$\frac{180}{\pi} = \frac{42}{r}, \quad r = \frac{42\pi}{180} = \frac{7\pi}{30}$$

### 3. (C)

Use the Pythagorean Theorem to find the hypotenuse and recognize the 30-60-90 triangle. That gives the reference angle to be $\pi/3$.

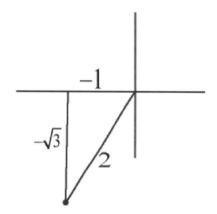

So $\theta = \pi + \pi/3 = 4\pi/3$.

### 4. (B)

Using the triangle in the diagram above

$$\sec\theta = \frac{1}{\cos\theta} = \frac{hyp}{adj} = \frac{2}{-1} = -2$$

### 5. (C)

First convert 36 degrees to radians

$$\frac{180}{\pi} = \frac{36}{r}, \quad r = \frac{36\pi}{180} = \frac{\pi}{5}$$

$$s = r\theta = 5\left(\frac{\pi}{5}\right) = \pi$$

### 6. (D)

$\sin\theta < 0$ means the y-coordinate is negative

$\cos\theta > 0$ means the x-coordinate is positive.

### 7. (A)

Only $7\pi/4$ is in the fourth quadrant.

### 8. (B)

$\sin(\pi/2) = 1$ and $\sin(3\pi/2) = -1$

$\sin(\pi/4) = \sqrt{2}/2$ and $\sin(3\pi/4) = \sqrt{2}/2$

$\sin(\pi/3) = \sqrt{3}/2$ and $\sin(4\pi/3) = -\sqrt{3}/2$

$\sin(2\pi/3) = \sqrt{3}/2$ and $\sin(5\pi/3) = -\sqrt{3}/2$

# 5. Data interpretation and statistics

The SAT® requires you to be able to interpret information displayed in various types of tables and graphs. But you are also expected to use that information to calculate or estimate a variety of statistics from those same tables and graphs.

## 5.1 Data Interpretation

This unit provides an overview of the various tables and graphs that you are likely to see on the test, along with some simple calculations that can be made such as fractions, percentages, and slope (yes, linear models show up in these problems as well).

### One way tables

Consider the life expectancy in the United States from 1930 through 1990.

| Year | US Life Expectancy (years)* |
|------|------------------------------|
| 1930 | 59.7 |
| 1950 | 68.2 |
| 1970 | 69.7 |
| 1990 | 75.4 |

*From the National Center for Health Statistics.

This table shows some improvement in life expectancy over time, presumably due to better living conditions and health care. But be careful: the data do not explain why life expectancy improved.

You might be asked to make calculations using these data, like the percent improvement in life expectancy from 1930 through 1970, which would be $\left(\dfrac{69.7-59.7}{59.7}\right)100 = 16.7\%$. Or the average

annual rate of change in life expectancy from 1930 through 1970, which would be

$\dfrac{69.7-59.7}{1970-1930} = \dfrac{10}{40} = .25$.

### One way frequency tables

Another type of one-way table is the one-way frequency table. For example suppose the number of television sets per family living in Smallville USA is given below:

| Number of TV sets | Number of families |
|-------------------|--------------------|
| 0 | 10 |
| 1 | 20 |
| 2 | 50 |
| 3 | 20 |
| 4 | 10 |

More elaborate calculations might be asked for this table (see the next unit 5.2), but suppose you are asked for the average number of TV sets per family. That calculation would be

$$\frac{10(0)+20(1)+50(2)+20(3)+10(4)}{10+20+50+20+10} = \frac{220}{110} = 2$$

## Two-way tables

| Year | US Life Expectancy (years)* | | |
|------|-------|-------|---------|
| | White | Black | Overall |
| 1930 | 61.4 | 48.1 | 59.7 |
| 1950 | 69.1 | 60.8 | 68.2 |
| 1970 | 71.7 | 64.1 | 69.7 |
| 1990 | 76.1 | 69.1 | 75.4 |

*From the National Center for Health Statistics.

Two-way tables provide more information and therefore more insight. This particular table enables you to see differences between life expectancy in races but does not explain the cause. You might be asked to compare the percent improvement in life expectancy for whites vs blacks from 1930-1970:

$$\text{Whites: } \left(\frac{71.7-61.4}{61.4}\right)=17\% \quad \text{Blacks: } \left(\frac{64.1-48.1}{48.1}\right)=33\%$$

## Line Graphs

Line graphs are pretty simple to read and interpret. In this example you might be asked where the rate of improvement in life expectancy was smallest, 1930-1950, 1950-1970, or 1970-1990. The rate of improvement is the slope and the slope is smallest in 1950-1970.

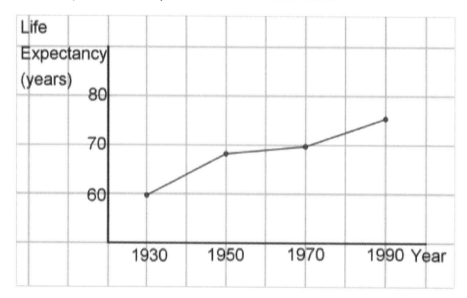

## Histograms

Histograms (bar graphs) are best for getting a quick impression of the underlying data without having to read details in a table. The first histogram below clearly illustrates that life expectancy rose during the period of 1930-1990.

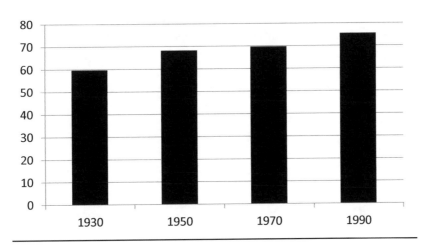

In just a glance, you can see from the histogram below that life expectancy has been rising over the period 1930-1990 and that life expectancy has been higher for whites than for blacks throughout those years.

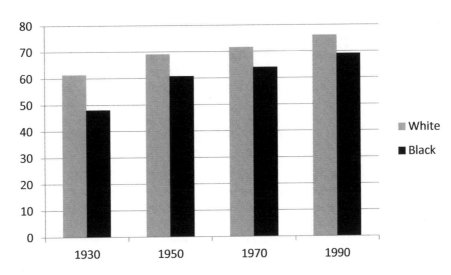

Scatter plots

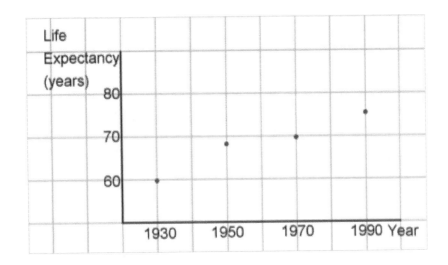

The same life expectancy data are shown in the scatter plot above. This type of graph is also useful for taking a quick look at trends in the data. On the SAT® these trends are often called **associations** (though in school you might have heard this called correlation). The scatter plot above illustrates a **positive association** because as time goes on the life expectancy increases. An association can be positive like the plot above, negative (if life expectancy were decreasing over time), or there might not be an association at all (if life expectancy was fluctuating over time with no particular up or down trend).

Line of best fit

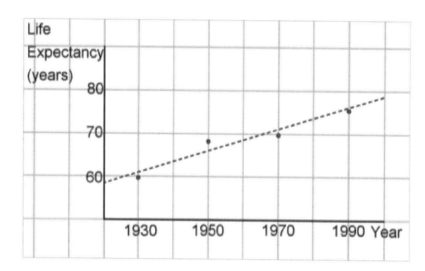

It is very common to have the calculator or graphing program calculate a "line of best fit" and draw that line along with the scatter plot. Do not worry about calculating the line; that is not required on the SAT®. In this case the calculator has given us the equation of the line of best fit as $y = 0.243x - 408.03$. A positive slope for the line of best fit indicates a **positive association**. Whereas a negative slope indicates a **negative association.** If the slope of the line of best fit is close to zero, this indicates **no association**.

Interpolation versus extrapolation

The line of best fit is very useful to estimate a hole in the data, which is called interpolation. Notice we only have data for odd number decades. If we wanted to estimate the life expectancy in 1940 we would plug 1940 into the equation of the line of best fit $y = 0.243(1940) - 408.03 = 63.39$. Our estimate for the 1940 life expectancy is 63.39 years.

However you must never extrapolate beyond the data given without stating the very critical assumption that life expectancy has a linear relationship with time. An extrapolation is valid only to the extent that that relationship holds. Using the line of best fit to extrapolate to 1993 we would expect the life expectancy to be 76.3 years. But the life expectancy in 1993 was only 75.5 years. That decrease was attributed to H.I.V.-related deaths.

How the calculator determines the line of best fit

You do not need to calculate the equation for the line of best fit but it is useful to know how the calculation is made. The computer program finds the line that is overall closest to the data points. Closeness is measured by comparing the predicted y-value using the equation of the line versus the actual y-value. This is done for every y-value in the scatter plot.

# 5.1 Practice problems on data interpretation
## calculator permitted

1. The table below shows the number of people without health insurance in AnyWhere, USA by age group.

| Age (years) | Number of uninsured |
|---|---|
| under 18 | 1,890 |
| 18-44 | 33,600 |
| 45-64 | 18,900 |

Of those under the age of 65 who are uninsured, what fraction are under 18?

A)   18/126

B)   1,890/54,390

C)   33,600/54,390

D)   18,900/54,390

2. Which of the scatter plots below shows a negative association?

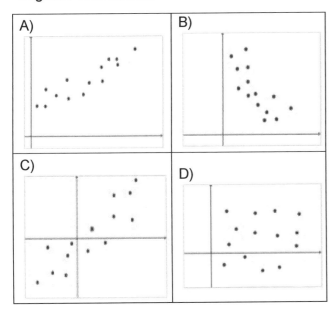

A)   A

B)   B

C)   C

D)   D

---

**Questions 3-5 refer to the following information.**

The table below shows cell phone ownership by grade and gender in Emily's school.

| Grade | Boys With Phone | Boys Without Phone | Girls With Phone | Girls Without Phone |
|---|---|---|---|---|
| 1 | 5 | 35 | 10 | 30 |
| 2 | 15 | 20 | 20 | 25 |
| 3 | 18 | 32 | 25 | 15 |
| 4 | 22 | 15 | 30 | 10 |
| 5 | 30 | 5 | 35 | 5 |

3. What fraction of third grade boys have cell phones?

A)   18/50

B)   18/32

C)   25/40

D)   22/37

4. If Emily's school consists of grades 1 through 5, what percent of the student population has cell phones?

A)   22%

B)   30%

C)   43%

D)   52%

5. What was the percentage decrease in the number of girls without cell phones from grade 2 through grade 4?

A)   25%

B)   50%

C)   60%

D)   83%

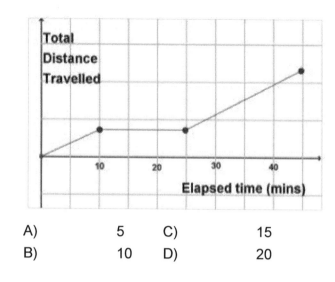

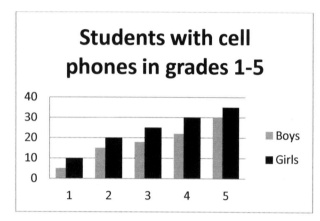

## Questions 6-7 refer to the following information.

The histogram below shows cell phone ownership by grade and gender in Emily's school.

**Students with cell phones in grades 1-5**

6. If there are 80 students in the third grade, approximately what percent of them have cell phones?

A)      35%

B)      50%

C)      65%

D)      80%

7. What conclusion can be drawn from the histogram?

A)      As fractions of the total student body, the fraction of girls with cell phones is larger than the fraction of boys with cell phones.

B)      More students in sixth grade than fifth grade have cell phones.

C)      Girls use cell phones more frequently than boys

D)      More girls have cell phones than boys

8. Alexandra started walking to her friend's house. She stopped to call and wait for an Uber car. Then she took the car to her friend's house. If the total trip took 45 minutes, approximately how many more minutes were spent in the car than were spent walking?

| A) | 5 | C) | 15 |
|---|---|---|---|
| B) | 10 | D) | 20 |

## Questions 9-10 refer to the following information.

The scatter plot below shows the number of households (in hundreds) in AnyTown USA with internet access by household income (in thousands). Also shown is the line of best fit.

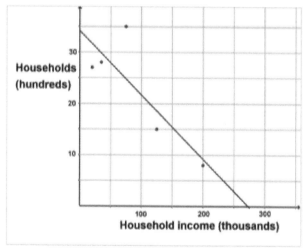

9. How many households with an income of $150,00 would be expected to have internet access?

| A) | 50 | C) | 150 |
|---|---|---|---|
| B) | 100 | D) | 200 |

10. The number of households with an income of $75,000 who have internet access is about how many more than predicted by the line of best fit?

| A) | 50 | C) | 150 |
|---|---|---|---|
| B) | 100 | D) | 200 |

# 5.1 Solutions to practice problems on data interpretation

1. (B)

2. (B)

A and C show positive associations. D shows no association.

3. (A)

$$\frac{18}{18+32} = \frac{18}{50}$$

4. (D)

$$\left(\frac{90+120}{90+107+120+85}\right)100 = \left(\frac{210}{402}\right)100 = 52$$

5. (C)

$$\left(\frac{25-10}{25}\right)100 = 60$$

6. (B)

$$\left(\frac{18+22}{80}\right)100 = 50$$

7. (D)

A) The histogram does not tell us how many boys and girls are in the school.

B) and C) are inferences that are not supported by the histogram

8. (B)

$$car - walk = 20 - 10 = 10$$

9. (C)

10. (B)

$$actual - predicted = 350 - 250 = 100$$

## 5.2 Statistics

In this unit we cover the various statistics that you are expected to calculate or estimate from the types of tables and graphs discussed in the previous unit.

This unit covers descriptive statistics, which are numbers that tell you something about a data set (set of numbers). The goal is to convey some general idea of what the data are like without having to look at every data point in the set.

### Measuring central tendency: mean, median, mode

Mean, median and mode tell you something about the center of the data set

### Mean

Standardized tests sometimes contain the phrase "average (arithmetic mean)." Don't let this confuse you. That phrase refers to the average, something you learned in grade school. It is the sum over the count. A simple example is:

> "Find the average (arithmetic mean) of 2, 3, -1 and 0." The sum is 4 and the count is 4. So the average is 4/4 or 1.

### Median

The value of the median depends on whether the count is odd or even. To find the median, list the numbers from smallest to largest. If the count is odd, the median is the middle number. If the count is even, the median is the mean of the middle two numbers.

> "Find the median of 5, -1, 6, 2, and 0." First, list the numbers from smallest to largest. The ordered list is: -1, 0, 2, 5 and 6. Next we notice that the count is odd (the count is 5). The median is the middle number, 2.

> "Find the median of 5, -1, 6, -3, 2, and 0." First, list the numbers from smallest to largest. The ordered list is: -3, -1, 0, 2, 5 and 6. Next we notice that the count is even (the count is 6). The median is mean of the middle two numbers, which is $\frac{0+2}{2} = 1$.

### Mode

The mode is the number that appears most frequently. Remember that there can be no mode at all, there can be one mode, or there can be more than one mode (this is called multi-modal). To find the mode(s), list the numbers from smallest to largest. The mode(s) are the numbers that appear most frequently.

> "Find the mode of 1, -2, 3, and 4." Every number appears once and so there is no mode.

> "Find the mode of 5, -1, 6, -3, 2, 0, and 6." First, list the numbers from smallest to largest. The ordered list is -3, -1, 0, 2, 5, 6, 6. The mode is 6 because it is the only number that appears twice.

> "Find the mode of 2, -1, 6, -3, 2, 0, and 6." First, list the numbers from smallest to largest. The ordered list is -3, -1, 0, 2, 2, 6, 6. The modes are 2 and 6 because they are the only numbers that appear twice.

The SAT® typically does not give you a list of numbers from which you are to calculate the mean, median or mode. Usually you are asked to calculate or estimate these from a table or graph. Consider the life expectancy in the United States from 1930 through 1990.

| Year | US Life Expectancy (years)* |
|------|------------------------------|
| 1930 | 59.7 |
| 1950 | 68.2 |
| 1970 | 69.7 |
| 1990 | 75.4 |

*From the National Center for Health Statistics.

For the four years given, let's find the mean, median and mode. The mean is the sum over count, which in this case is 273/4 = 68.25. The median is (68.2+69.7)/2 = 68.95, and there is no mode.

Another table that could be used is the one-way frequency table. For example suppose the number of television sets per family living in Smallville USA is given below:

| Number of TV sets | Number of families |
|-------------------|--------------------|
| 0 | 10 |
| 1 | 20 |
| 2 | 50 |
| 3 | 40 |
| 4 | 10 |

$$\frac{10(0)+20(1)+50(2)+40(3)+10(4)}{10+20+50+40+10}=\frac{280}{130}=2.15$$

Frequency tables may be a nuisance for calculating means but they are really convenient for medians and modes. For the median, cross out the top 50 numbers -- that brings you into the 2s. If you cross out the bottom 50 numbers that also brings you into the 2s. So the median is 2. The mode is obviously 2 because that appears most frequently.

Sensitivity of the mean, median and mode to changes in the data

Let's take the life expectancy data and add a data point for the year 2010 and the fictional life expectancy of 100 years. Now let's look at what happens to the mean, median mode from this fictional data set. The mean is sum over count, which is 373/5 = 74.5. Just that one data point causes the mean to jump by 5.5 years! But the median and mode remain pretty stable. The median becomes the middle number which is 69.7, a change of just 1.5 years, and there continues to be no mode.

**Measuring spread: range and standard deviation**

The range and standard deviation tell you something about how widely the numbers are spread about the center of the data set.

The range is simply the largest number in the data set (maximum value) minus the smallest number in the data set (minimum value).

The variance is the average of the sum of all the squared differences for each number in the data set from the mean of the data set. If $m$ is the mean of $n$ numbers,

$$\text{standard deviation} = \sqrt{\frac{1}{n}\left[(x_1-m)^2+(x_2-m)^2+(x_3-m)^2+...+(x_n-m)^2\right]}$$

Standard deviation is not something that you would ever have to calculate by hand. It could be given to you in a problem or you might be asked to compare standard deviations for data sets.

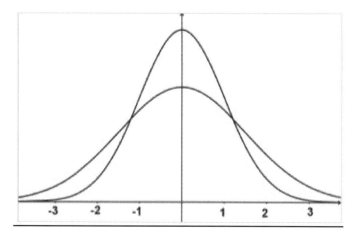

In the diagram above, two data sets are shown in the same frequency graph. In both cases, the graphs are symmetric about zero, which means that their means, medians and modes are all zero. Notice that although their measures of central tendency are the same, their ranges and especially their standard deviations are different. The taller curve has a small range and smaller standard deviation (it is more tightly arranged around the mean).

| 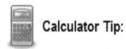 Calculator Tip: | To find the mean, median and standard deviation of the life expectancy data set, enter the data by using *stat-edit*. Then enter data values into L1. | To use a frequency table like the TV data set, enter data values into L1 and frequencies into L2. |
|---|---|---|

To find the mean, median and standard deviation of the life expectancy data set, enter the data by using *stat-edit*. Then enter data values into L1.

| NORMAL FLOAT AUTO REAL RADIAN MP | | | | | 1 |
|---|---|---|---|---|---|
| L1 | L2 | L3 | L4 | L5 | |
| 59.7 | ------ | ------ | ------ | ------ | |
| 68.2 | | | | | |
| 69.7 | | | | | |
| 75.4 | | | | | |

Next use *stat-calc-1var stats* to find the mean $\bar{x}$ ,median (Med) and standard deviation $\sigma_X$. You will need to scroll down.

NORMAL FLOAT AUTO REAL RADIAN MP

**1-Var Stats**
$\bar{x}$=68.25
$\Sigma x$=273
$\Sigma x^2$=18758.58
Sx=6.489221833
$\sigma x$=5.619830958
n=4
minX=59.7
↓Q1=63.95

To use a frequency table like the TV data set, enter data values into L1 and frequencies into L2.

NORMAL FLOAT AUTO REAL RADIAN MP

| L1 | L2 | L3 | L4 | L5 |
|---|---|---|---|---|
| 0 | 10 | ------ | ------ | ------ |
| 1 | 20 | | | |
| 2 | 50 | | | |
| 3 | 40 | | | |
| 4 | 10 | | | |

Next use *stat-calc-1var stats* to calculate the mean $\bar{x}$ ,median (Med) and standard deviation $\sigma_X$.

Use L1 for the List and *2nd-L2* for the FreqList. You will need to scroll down.

NORMAL FLOAT AUTO REAL RADIAN MP

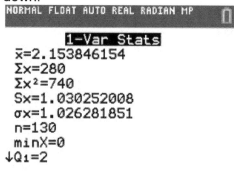

**1-Var Stats**
$\bar{x}$=2.153846154
$\Sigma x$=280
$\Sigma x^2$=740
Sx=1.030252008
$\sigma x$=1.026281851
n=130
minX=0
↓Q1=2

## Probability and conditional probability

On the SAT® probability is just another form of a fraction

$$\text{probability of an event} = \frac{\text{number of outcomes that include the event}}{\text{number of all possible outcomes}}$$

Consider the age and gender breakdown of students at AnyTown High School below.

| Age (years) | Number of students | |
|:---:|:---:|:---:|
| | Male | Female |
| 15 | 25 | 35 |
| 16 | 30 | 45 |
| 17 | 40 | 55 |
| 18 | 50 | 60 |
| TOTAL | 145 | 195 |

The probability of a student being male is just the number total number of males divided by the total student population, 145/(145+195) = 0.43. Likewise the probability of a student being 17 years old is just (40+55)/(145+195) = 0.30.

Sometimes you are asked to calculate a conditional probability (though the phrase "conditional probability" is not used). The probability that a 17-year old is male is 40/(40+55) = 0.42. This is called conditional probability because the probability is conditioned on the student being 17 years old. In other words, given that the student is 17 years old, the probability of being male is 0.42.

## Sampling and inference

The best way to know something about a population is to observe every member of that population. This is called a census. In the AnyTown High School above , that is exactly what happened. The complete records for the school were used to build the table shown. But a census can be very expensive when the population is large or difficult to observe. In that situation, it is more practical to take a survey. In a survey a subset of the population is observed and from the results of the sample an inference is made about the population as a whole.

For example suppose you want to know what residents of AnyTown USA think about their electrical service. Suppose you got a detailed map of AnyTown and visited every tenth house one day and interviewed the resident who answered the door. Would this sample be representative of the town? The answer is no, because it is **biased** and therefore any inference to the AnyTown as a whole would be invalid. You only interviewed residents who happened to be home on that day, eliminating any residents who were not home on that day from participating. The sample was biased, it was not representative of the population as a whole.

## Observational versus experimental studies

A survey is an observational study, meaning you observe how things are and record your observations. But in some situations it is better to conduct an experiment. Suppose you want to prove that the public drinking water is unsafe. The best way would be to randomly have some people drink bottled water while others drink public water. Over time, if the percentage of disease is higher in the public water drinkers is suggests that the water causes disease. If instead you had taken a sample of people, noted whether they were ill and asked what water they drank, this might show an association between public water usage and disease, but only an indication of possible causation.

# 5.2  Practice problems on statistics
## calculator permitted

**Questions 1-5 refer to the following information.**

The age and gender breakdown of students at AnyTown High School is shown below:

| Age (years) | Number of students | |
| | Boys | Girls |
| --- | --- | --- |
| 15 | 25 | 35 |
| 16 | 30 | 45 |
| 17 | 40 | 55 |
| 18 | 50 | 60 |
| TOTAL | 145 | 195 |

1.  What is the probability that a student chosen at random is a 16-year old girl?

A)      .09

B)      .13

C)      .57

D)      .60

2.  What is the probability that a student chosen at random is 17 years old?

A)      0.18

B)      0.22

C)      0.28

D)      0.32

3.  What is the probability that a 15-year old student chosen at random is a boy?

A)      0.40

B)      0.42

C)      0.45

D)      0.71

4.  How much more likely is an 18-year old student to be a boy versus a 17-year old student?

A)      0.01

B)      0.02

C)      0.03

D)      0.04

5.  If the students in AnyTown are representative of the 15 million high school students in the entire USA, what number of USA high school students would be expected to be 15-year old girls?

A)      1.1 million

B)      1.2 million

C)      1.4 million

D)      1.5 million

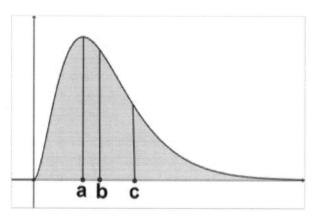

6.  In the frequency graph above, three points are shown (a, b, and c).  Which points could represent the mean, median and mode?

A)      a=mean, b=median, c=mode

B)      a=mode, b=median, c=mean

C)      a=mode, b=mean, c=median

D)      a=mean, b=mode, c=median

A histogram of the income (in thousands of dollars) versus number of households is shown below for AnyTown USA. For example, 27 households have an income of less than $25,000.

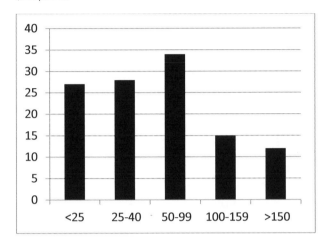

7. Which of the following could be the median household income for AnyTown USA?

A)          $20,000

B)          $35,000

C)          $60,000

D)          $110,000

8. If a household from AnyTown USA is selected at random, which of the following could be the probability that the household income is $100,000 or higher?

A)          0.09

B)          0.23

C)          0.31

D)          0.36

Danielle wanted to find out what the population of her town felt about constructing a new playing field at her school.

9. Danielle decided to stand at the door of the only grocery store in town, every day after school and all weekend for an entire week. She asked every person entering the store to share their opinion. What could improve Danielle's approach?

I. Have some friends stand with her at the grocery store

II. The following week, Danielle could stand at the post office and do the same thing.

III. Danielle could have her Mom stand at the grocery store when Danielle is in school.

A)          I only

B)          II only

C)          II and III only

D)          All are improvements

10. Which of the approaches below would give Danielle the most accurate measure of public opinion?

A) Place an advertisement in the local newspaper, asking people to send a text message to one number if in favor, or to another number if opposed.

B) From a list of property owners, send a questionnaire to every address, asking people to respond with their opinions by mailing a response in a pre-paid envelope.

C) Have all the students at her school interview their parents, and record their opinions.

D) Have the Town place the issue on the ballot during the upcoming local elections.

# 5.2 Solutions to practice problems on statistics

1. (B)

$$\frac{45}{145+195} = 0.13$$

2. (C)

$$\frac{40+55}{145+195} = 0.28$$

3. (B)

This is conditional probability.

$$\frac{25}{25+35} = 0.42$$

4. (C)

$$\frac{50}{50+60} - \frac{40}{40+55} = 0.45 - 0.42 = 0.03$$

5. (D)

$$\left(\frac{35}{145+195}\right)15,000,000 = 1,544,118$$

6. (B)

a is the mode because it represents the most frequent number

b is the median because about half the population of numbers lies below it and half lies above it.

c is the mean because the larger numbers pull the mean to the right of the medain.

7. (C)

To estimate the median, cross off the first 27 households in the far left category and balance that out by crossing off the 25 households from the two categories on the far right. The median must fall somewhere between $25,000 and $99,000. The $50,000-$99,000 category is larger so the median must fall in there.

8. (B)

$$\frac{15+12}{27+28+34+15+12} = 0.23$$

9. (D)

Although all have their flaws, each is an improvement over the original plan.

I. is an improvement because if Danielle is there alone, shoppers will walk past her while she is interviewing someone.

II. is an improvement because some people may buy their groceries elsewhere, or may be away that first week.

III. is an improvement because many people buy groceries while school is in session.

10. (D)

A. Some people do not subscribe to or buy the local newspaper. Many readers of the newspaper will probably not respond. Some people who have the local newspaper do not have cell phones or know how to use their cell phones to send text messages.

B. Only asking property owners excludes people in town who are renting. Also many people will treat the questionnaire as junk mail and throw it away.

C. Parents of school age children are undoubtedly more likely to favor the playground, versus other residents who do not have children attending school.

D. This restricts responses to residents who turn out to vote, but it is the best alternative because it is least biased and will probably produce the largest number of responses. Turning out to vote may not be expected to be related to opinions regarding school improvements.

**Before you do anything else, locate the practice PSAT® and SAT® tests that are published by the College Board**.  The Appendix of this book contains web links to the tests posted online and a reference to the book of official practice tests that you can buy.

If you have more than six weeks to prepare, start with Part One of this book and cover as many math topics as possible.  You could start by working on topics that you know are weaknesses, or you could use the Appendix of this book to find out which topics are likely to appear most frequently on the SAT®, or do some combination.  Topics in this book are mostly standalone and can be covered in any sequence.  For each topic, read the lesson, do the homework problems, and study the solutions to the problems that you got wrong or could not solve.

If you have less than six weeks to prepare, you should get started on practice tests right away.  The Appendix of this book tells you where you can find the practice tests and other supplementary materials.  The sections below provide some basic instruction on how to take the tests.

## Overview of the math sections

The SAT® contains two math sections.  Section Three is a no calculator section.  It contains 15 multiple choice problems followed by 5 grid-in problems.  On average, 75 seconds are allocated per problem.  A calculator is permitted on the other math section, Section Four.  The calculator section contains 30 multiple choice problems followed by 8 grid-in problems.  On average, 87 seconds are allocated per problem.

## Never leave a multiple choice problem blank

Your score on the SAT® depends only on the number of problems answered correctly.  So if you cannot finish the multiple choice problems or do not how to solve some of them, make sure to bubble in an answer anyway.  It can't hurt!  You could also bubble a guess for the grid-in problems, but a random guess has little chance of being correct.

## Use your time wisely

Within each math section, the multiple choice problems are arranged in order of difficulty, and then the grid-in problems are also arranged in order of difficulty.  Each problem, regardless of difficulty, is worth one point.  **This is the opposite of what you see in school, where the more difficult problems appear later in the test and are worth more points.**

The diagram below illustrates the best way for most people to allocate their time (students with a target of 750+ should disregard this advice).  Most of your time and effort should be spent making sure that you get the correct answer to problems that are within your range of ability to solve.  That means spending more time on the easy and medium level problems, and less or no time on the hard problems.

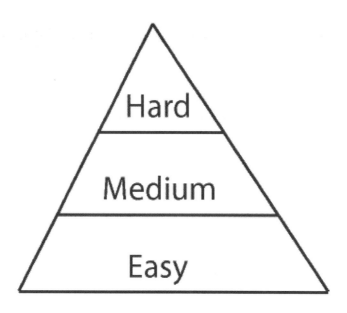

To accomplish this you should break off reading the harder problems that appear toward the end of each part of each section. Within each section, break off when the multiple choice problems become hard and go to the grid-in problems. When the grid-in problems become hard, you can stay with them or go back to the multiple choice problems. There are no restrictions on moving to different parts of the section, but of course you cannot look at problems outside the section.

## Estimate a target score and error rate

It is important to estimate a target math score for the SAT®. To do this, you could refer to your PSAT® or use the results of your first practice test to establish an initial target. Also try to use those materials to estimate your error rate, which is the number of problems solved incorrectly divided by the number attempted (read and solved, not guessed or left blank). Your target score and error rate determine the number of problems that you should attempt to solve next time (see below). Do not worry about the precision of your estimates ... you will revise them as you complete more practice tests.

## How many problems should you attempt (read and solve, not guess)?

Once you have target score and error rate estimates, use the table below to determine <u>approximately</u> how many problems you should attempt (read and solve, not guess or leave blank). Each SAT® has its own curve, so there is no fixed number of correct answers needed to achieve a particular score. More difficult tests have more generous curves and easier tests have less generous curves. Therefore the number of problems that you should attempt can only be estimated based on how the curve typically looks.

| Approximate Target Score | Error rate* | Number and percent of problems to be attempted (read and solved) |
|---|---|---|
| 750 | 5% | 56 (96%) |
| | | |
| 700 | 5% | 52 (90%) |
| | 10% | 55 (95%) |
| | 15% | 58 (100%) |
| | | |
| 650 | 5% | 44 (75%) |
| | 10% | 46 (79%) |
| | 15% | 48 (83%) |
| | 20% | 51 (88%) |
| | 25% | 55 (95%) |
| | | |
| 600 | 5% | 38 (65%) |
| | 10% | 40 (69%) |
| | 15% | 42 (72%) |
| | 20% | 45 (76%) |
| | 25% | 48 (83%) |
| | 30% | 52 (90%) |
| | 35% | 56 (96%) |
| | | |
| 550 | 5% | 31 (53%) |
| | 10% | 33 (57%) |
| | 15% | 35 (60%) |
| | 20% | 37 (64%) |
| | 25% | 40 (69%) |
| | 30% | 43 (74%) |
| | 35% | 46 (79%) |
| | 40% | 50 (86%) |
| | 45% | 54 (93%) |
| | | |
| 500 | 5% | 25 (43%) |
| | 10% | 27 (47%) |
| | 15% | 29 (50%) |
| | 20% | 30 (52%) |
| | 25% | 32 (55%) |
| | 30% | 34 (59%) |
| | 35% | 37 (64%) |
| | 40% | 40 (69%) |
| | 45% | 44 (76%) |
| | 50% | 48 (83%) |
| | 55% | 53 (91%) |

*The error rate is the number of problems solved incorrectly divided by the number of problems that were attempted (read and solved, not guessed or left blank).

To interpret the table above, if your target is 700 and you can move fast enough to attempt every problem, you can meet your target with a 15% error rate. If you have a 15% error rate but can only move fast enough to attempt half of the problems, your target would be 500. There are many lessons to be learned from studying the table above, but the most important lesson is that for most targets you do not have to attempt that many problems. **Most students will improve their score by attempting fewer problems (and reduce their error rate).** A broad summary of the detailed table above is given in the table below. For each practice test you take, keep track of the number of problems solved (not guessed) and your error rate. With each practice test, these numbers will change and you can experiment to find the tradeoff between speed and accuracy that works best for you.

**Approximate target scores, arranged by error rate and pace**

| Error rate | Pace | | |
|---|---|---|---|
| | Fast (95% attempted) | Moderate (75% attempted) | Slow (50% attempted) |
| Low (5%) | 750 | 650 | 550 |
| Moderate (15%) | 700 | 600 | 500 |
| High (25%) | 650 | 550 | 450 |

## Always follow this hierarchy when taking the test

For every math problem, always follow this hierarchy:

- Unless it is clearly outside your range, read the problem carefully
- Try to solve the problem using the math you learned in school
- If a calculator is allowed, set the problem up using your pencil then do the arithmetic on the calculator.
- If you cannot solve the problem using math, try using one of the seven techniques described later in this section.
- If you cannot solve a multiple choice problem by any means, try eliminating some answer choices.
- Always bubble an answer for multiple choice problems.

When you are taking the practice test, circle every problem that you were not able to solve (you need to do this to calculate your error rate). If it is a multiple choice problem, make sure that you bubble an answer.

## After taking each practice test

What will probably help you most is not the number of practice tests you take, but how much you learn from each practice. After every practice test, calculate your score, count the problems that you attempted to solve (these are the problems that you did not circle, see above) and calculate your error rate. Refer to the tables above to see what you might try to do to improve your score (by moving faster or moving more carefully). Take a look at the problems that you solved incorrectly and try to figure out your mistake by referring to the answer explanations provided by the College Board.

# Technique #1 -- Estimate rather than calculate

Some students stress out over the no-calculator section 3. If you need to review multiplication and long division take a look at the first lessons in this book. But for many multiple choice problems in the no calculator section, it is sufficient to estimate the answer rather than perform a calculation by hand.

| Sample problem | Use an estimate |
|---|---|
| Caroline wants to buy as many flowers as she can for Mother's Day. If she has $7.00 to spend and each flower costs 75 cents, how many flowers can she afford to buy (ignore any sales taxes)?<br><br>A)　　　　7<br><br>B)　　　　8<br><br>C)　　　　9<br><br>D)　　　　10 | Each <u>pair</u> of flowers cost $1.50, so four pairs would cost 4($1.50)=$6. After spending $6 Caroline would only have $1 left to spend, which means one more flower. That makes a total of 9 flowers. The answer is (C).<br><br>The pure math way is to do long division on 7.00/0.75. This gives you 9.33 flowers which would be rounded down to 9. |

# Technique #2 -- Backsolve (guess and check)

Sometimes the math needed to solve a problem may be just outside your range of ability or confidence to solve directly. If the problem is multiple choice, the answer is right there. It is among the four answer choices and "all you have to do" is find it.

As stated before, the best approach is the direct solution. Read the problem carefully, calculate the solution, and match your answer with an answer choice. If you are not able to calculate the solution, then backsolving is an option. To backsolve a problem, simply plug each of the answer choices into the original problem and see which one works. Many times the answer choices are ordered from smallest to largest (or largest to smallest). If that is the case, try the middle answer choice first. If it is not correct, go up or down from there.

Some problems are structured so that they cannot be backsolved, so this technique cannot be applied throughout the test. Also, backsolving takes time.

| Sample problem | Backsolve (guess and check) |
|---|---|
| What value of $x$ satisfies the equation<br>$2\|x-3\|=8$ ?<br><br>A)　　　　-7<br><br>B)　　　　-1<br><br>C)　　　　0<br><br>D)　　　　1 | Plug in answer choices.<br>(A) $2\|-7-3\|=2\cdot10=20$<br>(B) $2\|-1-3\|=2\cdot4=8$<br>(C) $2\|0-3\|=2\cdot3=6$<br>(D) $2\|1-3\|=2\cdot2=4$<br>The answer is (B). |

## Technique #3 -- Substitution

This is a popular technique to use instead of using algebra. Even when you know the algebra, substitution can be preferable. Let the A-students use algebra if they prefer it.

| Sample problem | Use substitution |
|---|---|
| A store clerk was asked to markup the price of a pair of shoes by 20%. Instead the clerk marked the price down by 20%. By what percentage does the price now have to be increased in order to be correct?<br><br>A)      20%<br><br>B)      33%<br><br>C)      40%<br><br>D)      50% | Assume the original price was $100. It was erroneously marked down to $80 when it should have been marked up to $120. Therefore the wrong $80 price must be increased by $40 to obtain the correct price of $120. This is a 50% increase over the wrong price. The answer is (D).<br><br>If you prefer algebra, assume the original price was x dollars. It was erroneously marked down to .8x dollars when it should have been marked up to 1.2x dollars. Therefore it must be increased by 1.2x -.8x=.4x dollars. The increase of .4x dollars is 50% over the wrong price of .8x dollars. The answer is (D). |

## Technique #4 -- Geometry guessing

Take full advantage of the fact that diagrams on the SAT® are drawn to scale unless otherwise indicated. When you see a diagram on the test and there is no warning that the diagram is not drawn to scale, especially in the multiple choice parts of the test, it is always an attractive target. Even if you cannot solve the problem, you can often take a good guess. Sometimes you can use your eyes to eliminate some answer choices and then take a guess Even when a diagram is not drawn to scale you can try to draw your own diagram to scale and take a guess based on that.

| Sample problem | Take a guess |
|---|---|
| In the diagram below, what is the measure (in degrees) of the angles marked X? 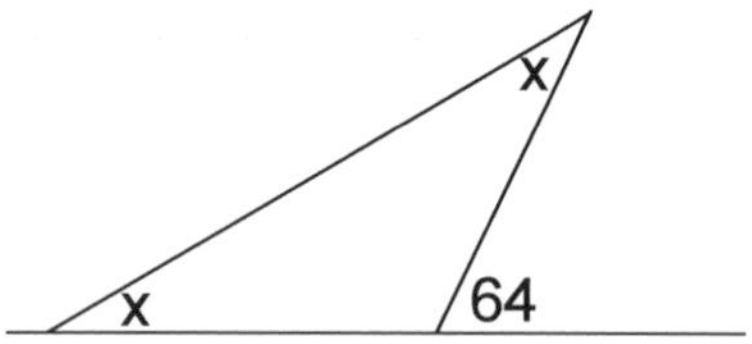<br><br><br><br>A)      12<br><br>B)      22<br><br>C)      32<br><br>D)      42 | The direct solution is to notice that the angle supplemental to the 64 degree angle is 116 degrees. The angles of a triangle must sum to 180, so we have the equation x+x+116=180, which gives x=32. The answer is (C).<br><br>Suppose you did not see how to solve the problem. It is fairly clear that the angle X is larger than 12 degrees, and a pretty good bet that angle X is less than 42 degrees. Having eliminated answer choices (A) and (D), you should take a guess from the remaining answer choices (B) and (C). |

## Technique #5 -- Use the graphing calculator

Obviously the graphing calculator can only be used in the second math section of the SAT®, Section 4, where it is allowed. What is surprising is how many students forget that the calculator can do much more than simple multiplication and division. The graphing calculator can be a very valuable tool if used with a little creativity, as shown below.

| Sample problem | Use your graphing calculator |
|---|---|
| 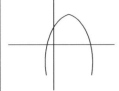<br><br>Above is the graph of the function<br>$y = ax^2 + bx + c$, where a<0, b>0 and c>-0.<br><br>Which of the graphs below could be the graph of the function $y = -ax^2 + bx + c$?<br><br>(A) 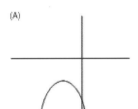   (B) 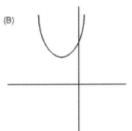<br><br>(C) 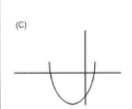   (D) 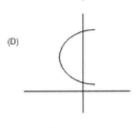 | The A-student might notice that the only difference between the two equations is the sign of the lead coefficient. So the new equation must open up and its y-intercept must remain the same. The only graph with those characteristics is (B).<br><br>However many students have difficulty with parabolas. So for them it is far better to use substitution and the graphing calculator.<br><br>Try values of a, b, and c in your graphing calculator until you have a graph that looks like the one on top. Let's say for example that you end up with $y = -x^2 + 3x + 5$ Enter this and check that it looks like the graph on top. Next put $y = x^2 + 3x + 5$ into your calculator and notice that it looks most like graph (B). |

# Technique #6 -- Roman numeral problems

Some of the problems on the test use the Roman numeral format. For this type of problem, treat each Roman numeral as a true-false question. Mark each Roman numeral as true or false, then match the pattern of your answers to the answer choice.

| Sample problem | Solve by marking true-false |
|---|---|
| Two sides of a triangle are each 5 units long. Which of the following statements MUST BE true?<br><br>I. At least two of the angles of the triangle are congruent.<br>II. The third side of the triangle must be less than 10 units long.<br>III. The triangle is equilateral.<br><br>A)       I only<br>B)       II only<br>C)       I and II only<br>D)       I and III only | I. True. If two sides of a triangle are congruent then the triangle is isosceles and at least two angles are congruent.<br><br>II. True. The triangle inequality states that any side of a triangle must be less than the sum of the other two sides.<br><br>III. False. The triangle could be equilateral, but it might not be.<br><br>The answer is (C). |

# Technique #7 -- Draw a picture

Some word problems can be solved easily if you read the problem carefully and draw a picture that matches the words in the problem. Sometimes students forget to draw a picture or try to solve the problem in their heads because they think that drawing will use up too much time. Although it may feel like it uses a lot of time, it really does not, and it will reduce the likelihood of making a very silly mistake that you will regret.

| Sample problem | Draw a picture |
|---|---|
| Sally drives south at the rate of 30 mph and at the same time Willy drives west at the rate of 60 mph. If Sally and Willy started at the same place at the same time, how far apart will they be after two hours?<br><br>A)       104 miles<br>B)       134 miles<br>C)       180 miles<br>D)       10,800 miles | After two hours Sally will have driven 60 miles and Willy will have driven 120 miles, so the picture looks like this:<br><br><br><br>It is now easy to see that we are interested in the hypotenuse of the right triangle.<br>$$60^2 + 120^2 = x^2$$<br>$$18,000 = x^2$$<br>$$134 = x$$<br>The answer is (B). |

# Guide to using this appendix

## Source materials

This appendix was built using the first six official SAT® practice tests and the first official PSAT® practice test (dated 2015). These tests may be found online, where they are free for downloading, or you can purchase a book containing the first four official practice SAT® tests.

If you purchase the book, The Official SAT Study Guide (ISBN 978-1-4573-0430-9), note that it contains only the first four official practice tests, bubble sheets and answer explanations. It does not contain answer keys or scoring grids for the tests. Those materials and the other official practice tests may be found online.

If you prefer to work with free online materials and prefer to practice using pencil and paper (this is my recommendation, because the SAT® is administered as a pencil and paper test), a good source for the official practice tests is the College Board web site. For official SAT® practice tests, see https://collegereadiness.collegeboard.org/sat/practice/full-length-practice-tests. Official PSAT® practice tests can be found at https://collegereadiness.collegeboard.org/psat-nmsqt-psat-10/practice/full-length-practice-tests. The 2015 practice PSAT® is listed on the web site as practice test 1 (the 2016 practice PSAT® is listed as practice test 2).

The College Board has partnered with Khan Academy, which takes more of an online approach to preparation. The Khan web site contains their own practice math problems organized by topic, online versions of the official practice tests, and other resources. If you are using the Khan web site but prefer to work with pencil and paper, you can find the same official SAT® practice tests at https://www.khanacademy.org/test-prep/sat/new-sat-tips-planning/new-sat-how-to-prep/a/full-length-sats-to-take-on-paper .

## Using problem references

Problem references are shown in the last column of the table below. They are structured as follows:

- For problems from the official SAT® practice tests, the format is:
  test number/section number/problem number.
  For example, 3/4/12 indicates the third practice test, section 4, problem 12.

- For problems from the 2015 official PSAT® practice test (called practice test 1 on the College Board web site), the format is:
  15/section number/problem number.

# Math topics in order of popularity

This is a list of math topics from this book, ordered from most popular to least popular. If you are having trouble with a particular topic, find it below and try some of the official practice problems after you have attempted the homework problems in this book. If you are interested in reviewing official practice tests by topic, find the topic below and look up the problem references. The previous page has an explanation of how to use the problem references.

| Math topic | Popular sub-topics | Problem references | | |
|---|---|---|---|---|
| 3.3  Linear equations and systems | Linear equations in one variable | 1/3/1 | 3/3/4 | 6/4/4 |
| | | 1/4/4 | 3/4/18 | 15/3/1 |
| | | 2/3/1 | 4/4/1 | 15/3/14 |
| | | 2/4/6 | 4/4/31 | 15/3/15 |
| | | 2/4/32 | 5/3/17 | 15/4/2 |
| | | 3/3/2 | 5/4/33 | |
| | Linear equations in two variables | 1/3/3 | 2/4/22 | 5/3/13 |
| | | 1/3/4 | 2/4/25 | 5/4/7 |
| | | 1/3/6 | 2/4/35 | 5/4/23 |
| | | 1/3/12 | 2/4/37 | 6/3/1 |
| | | 1/4/9 | 2/4/38 | 6/3/2 |
| | | 1/4/10 | 3/3/15 | 6/4/12 |
| | | 1/4/15 | 3/4/8 | 6/4/13 |
| | | 1/4/16 | 3/4/10 | 6/4/14 |
| | | 2/3/3 | 3/4/11 | 15/3/8 |
| | | | 3/4/22 | 15/3/9 |
| | | 2/3/12 | 4/4/5 | 15/4/4 |
| | | 2/3/16 | 4/4/21 | 15/4/11 |
| | | 2/4/1 | 4/4/32 | 15/4/24 |
| | | 2/4/3 | 5/3/8 | |
| | Systems of two linear equations | 1/3/9 | 3/3/9 | 5/4/6 |
| | | 1/3/11 | 3/3/19 | 5/4/12 |
| | | 1/3/18 | 3/4/24 | 6/3/6 |
| | | 1/4/19 | 3/4/30 | 6/4/10 |
| | | 2/3/9 | 4/3/3 | 6/4/11 |
| | | 2/3/20 | 4/3/19 | 15/3/3 |
| | | 2/4/34 | 4/4/6 | 15/3/5 |
| | | 3/3/6 | 5/3/18 | 15/4/5 |
| | | | | 15/4/29 |

| 3.2 Fractions and ratios | Operations on fractions | 1/3/7 | 3/4/7 | 5/4/9 |
| | Simplifying fractions | 1/3/8 | 3/4/9 | 5/4/31 |
| | Equations involving fractions | 1/3/13 | 3/4/14 | 5/4/32 |
| | Ratios | 1/4/2 | 3/4/19 | 5/4/37 |
| | Rates | 1/4//6 | 3/4/37 | 6/3/17 |
| | Unit Rates | 1/4/23 | 3/4/38 | 6/4/9 |
| | Unit conversion | 1/4/31 | 4/3/6 | 6/4/26 |
| | Direct and inverse variation | 2/4/2 | 4/3/10 | 6/4/29 |
| | | 2/4/4 | 4/4/3 | 6/4/31 |
| | | 2/4/11 | 4/4/11 | 6/4/35 |
| | | 2/4/15 | 4/4/33 | 15/3/2 |
| | | 2/4/23 | 4/4/34 | 15/3/14 |
| | | 2/4/31 | 4/4/35 | 15/3/16 |
| | | 3/3/5 | 5/3/15 | 15/4/6 |
| | | 3/3/15 | 5/3/19 | 15/4/7 |
| | | 3/3/17 | 5/4/3 | 15/4/17 |
| | | | | 15/4/22 |
| 3.4 Linear inequalities and systems | Linear inequalities | 1/4/11 | 2/4/21 | 5/3/16 |
| | Systems of linear inequalities | 1/4/18 | 3/4/31 | 5/4/13 |
| | | 1/4/28 | 3/4/36 | 5/4/25 |
| | | 1/4/32 | 4/4/16 | 6/3/14 |
| | | 2/3/8 | 4/4/17 | 6/4/5 |
| | | 2/4/9 | 4/4/19 | 15/3/7 |
| | | 2/4/12 | 5/3/7 | 15/4/27 |
| 5.2 Statistics | Mean, median, mode | 1/4/5 | 3/4/2 | 6/4/22 |
| | Range and standard deviation | 1/4/12 | 3/4/15 | 15/4/12 |
| | Probability | 1/4/14 | 3/4/32 | 15/4/13 |
| | Samples and inference | 1/4/27 | 4/4/9 | 15/4/15 |
| | | 2/4/13 | 5/4/14 | 15/4/16 |
| | | 2/4/16 | 5/4/15 | 15/4/20 |
| | | 2/4/18 | 5/4/22 | 15/4/23 |
| | | 2/4/19 | 6/4/7 | |
| | | 2/4/20 | 6/4/21 | |
| 3.7 Quadratic equations and their graphs | Standard form | 1/3/15 | 3/3/12 | 6/3/11 |
| | Vertex form | 1/3/16 | 3/3/13 | 6/3/13 |
| | Intercept form | 1/4/25 | 3/4/13 | 6/4/20 |
| | Quadratic formula | 1/4/30 | 4/3/15 | 6/4/27 |
| | Discriminant | 2/3/13 | 4/4/28 | 6/4/30 |
| | Completing the square | 2/3/17 | 5/3/3 | 15/3/13 |
| | Equating polynomials | 2/4/7 | 5/3/4 | 15/4/30 |
| | | 2/4/24 | 5/4/35 | 15/4/31 |

| 5.1  Data interpretation | Tables | 1/4/1 | 3/4/29 | 6/4/12 |
|---|---|---|---|---|
| | Histograms | 1/4/7 | 4/4/7 | 15/4/9 |
| | Scatter plots | 1/4/13 | 4/4/10 | 15/4/14 |
| | | 1/4/33 | 4/4/11 | 15/4/22 |
| | | 2/4/14 | 4/4/13 | |
| | | 3/4/1 | 4/4/22 | |
| | | 3/4/3 | 5/4/17 | |
| | | 3/4/20 | 6/4/8 | |
| 3.13  Functions | Notation | 1/3/10 | 3/4/16 | 5/4/34 |
| | Graphs and tables | 1/4/17 | 3/4/17 | 6/3/8 |
| | Combinations of functions | 2/4/10 | 4/3/2 | 6/4/25 |
| | | 2/4/26 | 4/3/4 | 15/3/10 |
| | | 2/4/33 | 5/4/2 | 15/4/1 |
| | | | | 15/4/21 |
| 2.3  Percentages | Percentage word problems | 1/4/20 | 3/4/27 | 6/4/6 |
| | Percentage change | 1/4/26 | 4/3/12 | 6/4/24 |
| | Increasing or decreasing a | 2/4/5 | 4/4//4 | 15/4/10 |
| | number by a certain percentage | 2/4/17 | 4/4/22 | 15/4/14 |
| | | 3/4/5 | 5/4/24 | 15/4/19 |
| 3.9  Higher order polynomials | Addition/subtraction/multiplication | 1/3/5 | 3/3/16 | 6/3/12 |
| | Graphing ratios (holes, | 1/4/29 | 3/4/6 | 15/3/12 |
| | asymptotes) | 1/4/36 | 3/4/33 | 15/3/17 |
| | Synthetic/long division | 2/3/15 | 4/3/18 | |
| | Finding zeros | 3/3/7 | 4/4/12 | |
| | Remainder theorem | 3/3/13 | 4/4/25 | |
| | Graphing (end behavior) | | | |
| 4.1  Graphs and equations of lines | Slope and y-intercept | 2/3/6 | 4/3/8 | 5/4/28 |
| | Parallel/perpendicular slopes | 2/4/27 | 4/3/20 | 6/3/5 |
| | Distance | 2/4/28 | 4/4/8 | 6/4/2 |
| | Midpoint | 3/3/8 | 5/3/1 | 6/4/3 |
| | | 3/4/26 | 5/4/11 | 15/4/8 |
| 3.12  Exponential growth and decay | Exponential models | 1/4/37 | 3/4/28 | 4/4/37 |
| | Base and rate | 1/4/38 | 4/4/13 | 4/4/38 |
| | Exponential versus linear models | 2/3/14 | 4/4/15 | 6/4/15 |
| | | 3/4/21 | 4/4/20 | 6/4/37 |
| 3.5  FOILing and factoring | FOIL | 2/3/4 | 5/4/8 | |
| | Factor | 4/3/5 | 5/4/30 | |
| | Perfect squares | 5/3/6 | 6/3/4 | 15/3/6 |
| | | 5/3/10 | 6/3/15 | 15/4/25 |

| 3.11 Exponents and radicals | Laws of exponents<br>Square roots<br>Laws of radicals<br>Simplifying expressions | 1/3/14<br>1/3/20<br>2/3/5<br>2/3/7 | 3/3/3<br>4/3/9<br>5/3/5<br>5/3/12 | 6/3/9<br>6/3/16 |
|---|---|---|---|---|
| 4.3 Triangles | Triangle Inequality<br>Similarity and congruence<br>Special right triangles | 1/3/17<br>2/3/18<br>3/3/18<br>4/3/16 | 5/3/20<br>5/4/19<br>6/3/18<br>6/4/16 | 15/3/4 |
| 3.8 Systems involving quadratic equations and inequalities | Equalities<br>Inequalities | 2/4/29<br>3/3/10<br>4/3//11 | 4/3/13<br>5/3/9<br>6/4/34 | 15/4/28 |
| 2.4 Averages | Using sums<br>Average rate of change<br>Relationship to slope | 1/4/22<br>3/4/35<br>4/4/29 | 5/4/24<br>6/4/6<br>6/4/24 | |
| 4.6 Solids | Volume<br>Surface area | 1/4/35<br>3/4/25<br>4/4/13 | 5/3/11<br>5/4/26<br>6/4/33 | |
| 3.10 Absolute value | Solving equations<br>Solving inequalities<br>Graphs | 1/4/8<br>4/3/1 | 4/4/26<br>6/4/28 | 15/4/3 |
| 4.4 Circles | Central and inscribed angles<br>Sectors<br>Equation of a circle | 1/4/24<br>2/4/36<br>3/4/34 | 4/4/24<br>4/4/36 | |
| 4.7 Trigonometric ratios | SOHCAHTOA<br>Complementary angles<br>Special right triangles | 1/3/19<br>3/3/20<br>3/4/23 | 4/3/17<br>15/4/26 | |
| 3.1 Distributing and common factor | Distributing<br>Common factor | 5/4/4<br>6/4/1 | 15/3/11<br>15/3/15 | |
| 3.6 Complex numbers | Operations on complex numbers<br>Powers of i | 1/3/2<br>2/3/11 | 4/3/14<br>6/3/3 | |
| 3.14 Transformations of functions | Translations<br>Reflections<br>Scale changes | 2/3/10<br>5/3/14 | | |
| 4.2 Angles and parallel lines | Complements and supplements<br>Congruence | 1/4/3<br>3/3/11 | | |
| 4.5 Polygons | Sum of interior/exterior angles<br>Quadrilaterals | 2/4/30<br>15/4/18 | | |
| 4.8 Radians and circles | Degrees/radians<br>Angles beyond the first quadrant | 2/3/19 | | |

Made in the USA
San Bernardino, CA
14 October 2017